CONTEMPORARY'S

American History 2

After 1865

Matthew T. Downey

McGraw Hill **Wright Group**

The **McGraw·Hill** Companies

Author

Matthew T. Downey received his Ph.D. in American History from Princeton University. He served as Director of the Clio Project in History-Social Science Education in the Graduate School of Education at the University of California, Berkeley. He also directed the U.C. Berkeley site of the California History-Social Science Project. He has taught at the University of Colorado, the University of California at Los Angeles, and Louisiana State University. Currently, he directs the Social Science Program and the William E. Hewitt Institute for History and Social Science Education at the University of Northern Colorado.

Reading Consultant

Grace Sussman, Ed.D.
   University of Northern Colorado

Senior Editor: Mitch Rosin
Executive Editor: Linda Kwil
Image Coordinator: Barbara Gamache
Cover Design: Tracy Sainz
Interior Design: Linda Chandler
Cartography and Graphics: Tim Piotrowski

Reviewers

Jeffrey J. Johll
   K–12 District Social Studies Supervisor
   Dubuque Community School District
   Dubuque, Iowa

Eleanor Nangle
   Social Studies Instructor
   Chicago, Illinois

Judy Novack-Hirsch
   Social Studies Instructor
   New York, New York

Brian Silva
   Social Studies Instructor
   Long Beach, California

Jill Smith
   Social Studies Instructor
   Giddings, Texas

About the Cover

The images on the cover include (from left to right): Martin Luther King, Susan B. Anthony, Ronald Reagan, Geronimo, Sally Ride, Franklin D. Roosevelt.

Photo credits are on page 380.

Wright Group

ISBN: 0-07-704438-X (Student Softcover Edition)
ISBN: 0-07-704437-1 (Student Softcover Edition with CD)
ISBN: 0-07-704516-5 (Student Hardcover Edition)
ISBN: 0-07-704517-3 (Student Hardcover Edition with CD)

Send all inquiries to:
Wright Group/McGraw-Hill
P.O. Box 812960
Chicago, IL 60681

Printed in the United States of America.

1 2 3 4 5 6 7 8 9 QUE 09 08 07 06

Contents

To the Student

This textbook is the second part of the story of the American people. It includes Reconstruction, Native Americans, industrialization, immigrants, cultural changes, world wars, statesmen, and soldiers.

The American story is not just one story, but many stories woven together. It is the story of ordinary people as well as the rich and famous. It is the story of politicians, merchants, farmers, sailors, servants, and frontier hunters. It is the story of people from different ethnic groups, races, and cultures that helped make America the country it is today.

American History 2 is the story of individuals as well as groups of people. This book includes biographies of men and women who left a mark on American society. Each chapter also includes firsthand accounts by individuals who lived at the time. These accounts are called primary sources.

Americans did not always agree. At times, America fought in wars to preserve democracy and freedom. While Americans are very different people, most have one thing in common. Most people, or their ancestors, came to America from somewhere else with the hope of finding a better life. The slaves were exceptions. They did not come on their own accord. Yet they, too, helped America become a better place in which to live.

The people included in this book helped shape the society in which you live. I hope it helps you understand that you can help shape the America of the future.

Matthew T. Downey

UNIT 1

REBUILDING AND EXPANDING

It was April 1865 and the Civil War was over. The North was expanding. The war had fueled the growth of its industries. Passage of the Homestead Act had sent people west to settle the Great Plains. The number of immigrants was increasing yearly. A railroad that would span the continent was being built.

The South had lost 360,000 men and much of its wealth. Half of its farm equipment and two-thirds of its livestock were destroyed. Miles and miles of railroad track had been torn up. How was the South to fit into the Union again?

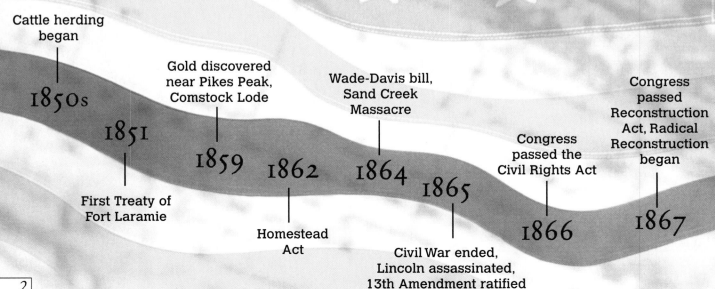

Cattle herding began

1850s

First Treaty of Fort Laramie

1851

Gold discovered near Pikes Peak, Comstock Lode

1859

Homestead Act

1862

Wade-Davis bill, Sand Creek Massacre

1864

Civil War ended, Lincoln assassinated, 13th Amendment ratified

1865

Congress passed the Civil Rights Act

1866

Congress passed Reconstruction Act, Radical Reconstruction began

1867

Why did people settle the Great Plains?

How did African Americans gain and then lose their rights?

How did westward expansion affect Native Americans?

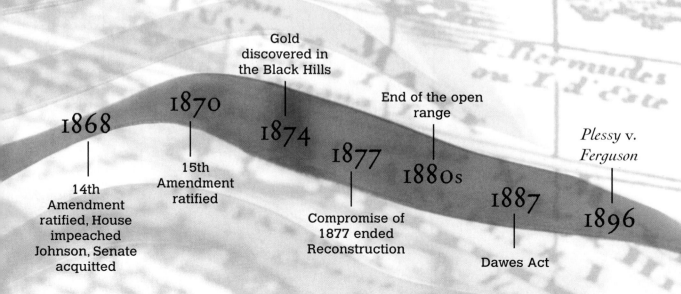

1868

14th Amendment ratified, House impeached Johnson, Senate acquitted

1870

15th Amendment ratified

Gold discovered in the Black Hills

1874

1877

Compromise of 1877 ended Reconstruction

End of the open range

1880s

1887

Dawes Act

Plessy v. *Ferguson*

1896

Chapter 1 RECONSTRUCTION

Getting Focused

Skim this chapter to predict what you will be learning.

- Read the lesson titles and subheadings.
- Look at the illustrations and read the captions.
- Examine the maps.
- Review the vocabulary words and terms.

Think about what you know about the Civil War. What do you think would be major problems in rebuilding the South after the war? Write at least four problems in your notebook.

Presidential Reconstruction

Thinking on Your Own

Read the vocabulary words. What words do you know? Write them in your notebook. Write a sentence for each word in your notebook.

The Civil War was over, and the nation was about to begin the task of **Reconstruction**. The question that the nation faced was straightforward: How were the Southern states to take their places in the Union? The answer was not simple.

Lincoln's Reconstruction Plan

Abraham Lincoln believed it was the responsibility of the president to oversee Reconstruction. By December 1863, he had a plan for Reconstruction. The main points of his plan were:

- Ex-Confederates who took an oath of allegiance to the United States would be given a **pardon**. This means they would be forgiven for supporting the Confederacy.
- Ex-Confederate officers and government officials would not be pardoned.
- When 10 percent of the voters in a state took the oath of allegiance, a new state constitution could be written, and elections for statewide offices could be held.

Those elected to Congress would then take their seats. The state would then be allowed to return to its place in the Union. Lincoln's plan did not give African Americans the right to vote.

focus your reading

What were the main points of Lincoln's Reconstruction plan?

Why did the Radical Republicans disagree with Lincoln?

What were the main points of Johnson's plan?

vocabulary

Reconstruction

pardon

Radical Republicans

Congressional Opposition

Many Republican members of Congress did not agree with Lincoln's plan. They believed that it was the job of Congress, not the president, to plan Reconstruction. The **Radical Republicans** also wanted land to be distributed to freed slaves and for freed slaves to gain the right to vote. The Constitution's framers never considered the possibility of secession. There was nothing in the Constitution about what to do if a state tried to secede. As a result, the president and Congress each had their own ideas about Reconstruction.

The Republican Congress created its own Reconstruction plan in 1864. It was called the Wade-Davis bill. The proposed law required that more than half of the voters in a state take the oath of allegiance. The bill also required the protection of rights for African Americans. Lincoln vetoed the bill.

New-York Daily Tribune.

Vol. XXV.....No. 7,504.   NEW-YORK, TUESDAY, APRIL 25. 1865.   PRICE FOUR CENTS.

PRICE FOUR CENTS.

RECEPTION
OF THE
REMAINS
OF
Abraham Lincoln
Sixteenth President of the United States,
IN THE CITY OF NEW-YORK
April 24, 1865.
———
SOLEMNITY OF THE OCCASION.
———
THE CORTEGE.
———
THE STREETS THRONGED
———
The Body in State at the City Hall.
———
A Requiem from 1,000 German Voices.
———
The Struggle to See the Corpse.

Lincoln's Death

On April 14, 1865, Lincoln, his wife, and some friends went to Ford's Theater to see the play *Our American Cousin*. During the play, John Wilkes Booth, who supported the Southern cause, shot Lincoln. The president was moved to a boarding house owned by William and Anna Petersen. The house was across the street from the theater. Doctors tended to a gunshot wound to the president's head. However, Lincoln died the next morning.

---

stop and think

How was Lincoln's Reconstruction plan different from the Wade-Davis bill? Write three sentences in your notebook to explain the differences.

The assassination of Lincoln shocked a nation already divided by the Civil War. Northern citizens mourned the death of the leader who had kept the nation together. African Americans thought they had lost the person responsible for their freedom. Even his enemies praised him.

Lincoln's coffin lay in the rotunda of the Capitol for several days. Citizens could come into the Capitol and walk around it. This is called "lying in state." Later his coffin was taken by horse-drawn carriage to the train station. Both the stand for the coffin, called a catafalque, and the carriage, known as a caisson, are still used today to honor fallen leaders.

A funeral train took Lincoln's body home to Illinois. Along the way, the tracks were lined with mourners. The whole nation was grieving. He was buried in Springfield, Illinois, on May 4, 1865.

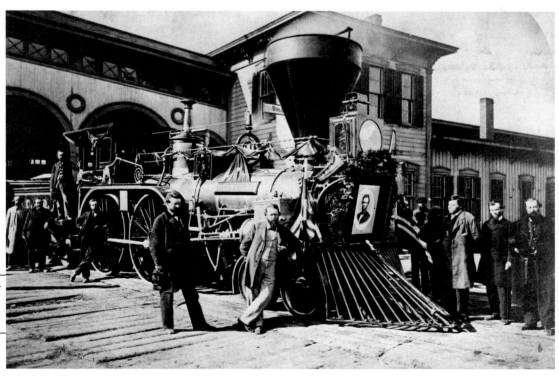

Abraham Lincoln's funeral train

Johnson's Reconstruction Plan

With the death of Lincoln, Andrew Johnson became president. He had been a senator from Tennessee before the Civil War. Johnson chose not to join with Tennessee when it seceded. In the election of 1864, Lincoln chose him as his vice president. Now Johnson was president. Like Lincoln, Johnson did not wish to punish the South. Johnson also believed that Reconstruction was the job of the president, not Congress. The following are the main points of Johnson's Reconstruction plan:

President Andrew Johnson

- Most ex-Confederates could swear allegiance to the Union and be pardoned.
- High-level ex-Confederate officials and military officers had to take an oath. They also had to personally ask the president for a pardon.
- States had to write new constitutions.
- State constitutions had to repeal secession and refuse to pay debts run up by the Confederacy.
- The states had to ratify the 13th Amendment to the U.S. Constitution, which abolished slavery.
- Once a constitution was written, a state could hold elections.

Like Lincoln's plan, those who were elected could then take their seats in Congress. The states would then be considered Reconstructed. Like Lincoln, there was no mention of African-American rights. There was one major difference between the two plans. Under Johnson's plan, there was no required number of voters who had to take the oath of allegiance.

Putting It All Together

Imagine you are a newspaper reporter writing about Reconstruction. In your notebook, write a two-line headline to describe Lincoln's plan. Then write a two-line headline about Johnson's plan.

Read a Primary Source

President Lincoln Is Dead

Elizabeth Keckley was born a slave in North Carolina. A talented seamstress, she was able to buy her freedom. She moved to Washington and in time became personal dressmaker and a close friend to Mary Lincoln. In her autobiography, *Behind the Scenes*, Keckley wrote about the death of President Abraham Lincoln. The excerpt below begins as a servant arrives at Elizabeth's home with a request from Mrs. Lincoln.

" 'I come from Mrs. Lincoln. If you are Mrs. Keckley, come with me immediately to the White House.'

"I hastily put on my shawl and bonnet, and was driven at a rapid rate to the White House. . . I was quickly shown to Mrs. Lincoln's room. . . .

"She was nearly exhausted with grief, and when she became a little quiet, I asked and received permission to go into the Guests' Room, where the body of the President lay in state. . . . No common mortal had died. The Moses of my people had fallen in the hour of his triumph. . . .

"Not-withstanding the violence of the death of the President, there was something beautiful as well as grandly solemn in the expression of the placid face. There lurked the sweetness and gentleness of childhood. . . . I gazed long at the face, and turned away with tears in my eyes and a choking sensation in my throat. Ah! never was man so widely mourned before. The whole world bowed their heads in grief when Abraham Lincoln died."

Elizabeth Keckley, *Behind the Scenes, or, Thirty Years a Slave, and Four Years in the White House.* G.W. Carleton (New York, 1868)

Radical Reconstruction

Thinking on Your Own

Read the Focus Your Reading questions. Write three predictions about what this lesson will include.

Under Johnson's plan, all the Southern states had ratified the 13th Amendment by December 1865, written new constitutions, and held elections. When the new Southern members of Congress appeared in Washington to take their seats, Northerners were alarmed. Southern voters had elected to Congress many former leaders of the Confederacy. Even the former Confederate vice president was elected. The Republican Congress refused to seat them. A new conflict between North and South had begun.

focus your reading

What were the main points of the Radicals' plan?

What did former slaves need after the Civil War?

How did Reconstruction affect women's rights?

vocabulary

black codes   impeach

civil rights   sharecropper

Southern Reaction, Northern Response

The fight was not only about elections to Congress. Across the South, ex-Confederates were being elected to state and local offices. As they regained power, they began to pass laws limiting what freed African Americans could do. These laws were known as **black codes**.

Under black codes, African Americans could not serve on juries, own guns, or gather in groups after dark. Under black codes, African Americans could do only certain jobs, like farm work; could be arrested if they could not prove they had a job; and had to sign labor contracts for a year at a time.

There was also a great deal of violence in the South against African Americans. To protect African Americans, Congress passed the Civil Rights Act of 1866. **Civil rights** are rights guaranteed to a person by law, like voting and equal protection. Johnson vetoed the Civil Rights Act, but Congress was able to override his veto. Later that year, Congress wrote the 14th Amendment to include rights for African Americans in the U.S. Constitution. Congress sent the amendment to the states to ratify.

stop and think

Think about what slavery was like. Then reread the black codes. Write in your notebook how the black codes were like slavery.

Johnson opposed both the Civil Rights Act and the 14th Amendment. In elections for Congress that year, Northern voters ignored Johnson. They sent many new members to Congress who sided with the Radical Republicans. Radical Republicans wanted to remake the South so that whites and the Democratic Party could not regain power.

The Radicals' Plan

The new Congress was quick to act and in 1867 passed the Reconstruction Act. Its main points were:

- The South was divided into five districts under military rule.
- Each state had to write a new constitution.
- African Americans were to be allowed to vote for delegates to the conventions that would write the new constitutions.
- All male citizens were to be guaranteed equal rights.
- All states had to ratify the 14th Amendment.

Once the conditions were met, a state could hold elections.

The fight between Johnson and Congress ended when the House

Johnson's impeachment proceedings in the House

of Representatives found enough evidence to impeach the president. Several charges were brought against him. The most serious was that he fired his secretary of state without the approval of Congress. Congress had passed a law that no cabinet member could be removed without its approval. His case was sent to the Senate for trial. Johnson was acquitted by one vote. President Johnson served out his term, but the real power to oversee Reconstruction now lay with Congress.

African Americans and Reconstruction

Politicians had specific views about Reconstruction. But what about the newly freed slaves? Life changed dramatically once they received their freedom. What did newly freed African Americans think about it? What did they want?

Sharecroppers' shacks were often small and provided basic shelter.

Former slaves needed the basics—food, shelter, clothing, and a way to earn a living. They also wanted education. In March 1865, Congress set up the Freedmen's Bureau to help former slaves. The bureau provided food, clothing, medical care, and helped former slaves arrange for work with plantation owners. But most of all, the bureau built schools for former slaves. It was not unusual to see an old person learning to read next to little children.

Adults and children attended school together.

stop and think

Suppose you were an African American who was now free. What would it be like? Describe in your notebook how you would feel being free.

The dream of many former slaves was to own land. Radical Republicans hoped to take land from former plantation owners and give it to freed slaves. However, this idea was too radical for most Republicans in Congress.

In the end, most African Americans became contract workers or **sharecroppers**. Contract workers signed agreements with white landowners to work for pay. Sharecroppers worked someone else's land in return for a share, or part, of the crop. They received seed, tools, food, and a house to live in. Landowners made sure a sharecropper family always paid more for the seed and other things than their share of the crop was worth. The family had to keep working for the landowner because they were never out of debt.

No Votes for Women

During Reconstruction, three important amendments were added to the U.S. Constitution. To rejoin the Union, the Southern states had to ratify them. These amendments established certain civil rights for African Americans, but they did not affect women's rights.

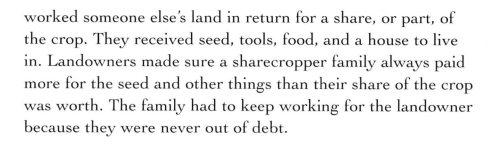

Reconstruction Amendments		
Amendment	Date Ratified	Purpose
13th Amendment	December 1865	Abolishes slavery
14th Amendment	July 1868	Defines citizenship and explains the rights of citizens; includes former slaves
15th Amendment	February 1870	Forbids states from keeping any male citizen from voting; includes former slaves

In the 1840s and 1850s, women had put aside their fight for the right to vote. Instead, they joined the fight to end slavery. Once the Civil War was over, these women expected to gain the vote as payment for their hard work. It did not happen. The 15th Amendment guaranteed the vote only to men. Women like Susan B. Anthony and Elizabeth Cady Stanton, who had worked so hard, were angry. It would take another 50 years of fighting for women to gain the right to vote.

Putting It All Together

One of the first rights given to African-American men was the vote. Women worked for over 100 years to gain the vote. In your notebook explain why being able to vote is an important right in a democracy.

Return of the South to White Rule

Thinking on Your Own

In your notebook write the title "Rights that Southern African Americans Lost." As you read, write facts that support the title.

Hiram R. Revels

In 1867, with the Radical Republicans in charge of Reconstruction, life in the South changed again. New state constitutions were written. New state legislatures were elected. For the first time, African-American men could vote. Between 1867 and 1877, they elected more than 600 fellow African Americans to the state legislatures. They also sent African Americans to Congress. Hiram Revels, from Mississippi, became the first African-American U.S. senator.

focus your reading

How did white Southerners react to Radical Reconstruction?

What was the Compromise of 1877?

How did Jim Crow laws affect African Americans?

vocabulary

lynch law   Jim Crow

popular vote   discriminated

electoral vote   segregation

Terror Against African Americans

Once the 14th Amendment was ratified, the black codes became unconstitutional. White Southerners could no longer restrict the rights of African Americans through laws. Instead, they used violence.

Secret societies like the Ku Klux Klan were founded. Members dressed in white sheets and rode through the dark of night. They broke into the homes of African Americans and dragged out men and boys. Some they beat and left for dead. Others they lynched. Lynching is putting someone to death,

The KKK was founded in 1865.

The practice of lynching spread throughout the South.

usually by hanging, without a legal trial. **Lynch law** ruled in the South. What had these African Americans done? Some tried to register to vote. Some started stores and other businesses. Some had done nothing. The idea behind the terror was to keep African Americans from trying to vote and better themselves.

African Americans were the biggest supporters of Republican candidates—both white and African American. Without African-American voters, white Democrats were easily elected to state and local offices. These Democrats took back the governments of the Southern states, one by one. By 1876, the South was firmly in the hands of Democrats, except for Florida, Louisiana, and South Carolina. They were still under military rule.

Compromise of 1877

By the 1870s, many Northerners were tired of Reconstruction. The nation's economy was not doing well. People were worried about having jobs and earning enough money to live. They turned away from the problems of African Americans.

In the presidential election of 1876, Republican Rutherford B. Hayes lost the **popular vote** to Democrat Samuel Tilden. But Hayes claimed that he had won the **electoral vote**. He based his claim on vote counts from Florida, Louisiana, and South Carolina. The votes were recounted and Democrats claimed victory.

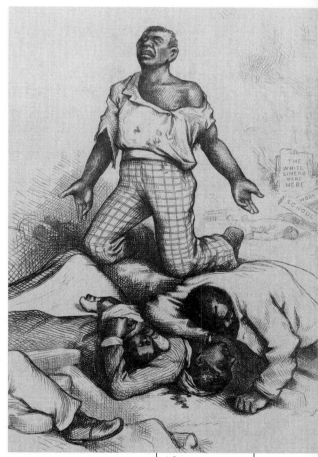

African Americans in the South felt abandoned by the North.

Congress set up a commission to settle the issue. The commission finally worked out a compromise. Hayes was named the winner. In return, he removed the last federal troops from the South. Reconstruction was over and so were the hopes and dreams of millions of former slaves.

"Jim Crow"

After Reconstruction ended, African Americans lost many of their new rights. Southern states passed what were called **"Jim Crow"** laws. These laws **discriminated** against African Americans in all parts of their lives. They could not work in factories. They could not eat in the same places as whites, or shop in the same stores. African-American children could not go to the same schools as white children. There were "whites only" and "blacks only" cars on railroad trains. There were even "whites only" and "blacks only" drinking fountains.

"Jim Crow" became a symbol of repression in the South.

One of the most important civil rights that African Americans lost was the right to vote. Southern states passed laws that took away this right.

African Americans protested their **segregation**. But in 1896, the U.S. Supreme Court upheld Jim Crow laws. In *Plessy* v. *Ferguson,* the Court said that "separate but equal" was constitutional. For example, as long as schools for whites and African Americans were the same, they were legal. In truth, no facility for African Americans was equal to what whites had, but the ruling lasted until 1954.

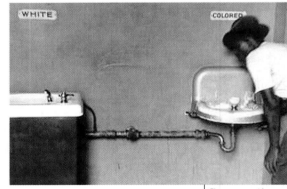

Segregation in the South lasted until the 1950s.

Putting It All Together

Reread the facts that you wrote in your notebook under the title "Rights that Southern African Americans Lost." Think about what you wrote. Choose what you think is the most important fact. Write three or four sentences that explain why it was so important.

Biography

Ida Bell Wells-Barnett (1862–1931)

Ida B. Wells did not start out to be a crusading journalist. She was born into a slave family in Mississippi in 1862. In 1876, Wells began a career as a teacher. She taught first in Mississippi and later in Tennessee.

Wells was never satisfied with the treatment of African Americans. She was only 22 when she sued a railroad. A conductor told her to give up her seat in a "white" section of a railroad car. She refused. When the conductor tried to remove her, she bit him. She was finally dragged off the train by three men. Wells filed a lawsuit against the railroad and won. The railroad appealed and the case was overturned in higher court.

As a teacher in Memphis, Tennessee, Wells was dissatisfied with the education African-American children received. She wrote a series of newspaper articles about the schools. Because of the articles, Wells lost her job.

Wells then joined some friends who owned and ran a local newspaper, *Memphis Free Speech*. It was the 1890s and violence against African-Americans in the South was common. Wells began a campaign to publicize the horrors of lynching. An angry mob attacked the offices of the newspaper.

Wells left Memphis, first for New York City and later for Chicago, but she did not stop her writing. In 1895, she published *A Red Record*. This was the first report on lynching in the United States. In addition, Wells began to give speeches about lynching. She helped organize anti-lynching societies around the nation.

In 1895, Wells married a Chicago lawyer and editor, Ferdinand L. Barnett. She continued to speak and write about lynching. Her research showed that between 1878 and 1898, some 10,000 African Americans were lynched.

Wells-Barnett also worked for women's rights. She founded the first African-American organization devoted to gaining the vote for women. She was also one of the founders of the National Association for the Advancement of Colored People (NAACP).

Chapter Summary

Once the Civil War was over, the Southern states had to return to the Union. President Lincoln began working on a plan for **Reconstruction** in 1863. His idea was to return the Southern states to the Union without punishing them. Some confederates would receive a **pardon**.

Andrew Johnson developed his own plan. Like Lincoln, Johnson did not want to punish the South. The **Radical Republicans** in Congress disagreed with both presidents. They thought that Reconstruction was the job of Congress. They wanted to see the South punished. Their plan included **civil rights** for African Americans. Johnson and the Radical Republicans fought over which plan to use. President Johnson was **impeached** by Congress in 1868, but he was acquitted.

Freed African Americans were facing hard times across the South. The federal Freedmen's Bureau helped. Many African Americans became **sharecroppers**.

White Southerners began to take out their anger over Reconstruction on African Americans. Secret societies like the Ku Klux Klan terrorized former slaves. **Lynch law** and **black codes** helped the whites reinforce **segregation**. **Jim Crow** laws in the South **discriminated** against African Americans. By the 1870s, white Democrats regained control of most Southern state governments.

In the presidential election of 1876, Republican Rutherford B. Hayes won the **electoral vote**, but not the **popular vote**. He was chosen as president in a deal with Southern Democrats, called the Compromise of 1877.

Chapter Review

1 Read your notes from the Thinking on Your Own sections. What surprised you about what happened during Reconstruction? Write a paragraph in your notebook.

2 Suppose you were writing a magazine article about Reconstruction. Choose one idea from this chapter and explain how Reconstruction failed for African Americans.

Skill Builder

Comparing and Contrasting Information

To compare means to look for things that are the same. *To contrast* means to look for things that are different. This chapter gives a great amount of information about Reconstruction. Much of it is about the different plans. One way to understand what was happening is to compare and contrast the plans. An easy way to do this is to make a table like the one below.

Plans for Reconstruction		
Lincoln's Plan	**Johnson's Plan**	**Congress's Plan**
Oath of allegiance for a pardon	Oath of allegiance for a pardon	Establish five military districts in the South
No pardon for officers and government officials	Oath of allegiance, ask president for a pardon for officers and government officials	No plan for officers
Write a new state constitution after 10% took the oath	Write new state constitutions	Write new state constitutions
No guarantee of rights	Repeal secession and refuse to pay Confederate debts	Guarantee equal rights to all male citizens
Hold statewide elections after a new constitution written	Hold statewide elections after a new constitution written	Hold statewide elections
No rights for African Americans	No rights for African Americans	Allow African Americans to vote for delegates to conventions to write new constitutions
No ratification requirement	Ratify the 13th Amendment	Ratify the 14th Amendment

Using the information in the table, answer the following questions:

1 Write one thing that was the same about the three plans.

2 Write one thing that was different between Johnson's plan and Congress's plan.

3 Write one thing that was different between Lincoln's plan and Johnson's plan.

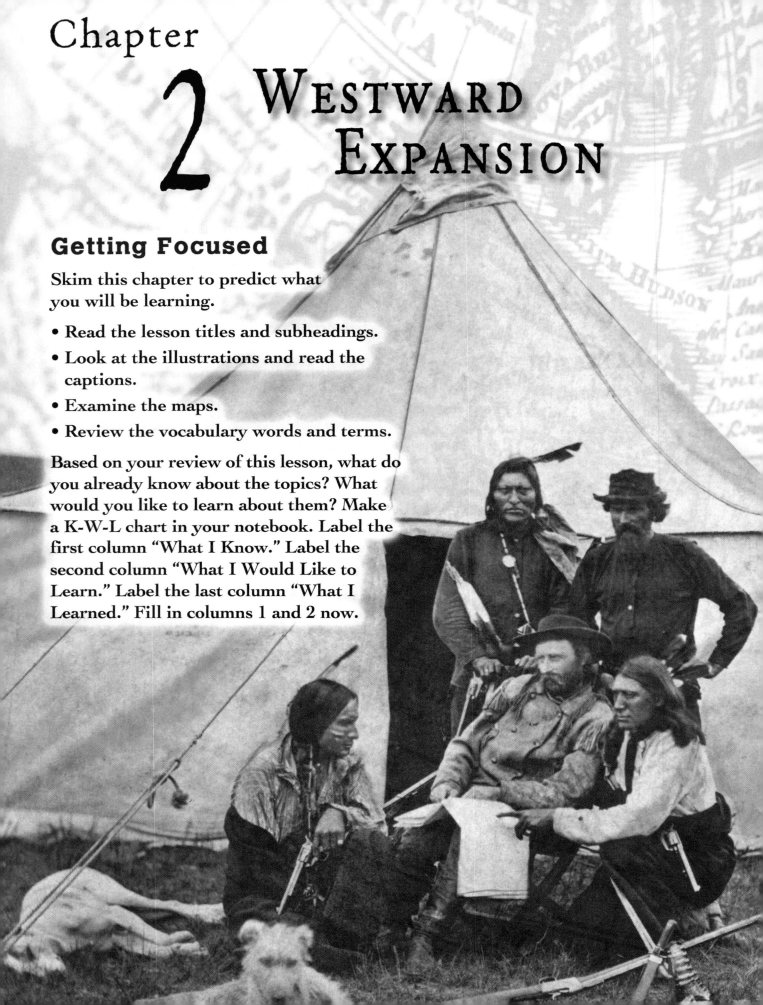

Chapter 2 WESTWARD EXPANSION

Getting Focused

Skim this chapter to predict what you will be learning.

- Read the lesson titles and subheadings.
- Look at the illustrations and read the captions.
- Examine the maps.
- Review the vocabulary words and terms.

Based on your review of this lesson, what do you already know about the topics? What would you like to learn about them? Make a K-W-L chart in your notebook. Label the first column "What I Know." Label the second column "What I Would Like to Learn." Label the last column "What I Learned." Fill in columns 1 and 2 now.

Miners and Ranchers

Thinking on Your Own

The period after the Civil War was a busy one for mining and cattle herding. As you read, make a list of important events in this lesson. Next to each event write the *who, what, where, why*, and *when* of the event.

In the 1830s and 1840s, people who went west traveled all the way to the Far West. They were looking for rich farmland in the Oregon Territory, or they were on their way to the gold fields in California. To get to either place, settlers passed through the Great Plains and over the Rocky Mountains. At that time, the Great Plains were called the Great American Desert. People did not think that crops would grow on the Plains. They thought the region was too dry for farming. People's ideas about the Plains and the mountains began to change in the 1850s.

"Pikes Peak or Bust"

"Pikes Peak or Bust" was the shout of men on their way to dig for gold in the Rockies. In 1858, gold was discovered at Cherry Creek—present-day Denver—in the Kansas Territory. People from the Far West and from the East made their way as fast as they could to the gold field. After the gold rush, the region where gold was found became the Colorado Territory.

The route to Pikes Peak was dangerous, and many people died searching for fortune.

Soon after, gold and silver were found in Nevada. Called the Comstock Lode, it was one of the richest silver and gold **strikes** ever. A **lode** is a source, or deposit, of ore. Throughout the 1860s and 1870s, gold and silver were found in the Dakota, Montana, and Idaho Territories.

Mining Camp to Boom Town

As soon as word of a gold or silver strike got out, people hurried to the site. Miners and shopkeepers often lived in

Mining towns, such as Goldhill, Nevada, grew near gold and silver strikes.

tents. A few people, sometimes women, set up cook tents and sold hot meals. Soon whole tent cities grew up near a gold or silver strike. If the strike turned out to be rich, wood buildings gradually replaced the tents. The tent city became a **boom town**. This is how Virginia City, Nevada, began. It rose from tents near the Comstock Lode.

The discovery of gold and silver quickened the settlement of the West. The population in the territories grew. People began asking for statehood. Nevada became a state in 1864, and Colorado in 1876. By 1890, North Dakota, South Dakota, Montana, and Idaho became states.

stop and think

Imagine you are new to Virginia City. All you see around you are tents. Write a letter back home explaining what you see. Describe where you eat and where you buy supplies. Share your letter with a partner.

Mining Companies

Over time, groups of wealthy men formed companies and bought out miners' claims. Miners went to work for the mining companies and drew paychecks. They earned little for their hard and dangerous work. Mine owners made millions of dollars from their investment.

Cattle Herding on the Plains

In the 1850s, there were no fences on the Plains. The land was **open range**. Millions of longhorn cattle roamed across the southern Plains. In the 1850s, some Texans decided that they could make money by selling the cattle. They hired cowhands to round up herds and take them to New Orleans for sale.

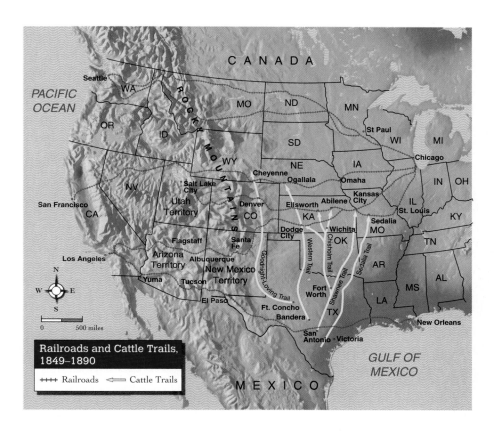

Railroads and Cattle Trails, 1849–1890

+++ Railroads   ⇐ Cattle Trails

Once the Civil War was over, the East seemed to be a better market for cattle. By the 1860s, railroads solved the problem of getting to the cattle market. Cowhands drove the herds to railheads. The first major **railheads** were Abilene and Dodge City, Kansas. At the railheads, the ranchers sold their cattle to buyers from Chicago. The cattle were then shipped in cattle cars to meatpacking plants in Chicago.

Getting the herds from Texas to Kansas took two to three months. The **cattle drive** was a long, dusty, and sometimes dangerous job. Twelve or more cowhands on horseback guided 2,000 or more head of restless cattle north.

The End of the Open Range

Texas ranchers had other customers besides meatpacking companies. They also sold their cattle to mining camps, the U.S. Army, and to people who wanted to start ranches farther north.

The cattle boom on the open range lasted until the 1880s. There were so many cattle for sale that the price dropped. At the same time, farmers were moving onto the Plains and putting up fences. The days of the open range and the long cattle drives were over.

stop and think

Think about the life of a cowhand. What do you think it was like on a cattle drive? Write about a day on a cattle drive. Share your ideas with a partner.

Cattle drives brought large numbers of cattle to railheads.

Putting It All Together

Both mining and cattle ranching changed in less than 40 years. Work with a partner to write one or two sentences explaining how mining changed. Then write one or two sentences explaining how cattle herding changed. Be sure to explain your answers.

Biography

Charles Goodnight (1836–1929)
Oliver Loving (1812–1867)

Not all cattle trails led to railheads in Kansas. The Goodnight-Loving Trail went from Texas, through the New Mexico Territory, to Denver, Colorado, and on to Cheyenne, Wyoming. The cattle on this trail were sold to the army, to miners, and to other ranchers.

The trail is named after Charles Goodnight and Oliver Loving. The two men were partners for two years. Loving was born in Kentucky but moved to Texas and ran cattle herds. Goodnight moved to Texas from Illinois in the 1840s to herd cattle.

While other Texans drove their herds north to Kansas, Goodnight saw an opportunity to the west. There were army posts in the New Mexico Territory. He believed that soldiers would like fresh beef. In 1866, Goodnight, Loving, and 16 cowhands set out with 2,000 head of cattle.

When they reached Fort Sumter in New Mexico, the men sold part of the herd. Much of it was to feed Native Americans on a nearby reservation. Loving sold the rest of the herd in Colorado. This was the beginning of the Goodnight-Loving Trail.

On the second cattle drive to New Mexico, Goodnight and Loving's herd was attacked by Comanches. Loving and another man left the herd to ride to the nearest fort. They were ambushed, and the two men separated. Loving fought off his attackers for three days. He finally escaped by swimming underwater past the Comanches. However, he was seriously wounded and died a few days later at the age of 55. After Loving's death, Goodnight continued to ranch in Texas until his death in 1929, at age 93.

Farmers on the Great Plains

Thinking on Your Own

What do you know about farming on the Great Plains? Write two or three phrases about farming. If you do not know anything about farming, look at the illustrations. Think about what they show. Write three things you notice about farming from the pictures.

Farmers began to settle on the Great Plains in the 1860s. In 1862, the federal government passed the Homestead Act. This act offered 160 acres to anyone who promised to live on and farm the land for five years. Men, single women, and widows could receive land under the act. Between 1862 and 1900, a half-million farms were started on the Plains.

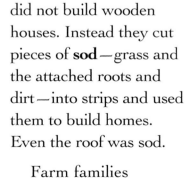

focus your reading

What was life like on a Great Plains farm?

Why was farming difficult on the Plains?

How did farming on the Plains change over time?

vocabulary

sod

technology

dry farming

Farm Life

Farmers often built sod houses on the Plains.

Life on these farms was hard. Winters were bitter cold and summers were blazing hot. Because there were few trees, farmers did not build wooden houses. Instead they cut pieces of **sod**—grass and the attached roots and dirt—into strips and used them to build homes. Even the roof was sod.

Farm families followed the routines of the seasons. The men and boys worked the

fields. The women, girls, and young children worked closer to the house. They grew vegetables in the garden. Many raised chickens and a milk cow. Cooking meals, sewing clothes, and making butter, soap, and candles were all women's work. Women also canned vegetables from the garden for winter meals. During spring planting and autumn harvest times, everyone went to work in the fields.

During planting and harvest times, farm families often joined together to get things done. They also got together to help one another build a house or a barn. One of the first buildings a community built was the school. Barn dances, church services, holiday picnics, and other social events, like quilting bees and parties, brought people together.

stop and think

Think about what life was like on a farm. Would you have moved to the Great Plains to start a farm? Explain why or why not. Write your answers in your notebook. Use the information in this lesson to support your opinion.

Social events were an important part of life on the Plains.

Farming on the Plains

Sod made strong houses, but it made farming on the Plains difficult. The grasses had long, tough roots that were hard to break apart. In addition, there was little rain on the Plains. To solve their problems, farmers bought new **technologies** and tried a new way to farm.

The first new technology was the steel plow. Steel is much harder than iron. The steel blades on the plow made it easier to break apart the ground. Grain drills allowed farmers to plant several rows of seed at once. Threshing machines made removing grains of wheat from the plant faster and easier.

One important invention was barbed wire. Farmers strung it between fence posts to mark off their land. The fences also kept cattle from roaming into fields. Barbed wire fences were one reason cattle ranching changed in the 1880s.

Barbed wire was patented in 1867.

Joseph Glidden invented a machine for mass-producing barbed wire.

Many places on the Great Plains were very dry. In those places, farmers used **dry farming** methods. They cut deep ditches between the rows of plants. Whatever rain fell could reach the roots of the plants more easily. Farmers also began raising crops like winter wheat. Winter wheat is planted in the fall and begins to grow in the spring when the ground still has moisture. It is harvested before the start of the hot summer.

Putting It All Together

Why was farming hard on the Plains? Make a T-chart labeled "Farming on the Plains." On one side write "Hard" and on the other side, "Easier." List two reasons why farming was hard. Then list ways that farmers were able to make it easier.

Native Americans and Western Expansion

Thinking on Your Own

Review the vocabulary list. As you read, try to figure out what each word means from its use in the sentence. You might have to read a couple of sentences before and after the sentence with the word in it. Write in your notebook what you think each word means. Compare the meaning in the Glossary with your meaning.

Some Native American Nations lived on the Plains for many centuries. Others were forced onto the Plains by the arrival of Europeans.

There were no horses in the Americas until the Spanish brought them to Mexico in the 1500s. As bands of Native Americans gained horses, they began hunting buffalo on horseback. Before then, they had hunted buffalo on foot.

focus your reading

Why were buffalo important to Plains Native Americans?

Why did Native Americans fight settlers and the U.S. Army?

How was the Dawes Act supposed to help Native Americans?

vocabulary

nomad   Americanize

reservation

The Plains Way of Life

Plains Native Americans depended on the buffalo for food, shelter, and clothing. They ate mostly buffalo meat. They sewed together buffalo skins, or hides, to make their clothes and their tepee coverings. The Plains Native Americans were **nomads**. They followed the buffalo herds as they wandered looking for grass to eat.

The Plains People also ate other foods. The women gathered nuts, berries, wild plants, and roots to add to meals. The Plains People were not farmers, but they depended on the land in order to live.

Clashes with Settlers

As early as the 1840s, settlers and Native Americans clashed. The settlers were on their way to the Oregon Territory. Their route lay through Native American lands.

In 1851, the federal government began making treaties with Native Americans in these areas. The government wanted land that could be traveled safely by wagon trains. In return, the government agreed to set aside lands for different Native American people. The U.S. Army would keep others out of these lands. The Native Americans would stay within these lands and not attack settlers on the Oregon Trail. Some chiefs distrusted the government. But in the end, they had little choice. Most chiefs signed the first Fort Laramie Treaty.

Sitting Bull

Broken Treaties and the Indian Wars

Peace did not last long. In the late 1850s, gold was found in Colorado on land given to the Cheyenne and Arapaho under the 1851 treaty. The U.S. Army forced the Native Americans off the land. Fighting lasted for several years between Native Americans and settlers. In 1864, Colorado militia attacked a large Native American camp that had surrendered to the United States. The attack has become known as the Sand Creek Massacre.

This set off a series of wars. Fighting between Native Americans and settlers and the army occurred during much of the 1860s. In 1867 and 1868, the federal government again asked Native

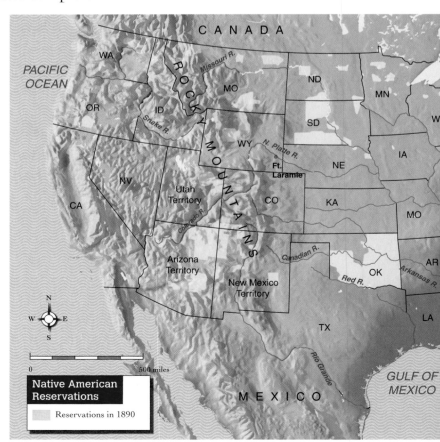

Native American Reservations

Reservations in 1890

Americans to come to Fort Laramie. This time government officials told the chiefs that they would have to go to **reservations** in the Dakota, Montana, Wyoming, and Indian Territories. Under the treaty, Native Americans would have these lands forever.

"Forever" only lasted until 1874. In that year, gold was discovered in the Black Hills in the Dakota Territory. By 1876, thousands of miners had set up camps. The Lakota and other Native American people attacked the trespassers.

William T. Sherman and the Sioux sign the Fort Laramie Treaty in 1868.

The fighting reached a turning point in the summer of 1876. A small group of Seventh Cavalry under Colonel George A. Custer was defeated by the Lakota and Cheyenne at the Battle of the Little Bighorn River. Custer disobeyed orders and attacked the Native Americans. His 264 soldiers were no match for more than 2,000 Native Americans. Angry about the massacre, the army pursued the Native Americans. Within one year, most of the Native Americans had returned to the reservations.

George Armstrong Custer

End of the Plains Way of Life

Ranchers and farmers wanted the land where the Native Americans wandered. The railroads, too, needed land for their track. But the railroads had another impact on Native Americans.

In order to feed the crews that laid the tracks, the railroads hired sharpshooters to kill buffalo. Railroads also brought sport hunters to the Plains. In all, some 13 million buffalo were killed in the years after the Civil War.

Without the buffalo, the Plains People lost their main source of food.

The Dawes Act

By the 1880s, a number of non-Native Americans were upset by the treatment of the Native People. These reformers asked the government to change its policies. They wanted an end to reservations and a way to help Native Americans become independent. The result was the Dawes Act. According to the law, reservation land was divided into small farms, each head of a family received 160 acres, and individuals received 80 acres. Unused land could be sold to non-Native Americans. Children were to be sent to special schools to learn American ways.

stop and think

Imagine you are Chief Sitting Bull of the Lakota. Write five bulleted notes that explain why Native Americans fought the settlers and the army. Share your notes with a partner. Are your ideas the same or different?

40,000 buffalo hides are stacked in Dodge City, Kansas, in 1878.

There were a number of problems with the Dawes Act. Plains Native Americans were not farmers. They were hunters. Much of the land that was given to them was not good for farming. Millions of acres were sold by Native People to whites. Under the Dawes Act, 138 million acres of land had been set aside for Native Americans. By 1934, whites owned more than half the land.

The purpose of the Dawes Act was to **Americanize** Native Americans. It did not work. Native Americans were still on land away from white society. There was only one way for Native Americans to become part of white society. They had to give up their language, religion, and customs, and move away from their people.

Putting It All Together

How was the Dawes Act supposed to help Native Americans? Make that idea your topic sentence. Then write a paragraph of three or four sentences to explain the Dawes Act. Share your paragraph with a partner. Ask if your paragraph has the most important information about the Dawes Act.

Read a Primary Source

Sarah Winnemucca (c. 1844–1891): Crusader for Native Americans

Sarah Winnemucca was born about 1844. Her grandfather and father were both chiefs of the Paiute Nation in western Nevada. The Paiutes, like other Native American people, were forced onto reservations by the U.S. government. Agents working for the government cheated them out of their food and other supplies. To help the Paiutes, Winnemucca published her autobiography *Life Among the Paiutes: Their Wrongs and Claims.* She then traveled around the country speaking out on behalf of the Paiutes.

reading for understanding

What did the Paiutes do to help themselves on their new reservation?

What was the $25,000 for?

What did Winnemucca think happened to the money?

66 The first work that my people did on the reservation was to dig a ditch, to put up a grist-mill and a saw-mill. . . . They dug about a mile; but the saw-mill and the grist-mill were never seen or heard of by my people, though the printed report in the United States Statutes . . . says twenty-five thousand dollars was appropriated. Where did it go? The report says these mills were sold for the benefit of the Indians who were paid in lumber for houses, but no stick of lumber have they ever received. My people do not own any timber land now. The white people are using the ditch which my people made to irrigate their land. This is the way we are treated by our white brothers. Is it that the government is cheated by its own agents who make these reports? 99

Sarah Winnemucca, (ed. Mrs. Horace Mann)
Life Among the Paiutes: Their Wrongs and Claims
(Boston: Cupples, Upham, and Co. 1883)

Chapter Summary

In the mid-1800s, people were looking at the Rocky Mountains and the Great Plains with new interest. Gold and silver **strikes** brought many people to the **boom towns** of Colorado, Dakota, Montana, and Idaho Territories. One of the biggest strikes was the Comstock **Lode** in Nevada. So many people moved to the West that six new western states were added to the Union between 1861 and 1890.

Among the first people to see opportunity on the Great Plains were cattlemen. The cattlemen rounded up the cattle on the **open range** and took them north on **cattle drives**. The cattlemen sold the cattle at railheads for shipment to meatpacking plants.

People thought the Great Plains were too dry to farm. The hard-packed **sod** was also a problem. But **dry farming** methods and new **technologies**, such as steel plows, made farming possible.

The losers in all this settlement were the Native Americans. At first, the federal government signed peace treaties and set up **reservations** to keep Native Americans separate from everyone else. The government wanted to **Americanize** Native Americans. The policy failed and many **nomadic** people lost their way of life.

Chapter Review

1 Go back to the K-W-L table in your notebook that you started at the beginning of this chapter. Fill in column 3, "What I Learned."

2 Read column 3 in your K-W-L table. What was the most important, the most interesting, or the most surprising fact you learned? Choose one idea and write a paragraph about it in your notebook. Explain why you think it is important, interesting, or surprising.

3 Imagine you are writing a report on westward expansion. You will write four sections entitled "Miners," "Ranchers," "Farmers on the Plains," and "Native Americans." Write three facts that should be included in each section.

Skill Builder

Using a Flowchart to Identify Cause and Effect

When you look for a cause, you are looking for why something happened. When you look for an effect of something that happened, you are looking for a result, or a change.

Example: Putting up fences on the open range changed cattle ranching.

Cause: putting up fences ⟶ **Effect:** a change in cattle ranching

Authors sometimes use certain words to signal cause and effect. Some words that signal a cause are *because, so,* and *since.* Some words that signal an effect are *then, as a result, result,* and *affect.* For example, Lesson 1 says: "Because there were few trees, farmers did not build wooden houses."

When you read, you can use a flowchart to help figure out causes and effects.

Cause: few trees ⟶ **Effect:** did not build wooden houses

Sometimes authors do not use signal words. You have to think about what you are reading to figure out what is the cause and what is the effect.

Read the following sets of sentences from this chapter. Create a cause-and-effect flowchart in your notebook for each set.

1. "In 1858, gold was discovered at Cherry Creek—present-day Denver—in the Kansas Territory. People from the Far West and from the East made their way as fast as they could to the gold field."

2. "Sod made strong houses, but it made farming on the Plains difficult. The grasses had long, tough roots that were hard to break apart."

3. "In order to feed the crews that laid the tracks, the railroads hired sharpshooters to kill buffalo."

2 UNIT

THE NATION IN THE LATE 1800S

By 1900, the United States had expanded from the Atlantic to the Pacific. It was a nation of small farms, giant factories and mills, and cities. The construction of railroads across the nation helped to change America. The growth of industry created great wealth for some and great hardship for others. Workers formed unions to fight for better working conditions. Farmers, too, joined together to fight the unfair practices of big business. Many of these workers and farmers were among the millions of immigrants who came to the United States in the 1800s.

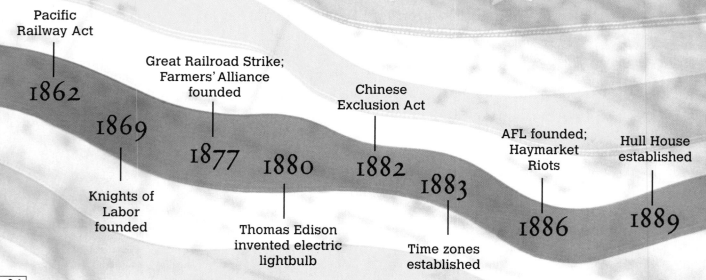

Pacific Railway Act

1862

1869
Knights of Labor founded

Great Railroad Strike; Farmers' Alliance founded

1877

1880
Thomas Edison invented electric lightbulb

Chinese Exclusion Act

1882

1883
Time zones established

AFL founded; Haymarket Riots

1886

Hull House established

1889

Why did so many people come to the United States in the 1800s?

Why did cities grow so quickly in the late 1800s?

How did industry power the growth of the United States?

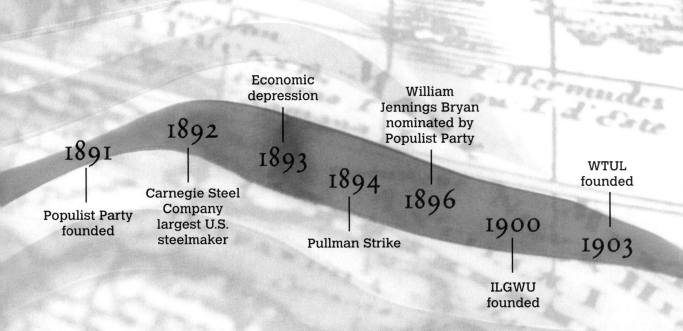

1891
Populist Party founded

1892
Carnegie Steel Company largest U.S. steelmaker

Economic depression
1893

1894
Pullman Strike

William Jennings Bryan nominated by Populist Party
1896

1900
ILGWU founded

WTUL founded
1903

Chapter

3 BUSINESS AND LABOR UNIONS

Getting Focused

Skim this chapter to predict what you will be learning.

- Read the lesson titles and subheadings.
- Look at the illustrations and read the captions.
- Examine the maps.
- Review the vocabulary words and terms.

Imagine working on the transcontinental railroad or in a factory in the late 1800s. Which job would you want? Write in your notebook a list of four reasons you would want the job.

The Growth of Railroads

Thinking on Your Own

Create a concept map for this lesson. Label the circle in the center "The Growth of Railroads." As you read the lesson, look for information about why and how railroads were built. Write the information in smaller circles. Use the vocabulary words.

Before the Civil War, there were no railroads west of the Mississippi River. The building of the transcontinental railroad brought great changes to America. Building a railroad cost a great deal of money. Investors were not interested in putting their money into railroads where few people lived. Most of the early railroads were built with money from local business owners and farmers. They were eager to have a way to transport goods quickly and easily.

focus your reading

How did the land grant system work?

Why was building the transcontinental railroad so difficult?

How did the growth of railroads help the nation?

vocabulary

land grant

transcontinental railroad

rail line

time zone

Steam engines brought goods to small towns like St. Peter, Minnesota, during the 1870s.

Early Railroads

In the 1830s and 1840s, most railroads were in the Northeast. These early railroads were short lines. In the 1850s, the United States government decided to help build railroads.

Congress wanted to speed the development of the Midwest. Railroads would do that by moving settlers, supplies, and farm products quickly, cheaply, and easily. Congress gave **land grants**, or gifts of land, to railroad companies. Those companies would then sell the land to settlers. The money from the sale was used to help pay the cost of building railroads.

The Transcontinental Railroads

The Pacific Railway Act of 1862 gave land grants to build a **transcontinental railroad**. The government gave the companies 10 square miles of land for each mile of track laid. The more track a railroad laid, the more land it would receive. This meant that the railroads would make more money from land sales.

Chinese laborers worked to build the Central Pacific Railroad.

The Central Pacific started from Sacramento, California. The Union Pacific began in Omaha, Nebraska. The Central Pacific workers had to work up, over, and through the Sierra Nevada mountain range. Pay was low and the work was dangerous. To find enough workers, the company hired men from China. These Chinese laborers dug and blasted their way through solid rock to create 18 tunnels. Once out of the mountains, they had to lay track across the desert.

Irish immigrants worked for the Union Pacific. Their work was mostly through the Great Plains. At Promontory Point, Utah, on May 10, 1869, the Chinese workers met the Irish workers. The Transcontinental Railroad was complete.

A National Network of Railroads

The 1870s and 1880s saw the combining of older railroads into new, longer ones. For example, the New York Central was bought by Cornelius Vanderbilt. He added it to his other railroads. The result was a huge system that stretched from New York State to Chicago, Illinois.

stop and think

What dangers did the Chinese workers face on the job? Research the topic in the library or on the Internet. Describe the dangers in your notebook.

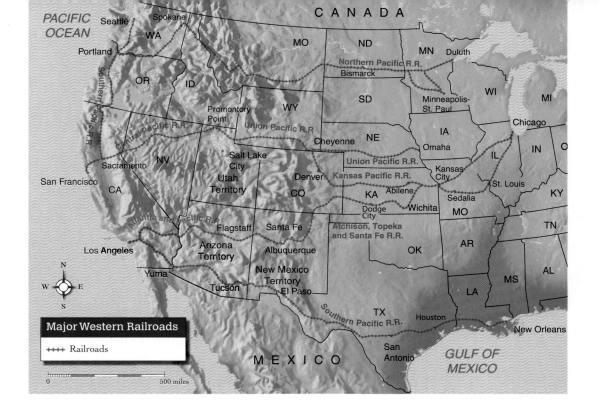

Major Western Railroads

+ + + + Railroads

0   500 miles

By 1890, a national network of railroads had been created. People and goods could travel from coast to coast completely by train. A factory in New England could ship its goods to stores in California. The costs of moving people and goods dropped. Towns and cities grew up along **rail lines**.

By 1900, Chicago was a major railroad city.

Time Zones

From the beginning of the nation until 1883, there was no standard time. It could be noon in St. Louis but another time in a town a few miles away. In 1883, the American Railway Association divided the United States into four **time zones**. The clocks in every place in a time zone were now set to the same time.

Putting It All Together

Choose one idea about how or why railroads were built from your concept map. Write a paragraph to explain this idea.

Biography

Leland Stanford (1824–1893)

Leland Stanford was one of the thousands of people who went to California during the gold rush of 1849. He did not go to dig for gold. He and five of his brothers opened and ran stores in the gold fields.

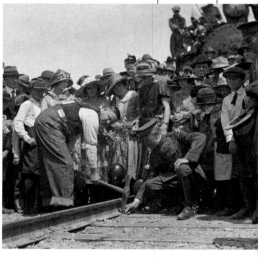

Stanford driving the final spike, May 10, 1869

The Stanfords were born and raised in Albany, New York. Leland was 28 and already a successful lawyer when he moved to California. When Stanford left for California, there was no transcontinental railroad. There were three ways to get there from the East. One way was overland by wagon train. Another was to sail down the East Coast, go west around the tip of South America, and sail north along the West Coast. Stanford took the third way. He went by ship to the isthmus of Panama, went overland to the Pacific, and then sailed north along the coast to California. Any of these ways could take four to six months. Stanford decided that a faster way was needed to move goods and people back and forth from east to west.

Stanford talked with three other businessmen in Sacramento—Collis Huntington, Mark Hopkins, and Charles Crocker. Together, they set up the Central Pacific Railroad in 1861 and sold shares in the corporation. Stanford was named president. In addition to stockholders' money, the "Big Four" used money from government land grants and government bonds to fund the railroad. On May 10, 1869, Stanford drove the final spike to celebrate the nation's first transcontinental railroad. The trip from Missouri to California now took only six days. Stanford had his faster route.

Stanford was also busy in California politics. He helped organize the Republican Party in the state in the 1850s and became governor in 1861. Californians elected Stanford to the U.S. Senate in 1885 and 1891. Stanford and his wife, Jane Lathrop Stanford, founded Stanford University in 1891. It was named in honor of their son Leland, Jr., who died at age 15. Today, the university is one of the world's leading educational institutions.

The Growth of Industry

Thinking on Your Own

Read the Focus Your Reading questions. Keep them in mind as you read the lesson. They will help you look for important information. As you read, make notes in your notebook to help you answer each question.

By 1900, the United States was fast becoming the greatest industrial nation in the world. Why? How did businesses go from small factories to giant mills? With the **mechanization** of production, large industries grew. Production in America went from skilled hand laborers to laborers tending large machines.

focus your reading

What five things do industries need in order to grow?

How did Andrew Carnegie build Carnegie Steel?

How did John D. Rockefeller build Standard Oil?

vocabulary

mechanization

industry

corporation

monopoly

horizontal integration

trust

vertical integration

How Did Industry Develop?

Industry is the name given to businesses involved in manufacturing, transportation, and communications. To develop into a large industry, such as steelmaking, there needs to be money to invest, natural resources, a market, a large workforce, and a transportation system. The national network of railroads was an important factor. Trains brought raw materials like coal, iron ore, and cattle to factories in the Midwest and Northeast. The factories produced mining equipment and farm tools like steel plows. The railroads carried these goods back across the nation to people eager to buy them. The late 1800s also saw a flood of new inventions and technologies. Some made work more efficient and cheaper, like the diesel engine, elevator, telephone, and typewriter. Other inventions made people's lives at home easier, like the lightbulb, electric-powered stove, and sewing machine.

One of the most important discoveries was how to use electricity. Thomas Edison figured out how to use electric power for light in 1879. The central power station was also his idea. Electric power was generated in one place and sent over wires to homes, factories, offices, and businesses. Some inventions helped create whole new industries.

Thomas Edison invented the lightbulb, phonograph, motion picture, and many other useful items.

The Steel Industry

One of the early industries to benefit from new technologies was the steel industry. Steel was much stronger than iron, but it was costly to manufacture. The price dropped greatly when a new production method was discovered. The new Bessemer process made it possible to produce steel cheaply.

When Andrew Carnegie first saw the Bessemer process in the 1870s, he was already a wealthy man. He had invested in businesses that made goods for the railroads. Carnegie realized that steel could transform the railroad business—and other businesses as well. In 1875, he built a huge steel mill near Pittsburgh, Pennsylvania.

Andrew Carnegie

Carnegie was correct. The demand for steel skyrocketed over the next few years. Thousands of miles of new steel railroad track were laid. Because steel was so strong, bridges were soon built of steel. With steel skeletons, buildings could be taller. Suddenly, skyscrapers were being built in city after city.

Carnegie continued to expand his business. By 1892, Carnegie Steel Company was the largest producer of steel in the United States. It was also one of the largest **corporations**. A corporation is a business that sells stock to shareholders and uses the money to invest in the business.

Braddoch, Pennsylvania, was home to Carnegie Steel.

The Oil Industry

John D. Rockefeller was important in the oil industry. Oil was not discovered in the United States until 1859. By 1863, Rockefeller decided that the oil business had great possibilities. He built his first oil refinery near Cleveland, Ohio. By 1870, his company was known as Standard Oil of Ohio. By 1880, Standard Oil owned 90 percent of the oil refineries in the United States. It bought out most of its competitors. If the company owned 100 percent of the oil companies, it would have been a **monopoly**.

John D. Rockefeller

"Big Business"

In building their wealth, men like Carnegie and Rockefeller created huge businesses. To do this, they set up new kinds of business organizations.

Rockefeller built his business through **horizontal integration**. First, he bought out other oil refining companies. To grow even more, Rockefeller and his partners set up a **trust**. Laws in some states prevented one company from owning stock, or shares, in another company. The goal of these laws was to prevent monopolies. The trust was meant to get around these laws.

Stockholders exchanged their stock in an oil company for shares in the trust. The trust then managed the oil company

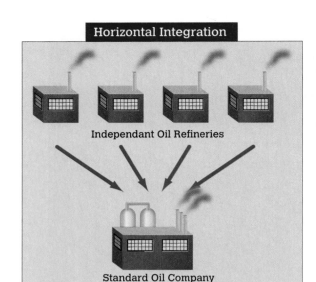

Horizontal Integration

Independant Oil Refineries

Standard Oil Company

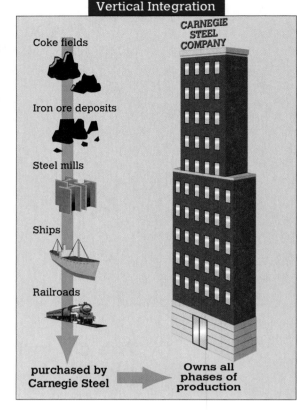

Vertical Integration

Coke fields

Iron ore deposits

Steel mills

Ships

Railroads

CARNEGIE STEEL COMPANY

purchased by Carnegie Steel

Owns all phases of production

and all the other companies in the trust. In all, 40 oil companies were part of the Standard Oil Trust. Rockefeller controlled the trust.

Andrew Carnegie built his corporation through **vertical integration**. Like Rockefeller, he bought competitors.

However, Carnegie also bought companies that provided raw materials and goods for his company. Steel is made from iron ore, so Carnegie bought iron mines. Coal fueled the furnaces that heated the iron, so Carnegie bought coal mines. These raw materials had to be shipped to his steel mills, and the finished steel had to be shipped to buyers. Carnegie bought railroads. In this way, Carnegie made sure Carnegie Steel always controlled the raw materials and transportation that it needed.

stop and think

Explain to a partner the difference between horizontal integration and vertical integration. Use the diagrams to help you. When you have your explanation clear and correct, write it in your notebook.

Putting It All Together

Imagine you are the owner of a small oil refinery. John D. Rockefeller has offered to buy you out. What would you do? With a partner, think of reasons to sell. Then think of reasons not to sell. Explain your decision in your notebook.

The Rise of Labor Unions

Thinking on Your Own

Many of the goals of the different labor organizations in the late 1800s were the same, but there were also differences. Create a table with three columns in your notebook. Label the columns: "Knights of Labor," "AFL," and "WTUL." As you read, list the goals of each union in these columns.

As early as the 1830s, some factory workers in the United States tried to organize labor unions. These early efforts did not last. Most workers were scared of losing their jobs and did not join the early unions. By the 1860s, however, workers were beginning to see the value of labor unions. No longer could they talk directly to their bosses. Workers reasoned that their demands would have more of an impact if they came from large unions.

focus your reading

What were the goals of the Knights of Labor?

What were the goals of the AFL?

What caused the major labor strikes of the late 1800s?

vocabulary

industrial union

craft union

collective bargaining

strikebreakers

This poster, in German and English, announces a meeting before the Haymarket Riot of 1886.

The Noble Order of the Knights of Labor

The first successful labor organization was the Knights of Labor. The Knights were a secret organization, made up of skilled craftworkers. In 1869, several lodges organized an **industrial union**. This means both skilled and unskilled workers within the same industry could be members. For example, a train conductor and a train cleaner would both be members of an industrial railroad union.

Attention Workingmen!

GREAT

MASS-MEETING

TO-NIGHT, at 7.30 o'clock,

AT THE

HAYMARKET, Randolph St., Bet. Desplaines and Halsted.

Good Speakers will be present to denounce the latest atrocious act of the police, the shooting of our fellow-workmen yesterday afternoon.

Workingmen Arm Yourselves and Appear in Full Force!

THE EXECUTIVE COMMITTEE.

Achtung, Arbeiter!

Große

Massen-Versammlung

Heute Abend, 8 Uhr, auf dem

Heumarkt, Randolph-Straße, zwischen Desplaines- u. Halsted-Str.

Gute Redner werden den neuesten Schurkenstreich der Polizei, indem sie gestern Nachmittag unsere Brüder erschoß, geißeln.

Arbeiter, bewaffnet Euch und erscheint massenhaft!

Das Executiv-Comite.

Frank J. Ferrell addresses the Knights of Labor in Richmond, Virginia.

The Knights welcomed African Americans, women, and immigrants as members. Among their goals were the eight-hour workday, equal wages for women, and an end to child labor. A violent strike caused many members to leave the organization. By the 1890s, the Knights had disappeared.

The American Federation of Labor

The American Federation of Labor (AFL) was more successful than other labor groups. The AFL was not one union, but groups of craft, or trade, unions. A **craft union** has only skilled workers as members. The AFL was founded by 20 individual craft unions in 1886. They decided that there was power in numbers. For example, construction companies employed carpenters. If all the companies dealt with the AFL rather than individual carpenters' unions, the workers thought they would be more successful in achieving their demands.

Samuel L. Gompers, the president of the Cigar Makers Union, was elected president of the AFL. He served from 1886 to 1894 and from 1895 to 1924. Gompers favored **collective bargaining** over strikes. Collective bargaining is an attempt to negotiate contracts between workers and employers. The goals of the AFL were the eight-hour workday, higher wages, safer working conditions, and benefits for injured workers.

Watermelon was a popular treat at Labor Day picnics.

stop and think

Imagine you are a member of the AFL. You are working 10-hour days. Write a paragraph explaining why workers should have an eight-hour workday. Share your paragraph with a partner. Discuss the reasons you each gave to support an eight-hour workday.

African Americans, women, and immigrants had no place in the original AFL. The AFL still exists. In 1955, it joined with the Congress of Industrial Organizations (CIO), and together they became the AFL-CIO.

Strikes

The nation was going through difficult economic times in the late 1800s. Some companies were cutting wages and increasing working hours. Workers called for strikes.

The strike was the major tool that workers had against their employers. If workers were unsuccessful in getting higher wages or better working conditions, they tried to close down the company. They refused to work and set up picket lines in front of the business. They wanted to keep **strikebreakers** from entering and going to work. Strikebreakers are people hired to replace workers who are on strike.

Strikes often became violent when tempers flared.

Companies hired recent immigrants or African Americans as strikebreakers. Companies also asked the government to send troops to open factories or rail lines to nonstriking workers. If a strike was not already violent, the arrival of troops could lead to violence.

Women Workers and Unions

Up until the late 1800s, educated women who worked outside the home were often teachers and nurses. In the 1890s, women began working as secretaries in offices or as department store clerks. Often, immigrant women found jobs as servants or in factories.

Women and men sew garments in an east coast factory.

In 1900, workers in the women's clothing industry founded the International Ladies Garment Workers Union (ILGWU). In 1903, the Women's Trade Union League (WTUL) was founded to unionize women in the laundry, garment, and telephone industries. The goals of the WTUL were similar to the goals of the AFL: an eight-hour workday, a minimum wage, and an end to child labor.

Putting It All Together

Read the three columns you made with the goals of the Knights of Labor, the AFL, and the WTUL. Notice which goals are the same and which are different. Write a sentence stating the goals that are the same. Write a sentence stating the goals that are different. Take turns with a partner and quiz each other on the goals of the different unions.

Read a Primary Source

Samuel L. Gompers (1850–1924)

Samuel L. Gompers came to the United States from London in 1863. At the young age of 13, he was already a cigar maker. In New York, he joined the Cigar Makers Union and, in time, became its president. Gompers was one of the founders of the American Federation of Labor. The following is from a speech Gompers gave in 1890 about an eight-hour workday for skilled workers.

What Does the Working Man Want?

"We want eight hours. . . . We have been accused of being selfish, and it has been said that we will want more; that last year we got an advance of ten cents and now we want more. We do want more. You will find that a man generally wants more. . . . You ask a workingman, who is getting two dollars a day, and he will say that he wants ten cents more. Ask a man who gets five dollars a day and he will want fifty cents more. . . . We live in the latter part of the Nineteenth century. In the age of electricity and steam that has produced wealth a hundred fold, we insist that it has been brought about by the intelligence and energy of the workingmen, and while we find that it is now easier to produce, it is harder to live. We do want more, and when it becomes more, we shall still want more. [Applause] And we shall never cease to demand more until we have received the results of our labor."

Samuel L. Gompers,
Reprinted in the *Louisville Courier Journal*,
May 2, 1890

---

reading for understanding

What argument do people use against giving workers an eight-hour workday?

What does Gompers say about this argument?

According to Gompers, how has the nation's wealth been produced?

Chapter Summary

One of the most important changes in the mid-1800s was the growth of railroads. The federal government gave **land grants** to railroad companies. In 1862, the Central Pacific and the Union Pacific Railroad began to build a **transcontinental railroad**. The Central Pacific started in California. The Union Pacific began in Nebraska. The two railroads joined at Promontory Point, Utah. By 1900, **rail lines** crisscrossed the United States from one **time zone** to another.

Both railroads and scientific discoveries helped the **mechanization** and growth of **industry**. Large **corporations** were created.

Andrew Carnegie created the Carnegie Steel Company through **vertical integration**. John D. Rockefeller built his Standard Oil Company through **horizontal integration**. Standard Oil owned so many oil companies that it was almost a **monopoly**. Rockefeller set up a **trust** to manage additional oil companies.

The late 1800s saw the rise of labor unions. The first large national labor organization was the Knights of Labor. It was an organization of both skilled and unskilled laborers, called an **industrial union**. The American Federation of Labor (AFL) was founded as a **craft union**. It used **collective bargaining** to try to gain its workers' demands. When workers called for strikes, employers called in **strikebreakers**.

Chapter Review

1 Make a list of things you want in an ideal job. Compare your list to what union members fought for in the 1800s. Write three or four sentences that compare your list to workers' demands in the 1800s. Talk with a partner about how much jobs have changed since the late 1800s.

2 The creation of time zones was important to the economy. Write a short editorial to convince people that time zones are necessary. Use information from the chapter to support your arguments.

Skill Builder

Analyzing a Table

Tables are useful tools for sorting information. Tables often present information that is not included in the text. The table shown below, "Major Strikes of the Late 1800s," lists basic information about important strikes. Column 1 lists the types of information that you will find in each row. Columns 2 through 5 list each of the major strikes.

This table is also set up to allow you to compare and contrast information. Suppose you want to compare the causes of the Haymarket Riots with the causes of the Pullman Strike. Read down column 1 to row 4, "Causes." Then read down column 2, "Haymarket Riots," and column 5, "Pullman Strike," to row 4.

1 What company did workers strike in the Homestead Strike?

2 What was the cause of the Great Railroad Strike of 1877?

3 Were the effects of the Haymarket Riots and the Homestead Strike the same or different? Explain your answer in two or three sentences.

Major Strikes of the Late 1800s

Strike	Great Railroad Strike	Haymarket Riots	Homestead Strike	Pullman Strike
Year/City	1877 Began in Martinsburg, West Virginia, and spread through the Midwest	1886 Haymarket Square, Chicago, Illinois	1892 Homestead, Pennsylvania	1894 Pullman, Illinois
Industry/Company	Baltimore & Ohio Railroad	Factory works across Chicago	Carnegie Steel Company	Pullman Company (made railroad cars)
Causes	Workers protested wage cuts by the railroad.	Workers protested police actions against an earlier local strike.	The company demanded a wage cut and a 70-hour work week.	The company cut wages and fired the union leader.
Effects	• Workers destroyed rails, train stations, and train cars. • Federal troops were called in to end the strike. The strikers went back to work.	• Seven police were killed by a bomb. • Seven radicals tried, sentenced to death; four were hanged. • The public tied the riots unfairly to the Knights of Labor.	• Several workers and private guards were killed. State militia broke up the strike. • Strikers went back to work; the union broke up.	• Chicago had no trains for 2 months; 27 states had partial or no train services. • Federal troops broke up the strike; 22 strikers were killed.

Chapter 4

A Time of Hope and Hardship

Getting Focused

Skim this chapter to predict what you will be learning.

- Read the lesson titles and subheadings.
- Look at the illustrations and read the captions.
- Examine the maps.
- Review the vocabulary words and terms.

Write three or four sentences in your notebook to explain how the chapter title and the lesson titles might be related.

Immigrants in Search of Better Lives

Thinking on Your Own

Think about immigration to the United States today. In your notebook, write as many ideas about modern immigrants as you can think of in two minutes. When you have finished, sort your ideas into categories. Possible categories might be "Why People Come," "Where They Live," or "What Kind of Work They Do."

Between 1820 and 1920, more than 33 million people moved to the United States. These **immigrants** came from other countries to make a better life for themselves and their families. Immigrants are people who move from one country to settle in another.

Railroads sold land in the West to immigrant farmers.

Old Immigration and New Immigration

Historians divide American immigration in the 1800s into **Old Immigration** and **New Immigration**. Members of the "Old" group came to the United States between 1840 and 1890. Most of these people came from northern and western Europe. Beginning in the 1850s, several thousand Chinese also came.

The New Immigration grew rapidly after 1890. Many of these people came from southern and eastern Europe. This group also included people from Mexico, other nations in Latin America, and Japan.

PRODUCTS WILL PAY FOR LAND AND IMPROVEMENTS!

MILLIONS OF ACRES

IOWA AND NEBRASKA LANDS

FOR SALE ON **10** YEARS CREDIT

BY THE

Burlington & Missouri River R.R.Co.

AT 6 PER CT. INTEREST AND LOW PRICES.

Only One-Seventh of Principal Due Annually, beginning Four Years after purchase.

20 PER CENT. DEDUCTED FROM 10 YEARS PRICE, FOR CASH.

LAND EXPLORING TICKETS SOLD

and Cost allowed in First Interest paid, on Land bought in 30 days from date of ticket.

Address GEO. S. HARRIS, LAND COMMISSIONER,

or T. H. LEAVITT, Ass't Land Comm'r, Burlington, Iowa.

Or apply to

FREE ROOMS for buyers to board themselves are provided at Burlington and Lincoln.

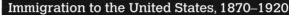

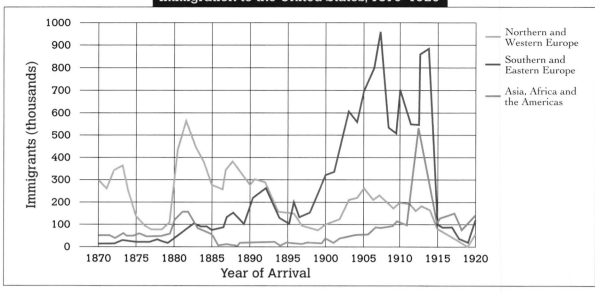

Immigrants (thousands) / Year of Arrival

Legend:
- Northern and Western Europe
- Southern and Eastern Europe
- Asia, Africa and the Americas

Pushing Immigrants

The New Immigrants were very different from the native-born Americans. Most were even different from the Old Immigrants in their clothing, religion, and languages. Both Old and New Immigrants shared many of the same reasons for coming to America.

The reasons that forced people to leave their native countries are called **push factors**. Among the push factors were poverty, lack of religious freedom, political oppression, and injustice.

In many countries, small farms could no longer support large families. Farm crop prices had dropped. Without work and an income source, these people had no reason to stay in their native countries.

Religious persecution also forced people to leave their homelands. In Russia and Poland, Jews were not allowed to practice their religion. Many left for the United States.

Asia
Alaska
Canada
7,876,122
Canadian Immigrants 820,669
10,961,744 Total
Europe
Japan 28,409
Angel Island
United States
Ellis Island
3,085,622
China
243,860 Asian Immigrants Total
Latin American Immigrants 91,792
Africa
215,451
Mexico
PACIFIC OCEAN
South America
ATLANTIC OCEAN
Australia

Old and New Immigrants, 1870–1900

N / W / E / S

Pulling Immigrants

Democracy, freedom of religion, and economic opportunity are three of the reasons that brought people to the United States. These are called **pull factors**. They pulled, or attracted, people to move to the United States.

Some Europeans thought the streets were "paved with gold." Many immigrants would agree with the Greek street vendor whose brother had written that in America "fortunes could easily be made."

Spreading Out Across the Nation

Immigrants from Europe arrived in port cities on the East Coast. Many of the newcomers, including women and children, went to work in Northeast factories. The men took work as bricklayers, carpenters, street vendors, or whatever work they could find.

On board the *Olympic* in 1915, immigrants catch a glimpse of the Statue of Liberty in New York Harbor.

Those who could afford the train fare continued west. Some went as far as Detroit and Chicago. There, they found work in new factories. In the late 1800s, immigrants provided the labor that grew the nation's industries.

Tenement life was difficult for children who often sewed piecework clothing to make money.

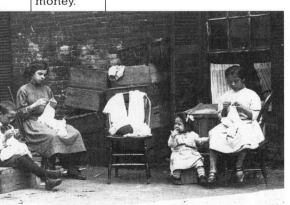

Many immigrants took advantage of the Homestead Act to start farms. This act made it possible to get free government land on the Great Plains.

Chinese and Japanese immigrants arrived in port cities like San Francisco and Seattle on the Pacific Coast. They settled mainly in the West. Many became farmers or worked in construction. Mexicans settled in the Southwest and became farm workers.

stop and think

Make a T-chart in your notebook. Label one side "Push Factors," and label the other side "Pull Factors." List the push and pull factors that you just read about.

Reactions of Native-Born Americans

Not all native-born Americans welcomed immigrants. The newcomers were "different." They spoke their own languages and had their own customs and traditions. Many newcomers were Roman Catholic. Some were Jewish, and Asian immigrants often were Buddhist. At the time, most native-born Americans were Protestant. Some native-born people feared that the immigrants would greatly change American society and traditions.

Angel Island was the port of entry for Chinese immigrants arriving in California.

Many members of the labor unions feared that immigrants would harm workers. Immigrants were willing to work for lower wages than native-born workers. Companies also hired immigrants as strikebreakers.

Many native-born Protestant Americans disliked immigrants. These **nativists**, as they are called, wanted to keep immigrants, especially Catholics and Jews, from coming to the United States. As a result of their activities, Congress passed the first immigration law in 1882. The Chinese Exclusion Act halted immigration from China for 10 years. The Chinese protested the policy, but it did no good.

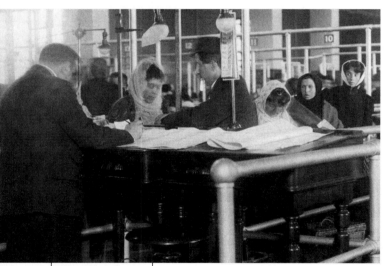

Ellis Island was the gateway to a new life for immigrants arriving in New York.

Putting It All Together

Read the lists that you made at the beginning of the lesson. How do your ideas about modern immigrants compare with the immigrants who came to the United States in the late 1800s and early 1900s? Choose one idea and write a paragraph to compare then and now. Choose (1) reasons for immigration, (2) regions where immigrants settle, or (3) work.

Cities: Crowded, Noisy, and Exciting

Thinking on Your Own

Read the subheadings in the lesson. Turn each one into a question. Write each question in your notebook. Answer the questions as you read.

In 1840, there were 131 cities in the nation. By 1900, the number had increased to 1,700. How did this spectacular growth happen? By 1920, more than half of all Americans lived in cities.

focus your reading

Why did people move to the cities?

What was life like in cities?

What were the problems that cities had?

vocabulary

class	settlement house
suburb	political machine
tenement	party boss
sanitation	

Growing Cities

Farm machines were replacing farm workers. Falling farm prices caused some farm families to lose their farms. Factories, mills, and other city businesses needed workers. People from the countryside were pushed to cities in search of work.

Cities also attracted people because cities were exciting. There were streetlights, tall buildings, department stores, and streetcars. For fun, people could see a vaudeville show or a movie.

Immigrants also contributed to the growth of cities. Cities were where the jobs could be found. Many jobs were low-paying and city life was hard for immigrants.

In 1909, crowded streets were a problem in Chicago.

The Development of Neighborhoods

The growth of industry in the United States divided people into the wealthy, a growing middle **class**, and the very poor. The very wealthy lived in the city centers. They built large homes taken care of by servants, wore elegant clothes, and went to the opera and the theater. They owned horses and carriages.

Suburban homes in 1905 were very comfortable.

The middle class was growing. New industries like railroads and new businesses like department stores created new kinds of jobs. One such job was manager. Teachers, doctors, lawyers, social workers, sales clerks, bank tellers, and people who worked for the government were all part of the middle class. A growing number of middle-class families moved to new neighborhoods at the edge of cities. New streetcar lines connected these **suburbs**, or residential areas, to places of work downtown.

Tenement life was cramped and difficult.

The working class were the poorest people. Some worked building the new skyscrapers, digging subway tunnels, or in factories. The working class lived farthest from the city center. Their neighborhoods were close to the factories, railroad yards, and slaughterhouses. The Chinese lived in one section of a city, the Irish in another. This is how names for neighborhoods like "Little Italy" and "Chinatown" started. In some cities, the working class lived in **tenements**. Tenements had no elevators, and some lacked running water. Families of six or more crowded into only one or two rooms.

The rapidly growing cities had serious problems. Fires gutted entire business sections in Chicago, Boston, and other cities. Sewage flooded basements and garbage piled up in the streets. Over-crowding and poor **sanitation** caused outbreaks of disease. Smoke and grime from burning coal polluted the air.

Two Reformers: Jane Addams and Jacob Riis

A number of reformers tried to clean up cities and help the poor. Jane Addams established Hull House, in Chicago, in 1889 to aid the poor and immigrants. It offered medical care, day care, and English classes. Single working women could live in Hull House's boardinghouse. Addams's work became the model for **settlement houses** in other cities. Settlement houses were privately run neighborhood centers that provided services for the poor.

Jacob Riis was a newspaper reporter in New York City. In 1890, he published *How the Other Half Lives* about working-class neighborhoods in New York. He was especially concerned about housing for the poor. His book alerted people to the need for change.

City Politics

As cities changed, city politics changed, too. One change was the rise of **political machines**. A political machine is a well-organized political party that controls a city's government. It rewards party workers by giving them city jobs. If an immigrant lost his job, he could ask the party for help. All the party asked in return was the person's vote. That is how a political party stayed in power in a city.

Political machines were run by **party bosses**. Many of the bosses were greedy and corrupt. Party bosses usually had city government jobs. Often they hired outside companies that had to give money to the boss to get a job. William "Boss" Tweed is an example of a corrupt official. He stole millions of dollars from New York City. He was finally arrested, tried, and sentenced to jail.

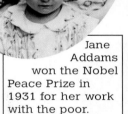

Jane Addams won the Nobel Peace Prize in 1931 for her work with the poor.

stop and think

Make a list of the things that were important to Riis and Addams. Next to each one, write how these things helped the poor. Compare your list and ideas with those of a partner.

Putting It All Together

In 1860, there were 800,000 people in New York City. Now it has almost 8.5 million people. List at least four things that can happen when a city grows so large. Use information from the lesson.

Read a Primary Source

The Triangle Shirtwaist Factory Fire

On March 25, 1911, 146 people died in the Triangle Shirtwaist Factory fire in New York City. The factory doors had been locked to keep employees from leaving and to prevent theft. The owners, Isaac Harris and Max Blanck, were indicted for manslaughter. During the 1911 trial, Kate Alterman, a ninth-floor worker, described the scene when the fire broke out. Public outrage over the horrific loss of life during the fire spurred the creation of new laws to protect worker safety, improve working conditions, and strengthen building codes.

reading for understanding

What were the factory workers' options for escaping the building?

Why were so many people unable to get out of the burning building?

How did female factory workers dress in the early 1900s?

"I wanted to go up Greene street side, but the whole door was in flames, so I went in hid myself in the toilet rooms and bent my face over the sink, and then ran to the Washington side elevator, but there was a big crowd and I couldn't pass through there. I noticed some one, a whole crowd around the door, and I saw the Bernstein, the manager's brother trying to open the door, and there was Margaret near him. Bernstein tried the door, he couldn't open it and then Margaret began to open the door. I take her on one side I pushed her on the side and I said, 'Wait, I will open that door.' I tried, pulled the handle in and out, all ways—and I couldn't open it. She pushed me on the other side, got hold of the handle and then she tried. And then I saw her bending down on her knees, and her hair was loose, and the trail of her dress was a little far from her, and then a big smoke came and I couldn't see . . . and I noticed the trail of her dress and the ends of her hair begin to burn."

Excerpt from:
The Triangle Shirtwaist Fire Trial. (New York City, 1911)

LESSON **3**

The Challenges of Farming

Thinking on Your Own

Make a T-chart in your notebook. Title it "Farming in the Late 1800s." Label the left side "What I Know." Label the right side "What I Am Learning." Fill in the left side of the chart before you begin to read. Fill in the right side as you read.

Farmers in the late 1800s were in trouble. As railroads opened new farm land in the West, farmers grew more crops than ever before. But the more wheat or corn they raised, the less money they made at harvest time. They made less because farmers in Canada, Argentina, and elsewhere were also growing more crops. The world's supply of food crops was greater than the demand from consumers. When supply exceeds demand, prices usually fall. The farmers' costs also declined, but not as fast as crop prices. Farmers tried to find a way out.

focus your reading

How did farmers use the Grange and the Farmers' Alliance to help themselves?

What was the Populist Party platform?

What was the main issue in the election of 1896?

vocabulary

Grange   Populist Party
cooperative   depression

On the other hand, the costs of running farms did not drop. Farmers paid high fees to the owners of grain elevators. Farmers had to use these tanks to hold their crops until they could be shipped. The railroads charged the farmers high prices to carry the crops to market. At the same time, farmers had less money to pay for machinery and other goods they needed.

The Grange

The **Grange** was set up in 1867 to help farmers in the South. It began as a way for farm families to get together socially.

The Grange also provided farmers with information about new farming methods. Within a few years, the organization of farmers spread through the Midwest and West. However, Grangers soon turned to political and economic action.

In some states, Grangers asked their lawmakers for help. They wanted laws passed to regulate the rates that railroads and grain elevators charged.

This 1873 poster for the Grange shows the benefits of membership.

To help themselves financially, Grangers formed **cooperatives**. A cooperative combined the buying and selling power of a group of farmers. If they bought machinery and goods together, farmers thought they could get lower prices. By combining their crops for shipment, farmers also hoped to get better rates from the railroads.

The cooperatives turned out not to be very successful. They were not big enough to have much power over buyers of crops or over the railroads. Courts also overturned some of the laws that were passed to help farmers. Grangers turned to a new organization for help.

The Farmers' Alliance first met in Pleasant Valley, Texas, in 1877.

The Farmers' Alliance

The Farmers' Alliance began in Texas in 1877. Local chapters were soon organized in the South, Midwest, and West. Instead of cooperatives, the Farmers' Alliance set up exchanges. These were similar to cooperatives, but more successful. The Alliance had more members, but the results were still far from enough to help the farmers.

In 1890, a group in the Kansas Farmers' Alliance decided that greater political action was needed. They founded the People's Party. Alliances in Nebraska, South Dakota, and Minnesota also founded their own political parties. The state parties nominated candidates for state offices and for Congress in the 1890 elections. When the votes were counted, the new parties had been very successful. They elected members to the U.S. House and to the Senate. Their candidates were the majority in four state legislatures.

Populism

State parties came together in 1892 and founded a national People's Party. It became known as the **Populist Party**. *Populist* is another word for *people*. The Populist Party demanded the following: unlimited coinage of silver, income tax, eight-hour workday, limits on immigration, government ownership of railroads, direct election of U.S. Senators, and a secret ballot for elections.

The new party met in 1892 and nominated James B. Weaver for president. During the campaign, Populists tried to appeal to Northern factory workers. But the workers continued to vote for Democratic or Republican candidates. On election day, the nation elected President Grover Cleveland, a Democrat, to a second term.

Gold Versus Silver

By 1893, the nation was plunged into an economic **depression**. During a depression, business activity slows. People lose their jobs because factories and stores close. As a result, people buy less, and more businesses close. Prices for all goods, including food crops, fall.

Farmers suffered in the depression, as did factory workers, miners, other workers, and business owners. The Populist Party believed that coining more silver would help. Silver versus gold had been an important political issue since the 1870s.

stop and think

Why did farmers organize the Grange and the Farmers' Alliance? Write your ideas in your notebook. Check your answers with a partner to see if you left anything out. Add to your list if you need to.

Uncle Sam bicycles the country to bankruptcy on a silver dollar in this 1886 cartoon.

Until 1873, U.S. currency had been backed, or supported, by both gold and silver. This means that the value of U.S. money was set by the value of both gold and silver. In 1873, the United States adopted the gold standard. The value of a dollar from then on would be determined by the value of an ounce of gold. Farmers and silver miners protested. They wanted the United States to go back to buying silver and making silver dollars. They thought the economy would improve if more silver was added to the supply of money.

The Election of 1896

At its convention in 1896, the Republican Party supported the gold standard. The Democratic Party had strong supporters of both silver and gold. When the party met at its convention,

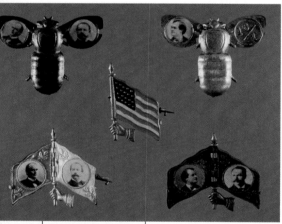

Campaign badges from 1896 show the Democrats' support for the silver standard and the Republican support for the gold standard.

members were split. Once William Jennings Bryan spoke, there was no debate. Bryan gave one of the most famous speeches of American politics. In closing, he thundered, "You shall not press down upon the brow of labor this crown of thorns; you shall not crucify mankind upon a cross of gold." The party and Bryan supported silver.

By *labor,* Bryan meant any worker, including farmers. The Democrats nominated Bryan, and so did the Populist Party, at its convention. Bryan faced Republican William McKinley. McKinley had the support of business leaders and Northern workers. As a result, McKinley easily won the election.

By 1900, the depression had ended. Farmers' financial problems eased. With better economic times, the appeal of the Populist Party faded.

Putting It All Together

Read the information on the T-chart you created at the beginning of this lesson. Choose a topic, like why farmers founded a political party or why farmers voted for Bryan. In your notebook, write a paragraph explaining what you learned about this topic.

Biography

Mary Elizabeth Lease (1850–1933)

Born in Pennsylvania, Mary Elizabeth Clyens moved to Kansas when she was 20 years old. She took a job as a teacher in Osage Mission. Three years later she married Charles L. Lease. By 1883, they were living in Wichita, Kansas, and had four children.

In 1885, Mary Lease became a lawyer. That same year, she also began her career as a public speaker. At that time, it was unusual for a woman to speak in public and to work for a political party. Lease did both.

Lease was an enthusiastic and fiery speaker who was much in demand. Her first efforts were for labor unions. She worked with the Union Labor Party and the Knights of Labor in Kansas.

From 1890 on, Lease turned her skills to helping the Farmers' Alliance and then the Populist Party. During the election of 1890, Lease crisscrossed Kansas giving speeches. She spoke 160 times in support of candidates of the Populist Party. Later she traveled through the South speaking to farmers about Populist Party issues.

At the 1892 Populist Party convention, Lease had an important duty. She gave the seconding speech for the presidential nominee, James B. Weaver. In 1893, Lease ran for U.S. Senate from Kansas but was defeated. Women could not yet vote in Kansas or in most of the United States.

In 1896, Lease left the Populist Party. She was against the nomination of William Jennings Bryan. She moved to New York and went to work for a newspaper. Until her death, Lease continued to speak out on issues, including women's right to vote.

Chapter Summary

The late 1800s and early 1900s saw a large rise in the number of **immigrants**. This **New Immigration** was different from the **Old Immigration** of the earlier 1800s. **Push factors** that drove people from their home countries were poverty, religious persecution, and political oppression. **Pull factors**, such as democracy, freedom of religion, and economic opportunity, attracted people to the United States. **Nativists** tried to limit immigration.

Most immigrants moved to cities. People lived in neighborhoods divided by social **class**. Many middle-class families lived in **suburbs**. The working class lived in **tenements** in poor neighborhoods. To aid immigrants, **settlement houses** were founded in some cities.

Cities had many problems including poor **sanitation**, fires, and pollution. Many big cities were run by **political machines**. These groups controlled city government. Some of the **party bosses** who headed the machines were corrupt.

Farmers were suffering hard economic times at the end of the 1800s. The **Grange** tried to help by forming **cooperatives**, but they were unsuccessful. Farmers who belonged to the Farmers' Alliance founded the **Populist Party** to elect lawmakers who supported them. In 1896 during a serious economic **depression**, the party nominated William Jennings Bryan for president.

Chapter Review

1 The chapter is titled "A Time of Hope and Hardship." Immigrants had great hopes about coming to the United States. Once here, they also suffered great hardship. Write a paragraph to explain the hope and hardships of immigrants.

2 Think of a city as a big circle. Make a diagram to show where different groups of people lived in a typical big city at the end of the 1800s and the early 1900s.

3 Use the list you made in Lesson 2 to write a paragraph that compares the social classes.

Skill Builder

Outlining Information

An outline is like the skeleton of a piece of writing. It lists the basic information in the piece. Making an outline is a good way to organize information when you study. To make an outline, look for the main idea—the most important information—in a section. Then look for the details that support it.

An outline has a standard format of levels, letters, and numerals. Each level is indented.

I. Main ideas are listed with Roman numerals.
    A. The most important details are listed with capital letters.
        1. Less important details are listed with Arabic numerals.

An outline for part of Lesson 1 looks like this:

I. Pushing Immigrants
    A. Poverty
        1. Families grew and farms were too small.
        2. Prices for crops dropped.
    B. Lack of religious freedom
        1. Jews were persecuted in Russia and Poland.
    C. Political oppression, or injustice

This outline lists the basic information in the section "Pushing Immigrants." It makes it easy to answer the question "What are the three main reasons immigrants left their home countries?" Answer: "Immigrants left their home countries because of poverty, lack of religious freedom, and political oppression."

1 Outline "Spreading Out Across the Nation," page 57.

2 Outline Lesson 2. Use each subheading in the lesson as a main idea. Your outline will have Roman numerals I through IV for main ideas. The number of other lines in your outline will depend on how many supporting details you list.

UNIT 3

IMPERIALISM AND REFORM

By 1890, the United States extended from the Atlantic Ocean to the Pacific. Industry was expanding. The nation's population was growing. Political and business leaders now looked beyond the nation's shores. Where could they sell U.S. goods? Where could they get raw materials to make more goods? The answers started the nation on the road to overseas empire.

At the same time, problems at home continued to grow. Cities became more crowded. Working conditions became worse. However, federal, state, and city governments were slow to act. There was also the issue of the rights of African Americans and women. To force change, reformers took their causes to the public.

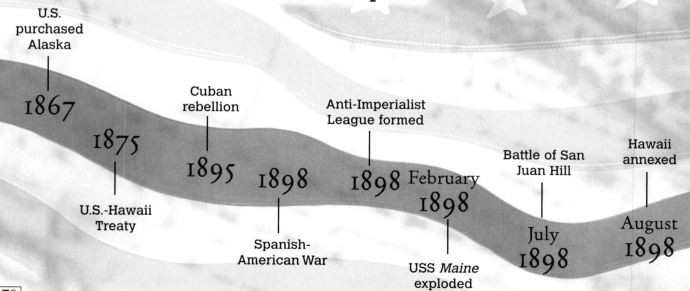

U.S. purchased Alaska
1867

1875
U.S.-Hawaii Treaty

Cuban rebellion
1895

1898
Spanish-American War

Anti-Imperialist League formed
1898

February **1898**
USS *Maine* exploded

Battle of San Juan Hill
July **1898**

Hawaii annexed
August **1898**

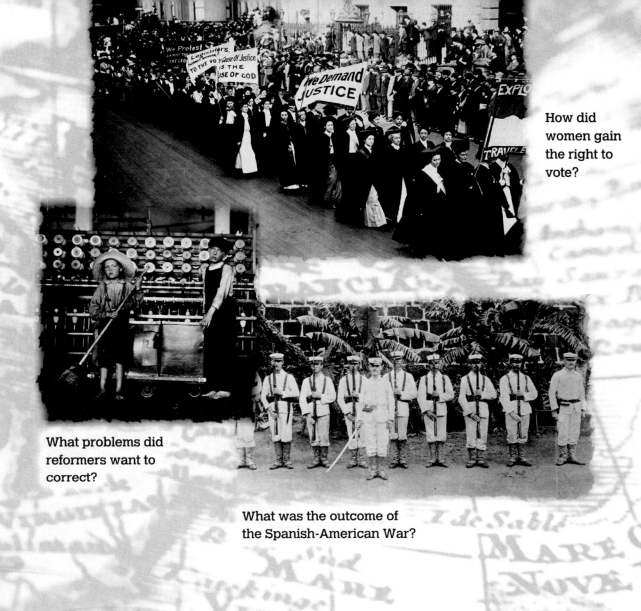

How did women gain the right to vote?

What problems did reformers want to correct?

What was the outcome of the Spanish-American War?

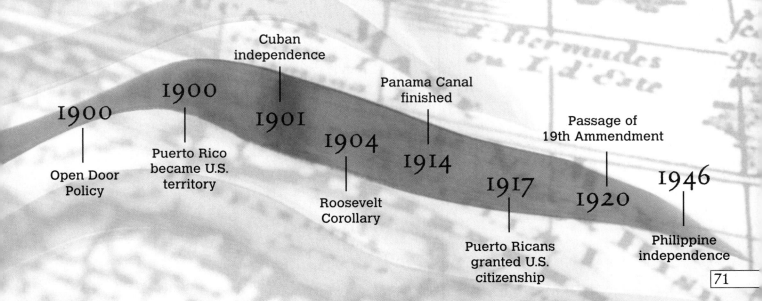

1900
Open Door Policy

1900
Puerto Rico became U.S. territory

Cuban independence
1901

1904
Roosevelt Corollary

Panama Canal finished
1914

1917
Puerto Ricans granted U.S. citizenship

Passage of 19th Ammendment
1920

1946
Philippine independence

Chapter 5

THE U.S. AS A WORLD POWER

Getting Focused

Skim this chapter to predict what you will be learning.

- Read the lesson titles and subheadings.
- Look at the illustrations and read the captions.
- Examine the maps.
- Review the vocabulary words and terms.

What do you think this chapter is about? Write three or four sentences to state your ideas in your notebook.

The Race for Empire

Thinking on Your Own

Practice your outlining skill. Review How To Make an Outline on page 69 of Chapter 4. As you read this lesson, create an outline of the information. Use your outline to study the lesson. Be sure to include all the vocabulary words.

European nations like Great Britain and France already had empires. The 13 colonies that became the United States had once been part of the British Empire. In the late 1800s, the United States set out to build its own empire.

focus your reading

Why did Americans want to build an empire?

How did the United States gain Hawaii?

Why did the United States build up its naval power?

vocabulary

imperialism

tariff

annexation

Policy of Imperialism

By the 1890s, overseas expansion and **imperialism** appealed to many Americans. Imperialism includes the governing of weaker nations or colonies by more powerful nations. People realized that the United States had become a powerful nation. It was the world's leading producer of steel and oil, and it had more miles of railroad than any other country. Farmers and ranchers had largely settled the frontier. The United States extended from the Atlantic Ocean to the Pacific. The army had the Native Americans penned up on reservations. Many Americans thought it was time for the United States to become a world power.

Merchant vessels like the *Valesia* were important in opening overseas markets.

The United States needed new markets for the goods it produced. As the nation grew, more crops and more goods were produced than Americans could use. This problem resulted in the hard economic times of the 1870s and 1890s. Overseas markets would allow the economy to continue growing.

Racist ideas about Anglo-Saxon superiority also helped support overseas expansion. Many Americans believed that Christian, English-speaking nations were better than others. They thought it was the duty of Americans to bring their civilization to the "backward" people of Asia and the Pacific.

The Annexation of Hawaii

The United States took its first step toward expanding overseas shortly after the Civil War. Abraham Lincoln's Secretary of State, William H. Seward, dreamed of a great American Empire. In 1867, he signed a treaty with Russia to purchase Alaska—which the Senate approved. Hawaii came next.

The annexation of Hawaii was an important topic in 1897.

By the 1870s, settlers from the U.S. mainland were growing sugarcane on large plantations in Hawaii. In 1875, the planters signed a trade treaty with the United States. The treaty allowed them to sell their sugar in the United States without paying a tariff. A **tariff** is a tax on goods brought into a country for sale. All other foreign sugar was taxed.

Queen Liliuokalani

As a result, the non-native Hawaiian planters became very wealthy and powerful. In 1887, they forced the Hawaiian king to grant them control of the legislature. When he died in 1891, his sister Liliuokalani became queen. She tried to regain control of the government.

stop and think

In your notebook, make a timeline for the annexation of Hawaii. Share it with a partner. Quiz each other on how many years passed between each event.

In 1893, the planters forced the queen from office and applied for annexation by the United States. **Annexation** meant that the United States would take control of Hawaii. President Grover Cleveland refused. The planters declared Hawaii a republic. President McKinley, who supported imperialism, annexed Hawaii in 1898.

Protecting the American Empire

If the United States was going to build an empire, it had to be ready to defend it. This was the argument of both business leaders and naval officers. They believed the nation needed a modern navy. No one was more persuasive than Captain Alfred T. Mahan. His book, *The Influence of Sea Power Upon History, 1660–1783*, used historical examples to support his argument. Congress, agreeing with Mahan and the others, budgeted money to build a modern navy.

The Norfolk Navy Yard, VA, in 1907

Putting It All Together

Choose one section from your outline of this lesson. Use the section as a guide, and write a paragraph to explain what Lesson 1 is about. Share your paragraph with a partner.

The Spanish-American War

Thinking on Your Own

Create two flowcharts for this lesson. Make one to track the causes of the Spanish-American War. Create another flowchart to list the effects of the war. The Skill Builder in Chapter 2 explains how to use a flowchart to track causes and effects of events.

By the 1890s, Cuba and Puerto Rico were the last Spanish colonies in the Americas. The other Spanish colonies had been independent nations for at least 50 years. In 1895, Cubans rebelled again. José Martí led the revolt. The Spanish fought back. The Spanish set up camps to separate ordinary Cubans from the rebels. The Spanish sent 500,000 Cubans—men, women, and children—to the camps.

focus your reading

What were the causes of the Spanish-American War?

Where was the Spanish-American War fought?

What were the results of the Spanish-American War?

vocabulary

yellow press

front

guerrilla war

Prisoners break rocks in a Havana prison camp.

Going to War with Spain

News of the rebellion and the camps quickly reached the United States. Many Americans supported the Cuban uprising. Some supported it because they owned sugarcane plantations or other businesses in Cuba. Others supported the uprising because they believed in freedom and independence.

The **yellow press** fed Americans' concern over the Cuban revolution. Yellow press was the name given to newspapers that sensationalized the news. Both the *New York World* and the *New York Journal* used vivid headlines to sell newspapers. Both papers reported terrible conditions in the Cuban camps where almost half the people died.

The sinking of the USS *Maine* in 1898 brought war closer still. The battleship was anchored in Havana harbor on a friendly visit. Suddenly it exploded, killing 260 sailors and officers. At the time, investigators said a mine caused the explosion. Later investigations said that either coal dust or ammunition on the ship had exploded.

The USS *Maine* exploded in Havana harbor on February 15, 1898.

The yellow press, however, blamed the explosion on the Spanish. "Remember the *Maine*!" became the slogan. The United States demanded changes in how Spain governed Cuba. Spain agreed to some of the demands. However, Congress decided the changes were not enough. In April 1898, Congress declared Cuba an independent nation. Spain declared war on the United States, and the next day the United States declared war on Spain.

The War in the Philippines

The Spanish-American War was fought on two **fronts**: the Caribbean, and the Philippine Islands in the Pacific Ocean. A war front is a battle zone, or area of fighting.

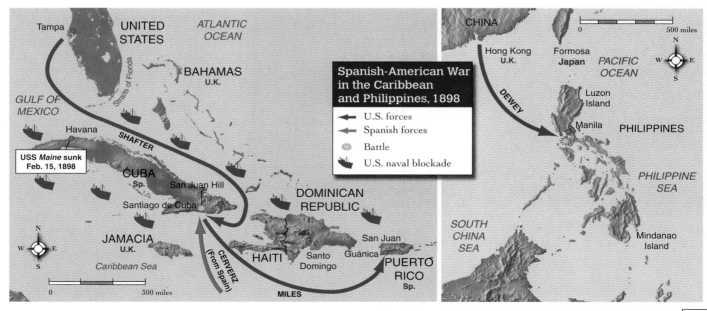

The first fighting took place in the Philippines. The Spanish had controlled the Philippines since the 1500s. On May 1, 1898, a U.S. fleet under Commodore George Dewey attacked a Spanish fleet in Manilla Bay. Most of the Spanish fleet was destroyed.

Filipinos had been fighting for independence from Spain for years. Under their leader Emilio Aguinaldo, the rebels now fought alongside U.S. troops. By August, they seized the capital of Manila and the main island.

The War in Cuba and Puerto Rico

The major fighting in the Caribbean took place in Cuba. A large Spanish fleet was at anchor in Santiago Harbor. In May 1898, the U.S. Navy blockaded the harbor.

A month later, 17,000 U.S. troops landed in Cuba near Santiago. Among the soldiers was the First Regiment of U.S. Cavalry Volunteers, known as the Rough Riders. They were commanded by Theodore Roosevelt. On July 1, 1898, he led his troops, along with African-American units, in a battle to capture San Juan Hill. The U.S. soldiers won the hill after a tough fight.

The Tenth Cavalry helped capture San Juan Hill, Cuba.

On July 3, the Spanish fleet tried to escape the blockade around Santiago Harbor. The U.S. Navy destroyed the Spanish fleet. Two weeks later, the city of Santiago surrendered. The war in Cuba was over.

U.S. troops were then sent to Puerto Rico. Spain had already granted Puerto Rico its own government. However, the United States took control of the island anyway.

Colonel
Roosevelt
and the
Rough Riders

The American Empire

On August 12, 1898, Spain agreed to a truce. The war ended after four months of fighting. Many of the dead were African American. About 25 percent of the soldiers who fought in the war were African American.

As a result of the war, Americans got their empire. The United States took possession of the Philippine Islands and Guam in the Pacific. In the Caribbean, it occupied Cuba and Puerto Rico.

Cuba was granted its independence in 1901. However, the United States insisted that Cuba lease Guantanamo Bay to the United States to use as a naval base. The United States also had the right to step in to safeguard Cuba's independence. United States businesses wanted to be sure that their investments in Cuba would be protected.

In 1900, Puerto Rico became a U.S. territory. Congress wrote its laws and appointed its government. In 1917, Puerto Ricans were given U.S. citizenship.

> **stop and think**
>
> Look at the maps of the Spanish-American War. What symbol shows U.S. forces? What symbol shows Spanish forces? How do you know where battles were fought? Write the answers in your notebook.

American soldiers watch over a boat in the Philippines during the fight for independence.

Congress intended to make the Philippines a territory also. However, Filipinos declared the Philippines a democratic republic. Under Aguinaldo, Filipinos continued their fight for independence—this time against the United States. The **guerrilla war** lasted until 1901, when Aguinaldo was captured.

Between 1898 and 1901, Americans hotly debated whether to grant the Philippines independence. On one side were anti-imperialists who supported independence. On the other side were Americans who thought the nation needed colonies in the Pacific. The imperialists won and a U.S.-led government was put in place. The Philippines did not gain independence until 1946.

Putting It All Together

Read the flowcharts you made of the causes and effects of the Spanish-American War. Write two questions about the causes of the war and two questions about the effects. Then work with a partner. Take turns asking and answering each other's questions.

Biography

Walter Reed (1851–1902)

Walter Reed was both a doctor and an officer in the U.S. Army. Reed was only 18 when he graduated from medical school at the University of Virginia. That same year, Dr. Reed moved to New York. He worked in various hospitals in Brooklyn. In 1873, he became an inspector for the Brooklyn Board of Health. Later he worked for the New York City Board of Health. In 1875, Reed joined the U.S. Army. Most of his first 18 years in the army were spent as a doctor on army posts. He served at forts in Arizona, Nebraska, Alabama, and the Dakotas.

In 1893, Major Reed was transferred to the Army Medical School in Washington, D.C. There, he studied typhoid fever. At that time, people thought typhoid was caused by breathing fumes from swamps and rivers. Because of his work we know that typhoid fever is caused by bacteria. In the 1890s, little was known about bacteria. Reed focused on typhoid because army bases had large numbers of typhoid cases. Reed's work helped the army to improve sanitation. As a result, the number of typhoid victims was greatly reduced.

The cause of yellow fever was also unknown. It sickened thousands of people every year in the southern United States and the Caribbean, including Cuba. More U.S. soldiers died from yellow fever in the Spanish-American War than from Spanish bullets. Major Reed's team proved that mosquitoes spread the disease. Their work was based on a theory of Dr. Carlos Juan Finlay. Reed and his group conducted experiments that proved Finlay's theory.

As a result of this work, public officials set out to destroy all puddles of water. Mosquitoes lay their eggs in water. Cuba, parts of the southern United States, and other areas in the Caribbean were freed from yellow fever. Controlling yellow fever made it possible to build the Panama Canal.

In honor of Major Reed, the Walter Reed Army General Hospital opened in 1909. Now called the Walter Reed Army Medical Center, it is located near Washington, D.C.

Imperialist Foreign Policy

Thinking on Your Own

As you read the lesson, list words in your notebook that you do not know. Try to figure out what each word means. Read a sentence or two before and after the sentence with the unfamiliar word. Think of a synonym that would make sense in the sentence?

While the United States debated what to do about the Philippines, it was also looking beyond those islands to Asia and Latin America. Everywhere U.S. businessmen looked, they saw new customers. Everywhere government leaders looked, they saw new power for the nation.

focus your reading

What was the Open Door Policy?

Why did the United States build the Panama Canal?

Why did Theodore Roosevelt propose the Roosevelt Corollary?

vocabulary

sphere of influence

isthmus

The Open Door Policy was debated in the media.

Open Door Policy

American sea captains began importing tea and silk from China in the 1780s. However, U.S. businesses were facing new competition. By the 1890s, Great Britain, France, Russia, Germany, and Japan controlled trade in vast areas of China. These regions were known as **spheres of influence**. The United States did not control any areas in China.

Business leaders were concerned about their trade with China. What if the other nations tried to force them out? Businessmen appealed to the federal government for help. Some government leaders were also concerned about the growing power of other nations in China. As a result, Secretary of State John Hay proposed the

Open Door Policy. This policy would allow all nations to trade with China on equal terms. European powers had mixed reactions to Hay's proposal. However, they did agree that China should not be carved up into colonies. Although Hay got less than he wanted, he declared his Open Door Policy a success.

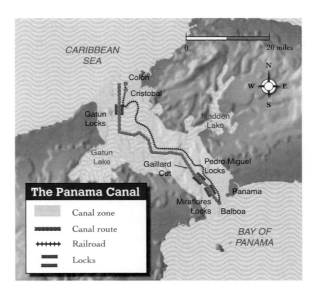

The Panama Canal

Canal zone
Canal route
Railroad
Locks

stop and think

Imagine you are Secretary of State John Hay. Write a letter stating your Open Door Policy, asking other nations to agree. First, work with a partner to come up with a list of reasons why other nations should agree. You may need to research the topic further in the library or on the Internet.

Building the Panama Canal

After the Spanish-American War, the United States had interests in both the Caribbean and the Pacific. To get from one to the other, ships had to sail around the southern tip of South America. A canal across the **isthmus** of Panama would be the ideal solution. An isthmus is a narrow strip of land joining two larger bodies of land.

In 1903, Panama was part of Colombia. When Panamanians rebelled, Roosevelt supported the rebels against Colombian troops. The new nation was grateful. It quickly agreed to lease to the United States a strip of land from the Pacific to the Caribbean. This 10-mile-wide strip became the Panama Canal Zone. In exchange for a 99-year lease, the United States agreed to pay Panama $250,000 per year.

President Roosevelt operates a steam shovel at Culebra Cut, Panama Canal.

Work began on the Panama Canal in 1904. At the beginning of the project, steps were taken to kill the mosquitoes that carried yellow fever. Within two years, they were gone from the Canal Zone. It took 10 years and 40,000 men to build the Panama Canal. The Panama Canal opened in 1914.

THE WORLD'S CONSTABLE.

Not everyone agreed with the Roosevelt Corollary.

Roosevelt Corollary

In 1823, President James Monroe warned European nations to stay out of the Western Hemisphere. His statement was called the Monroe Doctrine. In 1904, President Theodore Roosevelt expanded this policy with the Roosevelt Corollary.

Roosevelt stated that the United States would become the policeman of Latin America. He liked to quote the proverb "Speak softly and carry a big stick." The United States would decide when to step in to keep economic and political order. Roosevelt and later U.S. presidents used his corollary to intervene in the Dominican Republic, Cuba, Haiti, Nicaragua, and Panama.

Putting It All Together

Draw a cartoon to illustrate President Roosevelt's idea of the United States as the policeman of the Western Hemisphere.

Read a Primary Source

Anti-Imperialist League

Not all Americans agreed with the policy of imperialism. In 1898, a group of people formed the Anti-Imperialist League. *Anti-* means "against." The following selection is from its platform, or belief statement, published in 1899.

reading for understanding

In what other document will you find the phrase "life, liberty, and the pursuit of happiness"?

What does the Anti-Imperialist League say it will do in the election of 1900?

What event might Lincoln be discussing in his quote?

"We hold that the policy known as imperialism is hostile to liberty. . . . We regret that is has become necessary in the land of Washington and Lincoln to reaffirm that all men, of whatever race or color, are entitled to life, liberty, and the pursuit of happiness. . . .

"The United States have always protested against the doctrine of international law which permits the subjugation of the weak by the strong. A self-governing state cannot accept sovereignty over an unwilling people. . . . The United States cannot act upon . . . might makes right. . . .

"We shall oppose for reelection all who in the White House or in Congress betray American liberty in pursuit of un-American gains. We still hope that both of our great political parties will support and defend the Declaration of Independence in the closing campaign of the century.

"We hold, with Abraham Lincoln, that . . . 'Those who deny freedom to others deserve it not for themselves, and under a just God cannot long retain it.'

"We cordially invite the cooperation of all men and women who remain loyal to the Declaration of Independence and the Constitution of the United States."

Speeches, Correspondence, and Political Papers of Carl Schurz, vol. 6, ed. Frederick Barncroft. (New York: G.B. Putnam & Sons, 1913).

Chapter Summary

By the 1890s, government leaders and business owners were becoming supporters of **imperialism**. An early step in empire building was the **annexation** of Hawaii in 1898. A treaty eliminated a **tariff** on sugar sold to the United States.

In 1898, the United States went to war with Spain for three reasons. First, many Americans supported the Cuban uprising against Spain. Second, the **yellow press** stirred up emotions against Spain. Third, the USS *Maine* exploded and sank while in Cuba. The Spanish-American War was fought on two **fronts**—in the Caribbean and in the Pacific.

The United States took possession of Cuba, Puerto Rico, and the Philippines. Filipinos declared independence after the war but fought and lost a **guerrilla war**.

The Open Door Policy gave equal rights to all foreign nations trading in China. U.S. business and government leaders believed the policy was needed because of foreign **spheres of influence** in China.

In 1904, the United States began building a canal across the **isthmus** of Panama. The Panama Canal connects the Pacific to the Caribbean.

Chapter Review

1 Reread your predictions about the chapter. Now that you have studied the chapter, how close was your prediction? If necessary, revise your statement and write a summary of the chapter.

2 Decide whether you would have been an imperialist or anti-imperialist in 1900. Draw a cartoon about the annexation of the Philippines from your point of view—imperialist or anti-imperialist.

3 Why would a canal across Panama help U.S. trade? Write a paragraph that includes your reasons.

Skill Builder

Identifying the Sequence of Events

Sequence is the order in which something happens. When you follow step-by-step directions, you are following a sequence. The timeline at the beginning of each unit in this book is a sequence. It shows when events happened in time. Knowing the sequence of events in history can help you understand and remember them better.

There are two ways to identify the sequence of events. One is o look in the text for the dates of events. For example, the text lists 1898 as the date for the Spanish-American War.

There are also words that can help you figure out sequence. Following are some words that signal sequence:

first, second, third, fourth

one, two, three, four

next, now, then, later, soon, sooner

dates

The following tells the steps, or sequence, in which a ship goes through the Panama Canal. The signal words are in bold type.

A ship sails into a lock, and the back gate on the lock closes. **Then** the lock fills with water. **Soon** the ship floats to the top of the lock. **Next** the front gate on the lock opens. **Finally**, the ship sails out onto the lake.

Use the information from the chapter to determine the sequence of events.

1 Read the section "The Annexation of Hawaii" on pages 74–75. Which came first: Liliuokalani became queen or the trade treaty with the United States? In your notebook, write each word or date that signals the sequence of these events.

2 Read the section "The War in Cuba and Puerto Rico" on page 78. In your notebook, write each word or date that signals sequence.

Chapter 6

THE PROGRESSIVE ERA

Getting Focused

Skim this chapter to predict what you will be learning.

- Read the lesson titles and subheadings.
- Look at the illustrations and read the captions.
- Examine the maps.
- Review the vocabulary words and terms.

Progressives were reformers who wanted to improve government and life in general for Americans. Make a list of things in need of reform in 1890. Use information you have already read in this book as the basis for your list. Revise your list as you read the chapter.

Progressive Policies and Reforms

Thinking on Your Own

Make three columns in your notebook with the titles "Muckrakers," "Government Reforms," and "Social Reforms." Make a bulleted list of information for each column as you read.

About 1890, people who believed in reform and the improvement of society began to call themselves **progressives**. Some progressives wanted to see changes in the way government was run. Others wanted controls on big business. Still others wanted social reforms. In general, progressives were part of the white-collar middle class and the blue-collar working class. They supported (1) protection for individuals and (2) greater regulation of government and business.

focus your reading

What did the muckrakers write about?

What government reforms did progressives introduce?

What social reforms were passed in this era?

vocabulary

progressive   referendum

muckrakers   recall

direct primary   prohibition

initiative

The Muckrakers

Magazine writers focused public attention on the need for change. These journalists wrote about wrongdoing in business and government. President Theodore Roosevelt called them **muckrakers** because they uncovered ugly aspects of American life.

One muckraker was Jacob Riis. His book *How the Other Half Lives* publicized the unsafe and unhealthy living conditions of immigrants in New York City. He described the dark bedrooms, smelly basements, and filthy hallways of the tenement buildings. One two-room apartment housed a German immigrant family of nine people. "That day the mother had thrown herself out of the window, and was carried up from the street dead," Jacob Riis wrote. "She was 'discouraged' said some of the other women."

A Chicago meatpacking plant in 1906

Muckrakers attacked a wide range of problems. Lincoln Steffens wrote about corruption in city politics. Upton Sinclair wrote about unsafe and unhealthy conditions in the meatpacking industry. John Spargo used his writing to campaign for an end to child labor. Ida Tarbell wrote about the unethical business practices of the Standard Oil Company.

Government Reform

Progressives attacked corruption in both city and state government. Corruption included officials accepting bribes and party leaders or "bosses" buying votes at election time.

Some progressives wanted to break the power of the bosses and introduce efficiency into government operations.

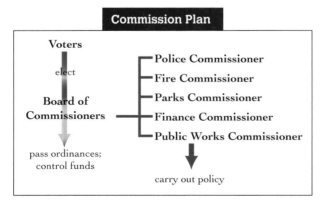

The result was the city commission plan and the city manager plan. Under the commission plan, city government was divided into departments with a commissioner in charge of each. These commissioners were experts in their fields, not politicians. The city manager was also a professional, not a politician. In 1901, Galveston, Texas, became one of the first cities to adopt the commission plan.

Other progressives wanted to see democracy expanded. They believed voters deserved more of a say in government. One change was the introduction of the **direct primary**. Under Governor Robert La Follette, citizens in Wisconsin began to vote directly for nominees for public office. Before that, there were no primary elections. Instead, Wisconsin's party bosses, at state conventions, chose the candidates to run for office.

Robert La Follette

Oregon also began using the direct primary. That state introduced three changes that Populists had long demanded: initiative, referendum, and recall.

- **Initiative:** A proposed state law or an issue is placed on the ballot to be voted on in the next election.
- **Referendum:** Voters are able to vote to accept or reject laws passed by the state legislature.
- **Recall:** Using recall, voters can remove an elected official from office between regular elections.

The biggest government change of the Progressive era was passage of the Seventeenth Amendment in 1912. Before this amendment, U.S. senators were elected by state legislatures. This often meant that party bosses made the decision about who was elected. The Seventeenth Amendment provides for the direct election of senators. This means that voters in a state were now able to vote for the candidate they wanted.

stop and think

In your notebook, write out the meaning of vocabulary words that tell about government reforms. With a partner, take turns quizzing each other about the meaning of each term.

Social Reforms

Several progressives wanted reforms to improve people's lives. The New York State Legislature passed the Tenement House Law in 1901. The law provided stricter building codes for the construction of tenement houses and addressed many of the concerns raised by Jacob Riis. Upton Sinclair's book about the meatpacking industry raised great concern about the health and welfare of ordinary citizens. In 1906, Congress passed the Meat Inspection Act and the Pure Food and Drug Act.

In the early 1900s, children still worked in factories and mines. The National Child Labor Committee was formed in 1904 to work for the abolishment of child labor. The Children's Bureau, a federal agency, was established in 1912 to investigate child labor and help to speed its end.

The Women's Christian Temperance Union marched in Washington, D.C., in 1909.

Prohibition, or the legal ban on selling alcohol, became an important social issue during the Progressive Era. Earlier attempts to ban alcohol were unsuccessful. By the early 1900s, alcohol was closely associated with corruption. Saloons in urban areas were often owned by politicians who gave away free liquor at election time.

Banning alcohol was a slow process, but several states had prohibition laws in place by 1906. The need to conserve grain for use in World War I gave prohibition a patriotic cause. In 1919, the Eighteenth Amendment outlawed the manufacture, sale, and transportation of intoxicating liquors.

Putting It All Together

Review the three-column list that you made at the beginning of this lesson. Add other information that you have learned from your reading.

The Progressive Presidents

Thinking on Your Own

Make a three-column table. Across the top write "The Progressive Presidents." Label each column with the name of one of the presidents in this lesson. As you read, fill in the table with the achievements of each.

The progressives were very successful in winning reform in state and local governments. For reform on the national level, they found a friend in President Theodore Roosevelt. Roosevelt became president in 1901 when President William McKinley was assassinated. One of Roosevelt's first acts in office was to go after trusts.

focus your reading

What three areas did Theodore Roosevelt work to reform?

What reforms did William Howard Taft support?

What reforms were passed during Woodrow Wilson's presidency?

vocabulary

square deal   conservation

bully pulpit

Theodore Roosevelt

This cartoon shows President Roosevelt as the lion tamer of Wall Street.

Many businessmen had followed John D. Rockefeller's example and set up trusts. Roosevelt did not think that all trusts were bad. He defined a bad trust as one that did business without considering what was good for the public. He wanted to regulate trusts, but not do away with them.

Roosevelt's first target was the Northern Securities Company. Set up in 1902, the company controlled all railroads from Lake Michigan to the Pacific. Northern Securities had no competition in the Northwest. The Supreme Court ruled that the company violated federal antitrust law and had to be broken up.

The coal strike of 1902 caused many problems for the country. Coal miners and owners disagreed about wages, the length of the workday, and the right to belong to a union. Roosevelt settled the coal strike. He called the agreement a "**square deal**," as it was fair to both sides. He liked to use the White House as a "**bully pulpit**," as he called it. He meant that it was a platform from which to present his views.

Conservation was important to President Roosevelt. He supported policies to conserve, or save, the environment, especially the western wilderness. Under Roosevelt, the U.S. Forest Service was established in 1905, and 100 million acres were protected as national forests. During Roosevelt's administration, 5 national parks, 51 federal wildlife reservations, and 150 national forests were set up.

President William Taft

William Howard Taft

In 1908, William Howard Taft ran as the Republican candidate. Taft easily defeated the Democratic candidate William Jennings Bryan. Progressive Republicans expected Taft to continue Roosevelt's policies. They were in for a big disappointment. Instead of continuing the policies of Roosevelt, Taft supported the conservative members of the Republican party in Congress.

Both the Republican and Democratic Parties tried to attract members of the Bull Moose Party.

During this period, many Americans felt that tariff protection would help the economy. Taft and the conservatives in the party wanted lower tariffs, but the liberal Republicans wanted higher tariffs. The bill that finally passed was the Payne-Aldrich Tariff. Although it lowered some rates, it kept most at a high level.

Like Roosevelt, Taft prosecuted antitrust cases. Roosevelt's administration prosecuted 43 antitrust cases in seven years. Roosevelt became known as a trustbuster. Taft's administration took twice as many cases to court in four years. The Sixteenth and Seventeenth Amendments to the U.S. Constitution were also passed during Taft's one term in office.

Over time, Roosevelt came to disagree with Taft's policies. Roosevelt and his supporters started the Progressive Party, and Roosevelt ran as its presidential candidate in the 1912 election. The Progressives and the Republicans split their support between Taft and Roosevelt. The result was the election of Democrat Woodrow Wilson.

Woodrow Wilson

As governor of New Jersey, Woodrow Wilson supported a number of progressive reforms in the state. He urged passage of similar progressive policies once he became president.

Wilson was opposed not only to big business, but also to big government. He wanted to lower the tariff and in 1913, the Underwood Tariff Act was passed. Also in 1913, Wilson asked Congress to pass the Federal Reserve Act that gave the federal government authority over the banking industry.

In 1914, Wilson asked Congress to set up the Federal Trade Commission. The FTC's mission was to look for unfair trade, or business, practices in the way companies operated.

Later in 1914, Congress passed the Clayton Antitrust Act. According to the law, companies could not charge one customer one price and another customer another price. In addition, one company could not stop another company from selling a third company's goods.

In the end, Wilson was more of a progressive than Theodore Roosevelt, and many of the reforms begun in Roosevelt's term were carried out in Wilson's term.

stop and think

Read the columns on your table of the achievements of Presidents Roosevelt, Taft and Wilson. Which one do you think was the most important? Talk over your idea with a partner. Then write a paragraph stating your idea and explaining your reasons.

President Woodrow Wilson

Putting It All Together

Read your table for the lesson. Write a paragraph that compares and contrasts two of the Progressive presidents.

LESSON 3

Women's Suffrage and Discrimination

Thinking on Your Own

Create a concept map for this lesson based on the word *prejudice*. Draw a circle in the center of your notebook page. Write *prejudice* in the circle. Draw lines with smaller circles for each idea in the lesson that is related to prejudice.

Not everyone benefited from the reforms of the late 1800s and early 1900s. Women were still the target of discrimination at work as well as in the voting booth. Immigrants from eastern and southern Europe, Catholics, Jews, Hispanics, Native Americans, and African Americans found few friends among the progressives. All three progressive presidents continued the earlier policy of **assimilation** of Native Americans and immigrants. Assimilation is when one cultural group is absorbed into another, larger group.

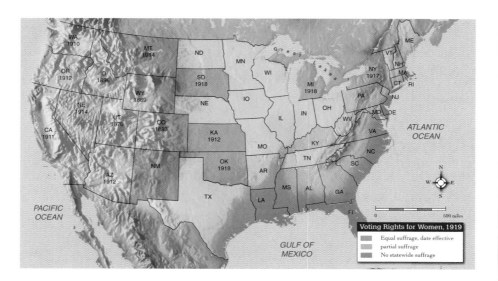

Suffragists protesting at the White House

Women's Suffrage

Women were angry when the Fifteenth Amendment did not give them the right to vote. Women **suffragists** did not give up. Gaining the right to vote for women became a goal for some progressives.

In 1869, women led by Susan B. Anthony and Elizabeth Cady Stanton formed the National Woman Suffrage Association (NWSA). The goal of the NWSA was passage of a constitutional amendment giving women the right to vote.

Another organization, the American Woman Suffrage Association, decided to focus on the states. The AWSA's goal was to get states to grant women the vote in state elections. In 1890, the two organizations combined and became the National American Woman Suffrage Association (NAWSA).

In 1915, Carrie Chapman Catt became president of the NAWSA. The final push for the vote was on. By then, 11 states had granted women the right to vote in state elections. Women used protest marches and hunger strikes to put pressure on President Wilson and Congress. In 1918–1919, Congress finally passed a constitutional amendment giving women the right to vote. Three-fourths of the states ratified the amendment in time for the 1920 election.

stop and think

Look at the map of voting rights for women. Find the states that had given women the right to vote before 1919. Think about what you know about life in the West in the late 1800s. Talk over your ideas with a partner. Then write a paragraph explaining why you think women first got the vote in the West.

African Americans, Native Americans, and Equality

At the end of the 1800s, a majority of African Americans still lived in the South. They were still denied education and **civil rights**. Civil rights are those rights guaranteed to citizens by the fact that they are citizens. This period in the South was a time of lynch law, loss of the right to vote, and legal case of *Plessy* v. *Ferguson*. This historic Supreme Court decision legalized segregation.

African-American leaders defined progress in different ways. Booker T. Washington was born a slave in Virginia in 1856. Through hard work, he was able to attend Hampton Institute, a college for African Americans founded in 1868.

Washington emphasized the need for African Americans to achieve economic independence. Political rights would come later. First, African Americans needed to earn a living.

Booker T. Washington

Some African Americans disagreed with Washington's emphasis on job training. They believed that political equality had to come first. Only then could African Americans achieve economic equality. The Niagara Movement, founded in 1905, supported this view. One of its leaders was W.E.B. Du Bois.

Du Bois at the office of the NAACP's *Crisis* magazine.

Du Bois attended Fisk University in Nashville, Tennessee. He then went to Harvard University and earned a master's degree and a doctorate. This was the first doctorate ever given by Harvard to an African American.

In 1909, Du Bois and others—African American and white—formed the National Association for the Advancement of Colored People (NAACP). Its goals included an end to segregation and racial discrimination. Among its targets were—and continue to be—voting, housing, jobs, and schools.

The Indian Agents' office in Spaulding, Idaho

Little was done to help Native Americans during the Progressive era. The process of assimilation begun in the 1880s continued. By 1911, many Native Americans feared that native cultures and traditions would be lost. However, it was not until the 1930s that any effort to allow Native Americans to continue their traditions became part of government policy.

Anti-Immigrant Discrimination

The reforms of the Progressive Era did not include everyone. By 1902, the Chinese were kept from entering the United States. In 1924, Congress passed a law ending all Japanese immigration.

Jews and Catholics were not barred from immigrating. But once in the United States, they faced prejudice. As more Jews arrived from eastern Europe, **anti-Semitism** grew. Anti-Semitism is discrimination against Jews.

In the late 1800s and early 1900s, Mexican immigrants added to the number of Hispanics in the United States. The first Mexican immigrants came in search of work. Later immigrants were pushed by the violence of the Mexican Revolution.

Like other immigrant groups, they found themselves living in poor sections of cities. Called **barrios**, these areas often had no running water, no paved streets, and no electricity. Mexicans learned to depend on one another for support.

El Paso, Texas, became the home of many Mexican immigrants.

Putting It All Together

In your notebook, state Booker T. Washington's idea of how African Americans could make progress. Then state W.E.B. Du Bois's view. Are these goals for progress the same or different from the goals of immigrants? Discuss the two ideas with a partner. Then decide which idea you agree with. Write a paragraph explaining why.

Biography

Carrie Chapman Catt (1859–1947)

Carrie Lane was born in Wisconsin. As a child, she moved to Iowa. She graduated from Iowa State College and became a teacher and later a principal in Mason City, Iowa. In 1883, she became the superintendent of the city's schools. This was an extraordinary job for a woman in the late 1800s.

Lane married twice. Her first husband, Leo Chapman, a newspaper editor and publisher, died a year after their 1885 marriage. In 1890, she married George W. Catt. By the time of her second marriage, she was already an organizer for the Iowa Woman Suffrage Association. After her marriage, she continued her work for women's suffrage. In 1895, Catt headed all organizing activities for the new National American Woman Suffrage Association (NAWSA). In 1900, she succeeded Susan B. Anthony as president of NAWSA and served until 1904.

In 1915, Catt was again president of NAWSA. She laid out a strategy that she called the "Winning Plan." NAWSA began an all-out push for an amendment to the U.S. Constitution giving women the right to vote. By 1918, the amendment had so much public support that the House of Representatives approved it. Catt then talked President Woodrow Wilson into supporting the amendment. He asked the Senate to approve it. The Senate, however, rejected it.

In the 1918 elections, NAWSA, under Catt's direction, went after senators who voted against the amendment. Two were defeated, just enough for passage. When the new Congress met in 1919, both houses passed the Twentieth Amendment. The states quickly ratified it.

Catt then turned her energies to a new organization, the League of Women Voters. She founded the group in 1920 to provide information about political, social, and economic issues to voters. The League continues its work today.

Read a Primary Source

The Niagara Movement: A Statement of Rights

The following list of demands was written by W.E.B. Du Bois for the Niagara Movement. Unlike Booker T. Washington and his supporters, members of the Niagara Movement wanted immediate change.

"First. We would vote; with the right to vote goes everything: Freedom, manhood, . . . the right to work, and the chance to rise, and let no man listen to those who deny this.

"We want full manhood suffrage, and we want it now, henceforth and forever.

"Second. We want discrimination in public accommodation to cease. Separation in railway and street cars, based simply on race and color, is un-American, undemocratic, and silly. We protest against all such discrimination.

"Third. We claim the right of freemen to walk, talk, and be with them that wish to be with us. . . .

"Fourth. We want the laws enforced against rich as well as poor; against Capitalist as well as Laborer; against white as well as black. . . . We want the Constitution of the country enforced. . . .

"Fifth. We want our children educated. . . . We want our children trained as intelligent human beings should be, . . . They have a right to know, to think, and to aspire.

"These are some of the chief things which we want. How shall we get them? By voting where we may vote, by persistent, unceasing agitation, by hammering at the truth, by sacrifice and work."

W. E. B. DuBois, *Address to the Nation*
(Harper's Ferry, West Virginia, 16 August, 1906)

reading for understanding

Restate, in your own words, each demand of the Niagara Movement.

Do you agree or disagree with the statement "with the right to vote goes everything"? Support your opinion with examples.

101

Chapter Summary

In the early 1900s, people who believed in political, economic, and social reform came to be known as **progressives**. **Muckrakers** used their writings to crusade for changes in government and the way businesses operated, an end to child labor, and safer working conditions, among other causes.

Wisconsin was the first state to adopt the **direct primary**. Another set of government reforms was pioneered in Oregon. That state adopted the **initiative**, **referendum**, and **recall**. **Prohibitionists** fought to ban alcohol.

Of the presidents who served in the early 1900s, Theodore Roosevelt is the best known for progressive policies. He earned the nickname "trustbuster" for his enforcement of antitrust laws. He settled a coal strike in 1902 with an agreement he called a **square deal**. Roosevelt also used the **bully pulpit** to end strikes and set up **conservation** programs to protect the environment.

Throughout the early 1900s, **assimilation** continued to be government policy toward Native Americans. **Suffragists** worked to gain the right to vote for women. African American leaders were divided over whether to seek economic independence or **civil rights**. Mexican immigrants, often living in **barrios**, did not benefit from reforms. Jews who immigrated faced **anti-Semitism**.

Chapter Review

1 Reread your list of reforms. Choose one reform. In your notebook, list all the information that you know about that issue.

2 Draw a cartoon to illustrate Theodore Roosevelt as the trustbuster who used the bully pulpit of the presidency.

3 Go back to your list of progressive reforms. Choose a reform. Imagine you are a muckraker reporting on the need for a particular reform. Write a title for an article that you might write about the need for that reform.

Skill Builder

How to Write an Effective Paragraph

Notice that the title says "effective paragraph." An effective paragraph is one that gets your point across.

An effective paragraph has:	
• a **topic sentence**	This is the main idea. The main idea is usually stated in the first sentence.
• **supporting details**	These explain, describe, or give examples about the main idea. A well-written paragraph has three to five sentences of supporting details.
• a **conclusion**	The final sentence is the conclusion. It summarizes the supporting details and restates the main idea.

Look at this example.

(1) Muckrakers investigated a number of similar problems. (2) Lincoln Steffens wrote about corruption in city politics. (3) Upton Sinclair wrote about unsafe and unhealthy conditions in the meatpacking industry. (4) Ida Tarbell wrote about the unethical business practices of the Standard Oil Company. (5) John Spargo used his writing to campaign for an end to child labor. (6) While each muckraker investigated a different issue, they found similar abuses and injustices.

- Sentence 1 states the main idea of the paragraph: The muckrakers investigated many different problems.
- Sentences 2 through 5 give examples of muckrakers and what they wrote about.
- Sentence 6 restates the main idea. This is one way to conclude a paragraph. The author could also have written: "The muckrakers investigated politics and business and found similar abuses and injustices in each."

1 Write a paragraph about a progressive reform. Use the ideas that you listed in number 1 under Chapter Review.

2 In Putting It All Together, pages 95 and 99, you wrote paragraphs. Did you include a topic sentence, supporting details, and a conclusion? Revise each paragraph to make it more effective.

4 UNIT

WAR, WEALTH, AND WELFARE

The years from 1914 to 1932 saw great changes in the United States. Americans lived through a war, strong prosperity, and economic troubles.

World War I began in 1914. America attempted to remain neutral but by 1917 declared war on Germany. The time of great prosperity was the 1920s. The decade is known as the "Roaring Twenties" and the "Jazz Age." The good times came to an end with the stock market crash of 1929. During the Great Depression, the nation endured a long period of hard economic times.

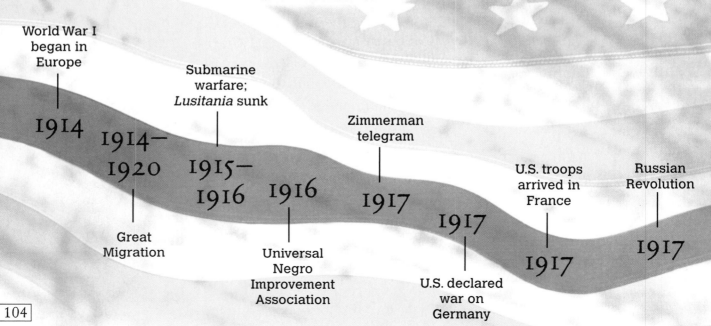

World War I began in Europe

1914

1914–1920

Great Migration

Submarine warfare; *Lusitania* sunk

1915–1916

1916

Universal Negro Improvement Association

Zimmerman telegram

1917

1917

U.S. declared war on Germany

U.S. troops arrived in France

1917

Russian Revolution

1917

How did the United States become involved in World War I?

What were the causes of the Great Depression?

$100 WILL BUY THIS CAR MUST HAVE CASH LOST ALL ON THE STOCK MARKET

Why were the 1920s called the "Roaring Twenties"?

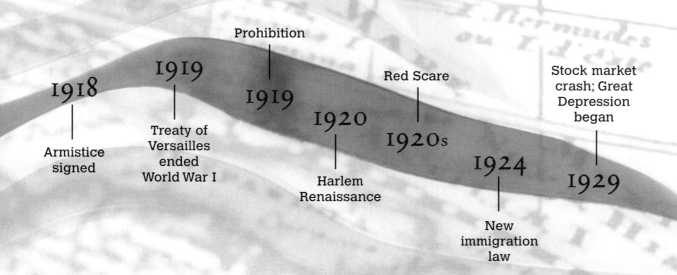

1918
Armistice signed

1919
Treaty of Versailles ended World War I

Prohibition
1919

1920
Harlem Renaissance

Red Scare
1920s

1924
New immigration law

Stock market crash; Great Depression began
1929

Chapter 7 WORLD WAR I

Getting Focused

Skim this chapter to predict what you will be learning.

- Read the lesson titles and subheadings.
- Look at the illustrations and read the captions.
- Examine the maps.
- Review the vocabulary words and terms.

Create three columns in your notebook. Label them, "The U.S. Enters the War," "The U.S. Fights the War," and "Problems After the War." As you read the chapter, write what happened, why, and how. Use words and phrases that will help you remember the most important information.

Lusitania
May 7 1915

Have been torpedoed send help.

War in Europe and U.S. Neutrality

Thinking on Your Own

Read each subheading. In your notebook, turn each subheading into a question that you can answer as you study the lesson. Be sure to look in the Glossary for the definition of any word in the vocabulary list that you do not know.

The Great War, later known as World War I, began in Europe in 1914. The United States proclaimed its **neutrality** and did not enter the war until 1917. Many Americans thought it was a European problem for Europeans to solve.

focus your reading

What were the causes of World War I?

Why did the United States adopt a policy of neutrality?

Why did the United States finally enter the war?

vocabulary

neutrality	ethnic group
nationalism	alliance

World War I in Europe

An arms race in Europe set the stage for World War I. European nations competed with each other to build the largest army or navy. Great Britain and Germany wanted the largest navy; Russia, France, and Germany wanted the largest army.

There were several long-term causes that eventually led to war. The arms race was driven by **nationalism**. Nationalism is a feeling of pride in and loyalty to one's nation. It was a very strong feeling among European nations. Nationalism also affected **ethnic groups** who did not have their own nation. One such group was the Slavs who lived in Austria-Hungary. They began to demand an independent country.

In 1916, antiwar demonstrators carry placards during a May Day parade.

WAR WHAT FOR?
FOR PROFITS
OF COURSE!

European Alliances, 1914

Allied Powers
Central Powers
Neutral Nations
Initial troop movements of Central Powers

For protection, European countries formed defensive **alliances**, or agreements. They agreed to come to one another's aid if attacked. The alliance formed by Austria-Hungary, Germany, and the Ottoman Empire became known as the Central Powers. Great Britain, France, and Russia were called the Allied Powers. Tensions in Europe were so high, an advisor reported to President Wilson in 1914, that "it only requires a spark to set the whole thing off."

There were also short-term causes of the war. The assassination of Austria-Hungary's Archduke Franz Ferdinand, in 1914, provided the spark. The archduke was killed by Gavrilo Princip, a Serbian nationalist. The Serbs supported independence for the Slavs. Very quickly, Austria-Hungary declared war on Serbia. This brought Austria-Hungary's allies—Italy and Germany—into the conflict. Serbia's allies—Great Britain, Russia, and France—then declared war against the Central Powers.

stop and think

World War I had both long-term and short-term causes. A long-term cause is one that has existed for a long time or builds up over a long time. A short-term cause is one that happens quickly or over a short time. In your notebook, list the causes of World War I. Next to each, mark "S" for short term or "L" for long term.

The United States Remains Neutral

Under President Woodrow Wilson, the United States adopted a policy of being neutral. The United States would not favor one side or the other. This was consistent with the nation's policy of "no entangling alliances," first stated by George Washington. The United States was determined to stay out of European affairs.

It was difficult for Americans to remain neutral in their thinking. They shared many traditions and values with the British. On the other hand, many Americans of German descent favored Germany. Many Irish Americans also sided with the Central Powers. They hoped that a British defeat would free Ireland from British rule.

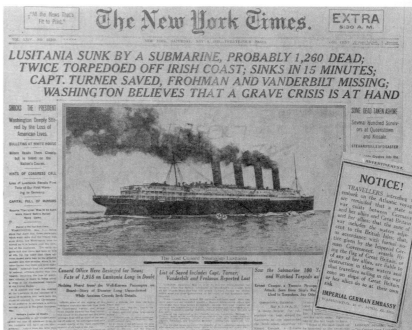

On May 7, 1915, a German torpedo sank the *Lusitania*, killing nearly 1,200 people, including many Americans.

However, the warring nations did not always respect neutrality. Great Britain blocked merchant ships from entering German ports. As a result, U.S. ships could not carry goods to Germany and the other Central Powers. German submarines, known as U-boats, attacked U.S. merchant ships sailing to Great Britain.

Even President Wilson found it difficult to be perfectly neutral. He issued several strong warnings to Germany about attacking merchant and passenger ships. Great Britain was also using its navy by blocking access to German ports. Wilson protested Britain's actions, but not vigorously. Wilson's two-sided approach did little to keep the U.S. neutral.

Steps to War

On May 7, 1915, Germans torpedoed the passenger liner *Lusitania* as it crossed the Atlantic. The loss of 128 American lives and approximately 1,000 European lives shocked

Americans and brought angry protests from President Wilson. Germany was afraid the United States would enter the war. To prevent the U.S. from joining the conflict, Germany announced that its submarines would stop attacking nonmilitary ships. Germany's pledge lasted less than a year.

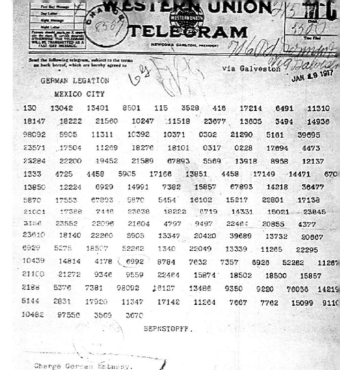

The turning point for America came in 1917. On February 1, Germany decided to begin unrestricted submarine warfare. Germany believed that they could conquer Britain before the United States entered the war. Several American merchant ships were torpedoed.

Once decoded, the Zimmerman telegram helped U.S. officials decide to join World War I.

The final push toward war came on March 1, 1917, when the Zimmerman telegram became public. In the telegram, a German foreign minister asked the German ambassador to Mexico to extend an offer. He wanted Mexico to declare war against the United States if the United States joined the war in Europe. In return, Mexico would receive New Mexico, Texas, and Arizona.

President Wilson addressed Congress on April 2, 1917.

Later that same month, German U-boats sank four U.S. ships. There was nothing to do but declare war. President Wilson went before Congress on April 2, 1917, and asked for a declaration of war against Germany.

Putting It All Together

In your notebook, make a timeline of the events that led the United States into World War I. Work with a partner to be sure you list all the dates and events.

Biography

Jeanette Rankin (1880–1973)

When President Wilson asked for a declaration of war, only 56 members of Congress voted "no." One of those members was Jeanette Rankin, a Republican from Montana.

Most American women could not even vote in local elections at the time. The Twentieth Amendment, giving women the right to vote, would not be ratified for another two years. But women in Montana could vote, thanks to the efforts of Rankin and the National American Woman Suffrage Association (NAWSA). In 1915, Rankin directed a campaign to gain the vote for women in Montana. The following year, Montanans elected her to the U.S. House of Representatives. Rankin was the first woman ever elected to Congress.

Jeanette Rankin was born outside Missoula, Montana. She graduated from the University of Montana in 1902 and went to graduate school at the Columbia School of Social Work in New York. In 1909, Rankin moved to Seattle and became a social worker. She also became active in NAWSA.

The people of Montana did not agree with Rankin's pacifist view on World War I. In 1918, she tried to gain the Republican nomination for Senator from Montana and was unsuccessful. Rankin returned to social work. In 1940, she ran again for the House of Representative and was elected. In 1941, she voted against joining World War II. She was the only member of Congress to vote "no" for a declaration of war against Japan.

Rankin did not run for public office again. However, she continued to speak out on issues related to women and to peace. In 1968, at the age of eighty-seven, she led a protest march in Washington, D.C. against the Vietnam War.

The Battlefield and the Homefront

Thinking on Your Own

What do you think the United States needed to do in 1917 to prepare for war? Write a list of things you think the nation had to do. As you read the lesson, decide how accurate your predictions are. Adjust your list to match what really happened.

The United States was now at war. The army needed more soldiers. The navy needed more ships. Factories had to produce war supplies rather than consumer goods. Farms had to grow more food.

focus your reading

Why were civil liberties an issue during the war?

What did civilians do to help the war effort?

How did U.S. forces help to defeat the Central Powers?

vocabulary

mobilize   dissent

draft   armistice

Great Migration

Mobilizing the Armed Forces

One of the first things that needed to be done was to **mobilize**, or prepare, the army and navy. The United States had a small army but needed a much larger one. In May 1917, Congress passed the Selective Service Act. All men aged 21 to 30 had to register for the **draft**. Almost three million men were called up for active duty.

Draftees report for duty at Camp Travis, San Antonio, Texas.

Mobilizing the Homefront

Congress had to mobilize the entire nation for war. It set up the Committee on Public Information to rally people in support of the war. Their goal was to convince the public that the war was justified. Congress also established the War Industries Board to organize the nation's industries. Factories had to switch from making consumer goods, like cars, to making war goods, like tanks and uniforms. The Food Administration oversaw the nation's farm output. The United States was feeding its own citizens, its soldiers, and also sending food to the Allies in Europe.

War bonds helped raise money for the war and increased patriotism.

All this pro-war activity led to a great deal of anti-German feeling. Germans were attacked by mobs. German was removed as a course from some schools. Sauerkraut was listed on menus and in grocery stores as "liberty cabbage."

Women often took the place of the men who went to war. More than one million women took jobs outside the home. African Americans were also hired to fill empty factory jobs in the North. From 1914 to 1920, around 500,000 African Americans moved north in what is called the **Great Migration**. These people were both pushed and pulled from the South. Southern

stop and think

How did the war benefit some people? In your notebook, list these groups and explain how they were helped. This is what is known as "unintended consequences." Talk with your partner about what this term means.

Producing munitions was an important part of the war effort.

tenant farmers and farm workers were pushed north because they made little or no money for their hard work. The possibility of paying jobs pulled many people northward.

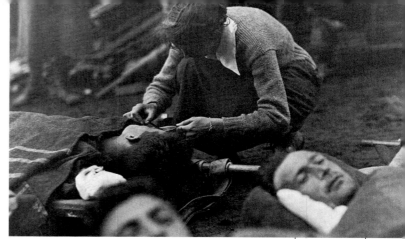

Women joined the Red Cross to help with the war effort.

In 1917, Congress passed the Espionage Act to punish anyone caught spying. At the time, the government worried about **dissent**, or expressing opposite views. In 1918, Congress passed the Sedition Act to discourage people from even speaking out against the war. These acts stifled civil liberties in the name of national security.

On the Battlefield

When U.S. soldiers arrived in France in June 1917, Europe had been at war for three years. The Allies were fighting the Central Powers on two fronts. The Western Front lay across France and Italy. The Eastern Front lay between the Central Powers and Russia.

In December 1917, Russia dropped out of the war. A revolution led by Vladimir Lenin had overthrown the czar. In March 1918, the new Russian government signed a treaty with Germany. Germany no longer had to fight on two fronts.

The invention of the tank, the machine gun, and poison gas changed how World War I was fought.

It could send all its troops to fight on the Western Front.

Germany used its new force to break out of the French lines. By June 1918, the Germans had pushed to within

40 miles of Paris. From June through mid-July, the Allies, including American troops, fought to keep the Germans from advancing any farther.

Then the Allies went on the offensive. From mid-July to the end of September, the Allies slowly advanced. Finally, they broke through the German lines during the seven-week Battle of the Argonne Forest. The German government asked for peace, and an **armistice** was signed at the 11th hour of the 11th day of the 11th month—November 11, 1918. The Treaty of Versailles officially ended the war on June 28, 1919.

Putting It All Together

Create a concept web for the "Effects of World War I on the Homefront." Review the lesson. As you read about an effect, add a line and write the effect in a smaller box.

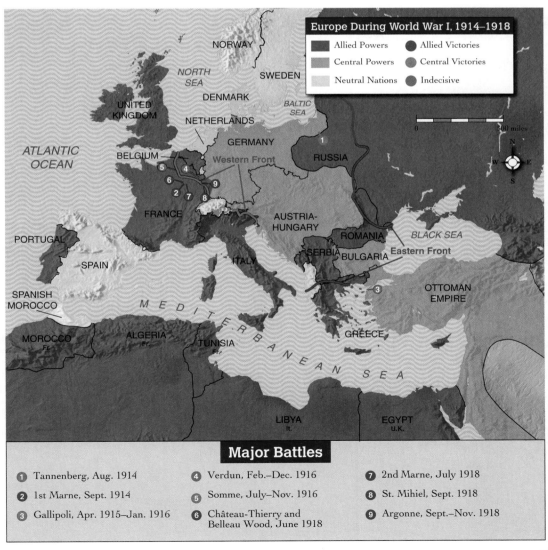

Europe During World War I, 1914–1918

- Allied Powers
- Central Powers
- Neutral Nations
- Allied Victories
- Central Victories
- Indecisive

Major Battles

1. Tannenberg, Aug. 1914
2. 1st Marne, Sept. 1914
3. Gallipoli, Apr. 1915–Jan. 1916
4. Verdun, Feb.–Dec. 1916
5. Somme, July–Nov. 1916
6. Château-Thierry and Belleau Wood, June 1918
7. 2nd Marne, July 1918
8. St. Mihiel, Sept. 1918
9. Argonne, Sept.–Nov. 1918

Read a Primary Source

Paying for the War

Waging war is very costly. One way the government paid for the war was by selling Liberty Bonds. For example, buying one $50 Liberty Bond was enough to vaccinate 666 soldiers against typhoid. The following is an ad from World War I. It urged everyone to buy Liberty Bonds to pay for the war.

Here is what your bonds will buy—

One $50 Liberty Bond will render 666 soldiers relatively safe from typhoid or will make 400 operations painless.

One $100 bond feeds a soldier for eight months.

Three $100 bonds clothe a soldier and feed him for one year in France.

One $500 bond supplies bicycles for the headquarters company of an infantry regiment.

One $1,000 bond buys six cases of operating instruments for a base hospital.

$1,500 worth of bonds will buy a motor ambulance.

Two $1,000 bonds buy a motor truck.

Three $1,000 bonds buy rifles for a field artillery battery.

$5,000 worth of bonds will equip a company of an infantry regiment with rifles.

$6,000 worth of bonds buys one liberty motor.

$9,000 worth of bonds will provide a rolling kitchen for field artillery brigade.

$10,000 worth of bonds fully equips three hospital wards of fifty beds each with beds made up and linen in reserve, chairs, tables, mirrors, foot tubs, 120 towels, pajamas, bath robes and towels.

$50,000 worth of bonds will construct a base hospital with 500 beds.

$100,000 worth of bonds will buy five combat planes.

Can you, with a free conscience, read the daily list of American casualties if you have not at least contributed to the provisioning of the men in American trenches?

There is no reader of PRINTERS' INK, man or woman, too poor to buy at least one Liberty Bond, one $50 or $100 bond, on the instalment plan if need be—**one dollar a week.**

This is the crisis, the decisive moment of the war. Subscribe today to the limit of your purse.

J. WALTER THOMPSON COMPANY
New York
Chicago Boston Detroit Cincinnati

Photographs by permission of Underwood & Underwood

FROM PRINTERS' INK, Issue of April 18, 1918.

After the War

Thinking on Your Own

Create a T-chart in your notebook. Label the left side "Fourteen Points." Label the right side "Treaty of Versailles." As you read, fill in the T-chart with the main points of each plan. Include facts from Lessons 1 and 2.

The war ended on November 11, 1918, with an armistice. The **kaiser**, or emperor, had been overthrown and the new German government asked for peace. In 1919, the Allies negotiated a peace treaty.

Woodrow Wilson's Proposal

President Wilson had his own idea of what peace should look like. He believed that there should be no winners or losers in the war. The future of the world depended on treating Germany and the other Central Powers fairly.

Wilson's peace plan was called the "Fourteen Points." It outlined a new world order based on freedom of the seas, free trade, arms reduction, and an end to secret treaties. Wilson also called

Citizens of Philadelphia celebrated the armistice on November 11, 1918.

for **national self-determination**. This would allow ethnic groups in Central Europe and Turkey to set up their own nations. Finally, he proposed a **League of Nations**, a new organization designed to help nations settle disputes peacefully.

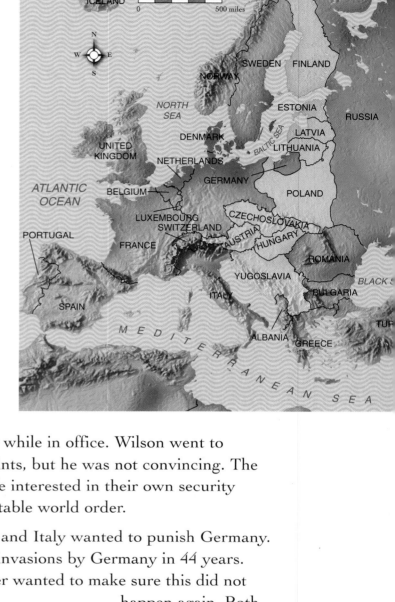

Europe After World War I

New Nations

0   500 miles

ICELAND

NORWAY   SWEDEN   FINLAND

NORTH
SEA   ESTONIA   RUSSIA

DENMARK   LATVIA

UNITED
KINGDOM   NETHERLANDS   LITHUANIA

ATLANTIC
OCEAN   BELGIUM   GERMANY   POLAND

LUXEMBOURG
PORTUGAL   SWITZERLAND   CZECHOSLOVAKIA

FRANCE   AUSTRIA   HUNGARY

SPAIN   ROMANIA

YUGOSLAVIA   BLACK S

ITALY   BULGARIA

ALBANIA   GREECE   TUR

MEDITERRANEAN SEA

Opposing Views at the Peace Conference

The Paris Peace Conference was the first time a United States president left the country while in office. Wilson went to promote his Fourteen Points, but he was not convincing. The other countries were more interested in their own security than in securing a more stable world order.

Great Britain, France, and Italy wanted to punish Germany. France had suffered two invasions by Germany in 44 years. The French prime minister wanted to make sure this did not happen again. Both France and Great Britain wanted **reparations**, or money, for their nations' losses in war. Along with the United States, these "Big Four" dictated peace terms to Germany and the other Central Powers.

Italy's Prime Minister Orlando, Britain's Prime Minister George, French Premier Clemenceau, and U. S. President Wilson (all seated) at the Paris Peace Conference.

stop and think

With which terms of the treaty would Wilson have disagreed? Choose one point. In your notebook, explain in a paragraph why Wilson would have disagreed with it. Share your paragraph with a partner.

The Treaty of Versailles ended World War I in 1919. The points in the Treaty of Versailles indicated:

- Germany accepted responsibility for the war.
- Germany would pay $33 million in reparations.
- Germany could keep only a small army and navy.
- Nine new nations were to be created from territory taken from the Central Powers.
- The League of Nations was to be created.

Rejection of the Treaty of Versailles

Wilson returned to the United States to urge the Senate to ratify the treaty. He he realized that the treaty had weaknesses, but he believed that the League of Nations could settle unresolved issues. Republicans, led by Senator Henry Cabot Lodge of Massachusetts, objected to the League. They were afraid that joining the League would mean that the U.S. would lose its **sovereignty**, or the ability to act on its own. They thought they would be committing the United States to go to war any time another nation was attacked.

The Senate voted several times and each time rejected the treaty. As a result, the United States never joined the League. Instead, it signed a separate treaty with Germany in 1921.

President Wilson spoke in St. Louis on September 6, 1919, to promote the League of Nations.

Putting It All Together

Think about how Wilson must have felt when the Senate rejected the Treaty and the League of Nations. Imagine you are Wilson. Write a journal entry describing your feelings.

Chapter Summary

World War I began in Europe in 1914. Its long-term causes were an arms race, **nationalism**, and the European system of **alliances**. Nationalism affected various **ethnic groups** who wanted their own independent nations.

At first the United States stayed out of the war, declaring a policy of **neutrality**. German U-boats torpedoed and sank U.S. ships and the ships of other nations carrying U.S. passengers. In 1917, the Zimmerman telegram and the sinking of more U.S. ships led to a declaration of war.

The United States had to **mobilize** for war. Congress set up a **draft** to register men for military service. Many jobs were filled by women and African Americans. The war was one cause of the **Great Migration** of African Americans from the South to the North. During the war, Congress also passed laws like the Sedition Act to deal with **dissent**.

The German **kaiser** was overthrown in 1918 and the war ended on November 11, 1918, with an **armistice**. During negotiations for the Treaty of Versailles, President Wilson proposed his Fourteen Point plan. This plan would have granted **national self-determination** to various European groups. He was outvoted on much of it because the Allies wanted to collect **reparations**. The Senate refused to approve the treaty because of the **League of Nations**. Senators were afraid the United States would lose its **sovereignty**.

Chapter Review

1   Review the table of long-term and short-term causes you made as you read the chapter. Choose the information in one column and write a paragraph to explain it.

2   Write a two-line headline about the declaration of war. Then write a two-line headline about the end of the war.

3   Design a poster to get people to buy Liberty Bonds.

Skill Builder

Understanding Sequence

Timelines are one way to show sequence. But sequence is more than the dates when events occurred.

Sequence is also the order in which things happened or should happen. For example, to change the cartridge in a printer, you have to follow certain steps. You cannot remove the cartridge before you open the printer. In the same way, you cannot surf the Internet before you log on.

Events in history happened in a certain order, too. For example,

> After a Serbian assassinated Archduke Franz Ferdinand, Austria-Hungary declared war on Serbia. Russia came to the aid of its ally, Serbia. Germany then declared war on Russia. Next, Germany declared war on France, an ally of Russia. Finally, France and Great Britain declared war on Germany and its ally Austria-Hungary.

The dates in text can help you determine sequence. There are also words that can help you figure out sequence. The following are some words that signal sequence:

first, second, third, fourth	months of the year
next, now, then, later	soon, sooner
days of the week	last, finally

1 Look at the example on this page. In your notebook, write all the signal words for sequence in this example.

2 Go back to pages 109 and 110 to the subheading "Steps to War." In your notebook, write all the signal words and dates that help you figure out the sequence for going to war.

3 Write a paragraph that describes the sequence in which you do something. Use some of the sequence words in the list.

Chapter
8 BOOM OR BUST

Getting Focused

Skim this chapter to predict what you will be learning.

- Read the lesson titles and subheadings.
- Look at the illustrations and read the captions.
- Examine the maps.
- Review the vocabulary words and terms.

The chapter title is "Boom or Bust." Make a T-chart in your notebook. Label one side "Boom" and the other side "Bust." Look through the chapter and choose three illustrations that you think show the boom, or good times. Then go through and find three illustrations that show the bust, or bad times.

The Roaring Twenties

Thinking on Your Own

People in the 1920s were just getting used to having movies and radio. Think about what your life would be like without movies, television, cable, and the Internet. Then write a paragraph describing a day in your life without these items. When describing an item, try to include words from the vocabulary list.

World War I ended in 1918. However, life for Americans did not return to what it was like before the war. They faced the new threats of **communists** and **anarchists**. In the election of 1920, Warren G. Harding said the nation needed a "return to normalcy." The Republican candidate for president captured the nostalgic mood of Americans perfectly. He won the election easily.

focus your reading

Why was there anti-immigrant feeling in the 1920s?

How did Americans' lives change in the 1920s?

What was the Harlem Renaissance?

vocabulary

communist

anarchist

quotas

consumer

mass production

assembly line

installment credit

racism

The Red Scare

The Russian Revolution of 1917 forced the czar, or ruler, from power when a new government took over. The new government was headed by communists—people who support a state-run economy. The fear that communists, also known as reds, would try to take over the United States became known as the Red Scare.

Anarchists—those who rebelled against any form of government—tended to be immigrants. A series of bombings by anarchists after WWI and the Red Scare led to a wave of anti-immigrant feeling in

Sacco and Vanzetti

the 1920s. In 1921, Nicola Sacco and Bartolomeo Vanzetti, two anarchists, were put on trial for robbery and murder. Many believed their conviction was the result of their anarchist views. They were put to death in 1927.

In 1921 and 1924, Congress tightened immigration policies. It passed laws that used **quotas** to favor immigrants from northern and western Europe over those from eastern and central Europe. Congress also ended all immigration from Japan. There were no limits on immigration from Mexico, however. Mexicans continued to come in great numbers.

Consumer Economy

The word *roaring* in the "Roaring Twenties" applies to the economy of the 1920s. It grew consistently for much of the decade. **Consumers**, people who buy goods, began to demand more items to make their lives easier and more enjoyable. **Mass production**, the making of large amounts of goods by machines, answered the demand. Machines created an **assembly line**. For example, in an automobile factory, one person attaches the left door and another person puts on the right door. Mass production makes it cheaper to manufacture goods.

The Model T and the assembly line changed the way goods were produced in America.

Henry Ford used the assembly line to mass-produce automobiles. In 1910, the Ford Model T cost $950. By 1924, as a result of mass production, a Model T cost $300. This made automobiles affordable for millions of middle-class families. It also allowed people to move out of the cities and into the suburbs.

After the war, businesses began to spend great amounts of money to advertise their products. The first radio shows were broadcast in the 1920s. Commercials began to come into homes, offices, and stores. Radio ads sang the praises of toothpaste, detergent, coffee, and an endless list of products.

Flapper-style clothing was a drastic change from the earlier Victorian dresses.

Many middle-class families could not afford to buy all these things. For purchases like cars, refrigerators, and washing machines, there was **installment credit**. With installment credit, a person paid some money up front and then small amounts over time. Interest was added to the price. As a result, the purchaser always paid more than the original price of the product.

The Harlem Renaissance

African Americans moved north during the Great Migration. Within a few years, New York City's Harlem became home to thousands of African Americans. It was here that the Jazz Age and the Harlem Renaissance began. Jazz was one African-American art form that spread quickly to white audiences. Jazz grew out of blues and ragtime in New Orleans.

The Harlem Renaissance is the name given to the period in which African-American literature, art, and music flourished. The writers and artists of the Harlem Renaissance explored two main themes. One was pride in their heritage—both African and African American. The second theme was **racism**.

The music of Duke Ellington was popular during the 1920s.

Aaron Douglas became a well known painter and graphic artist during the 1920s.

Putting It All Together

This lesson describes political, social, and economic changes in the United States in the 1920s. In your notebook, create a table with three columns. Label the columns "Political," "Social," and "Economic." List the changes you read about. Include immigration laws, mass production, installment credit, and the Harlem Renaissance. Share your table with a partner and add topics.

Biography

Marcus Garvey (1887–1940)

African Americans in general did not share in the wealth of the 1920s. They faced discrimination in jobs, housing, and education. They were ready for the ideas of Marcus Garvey.

Marcus Mosiah Garvey was born in Jamaica, an island in the British West Indies. In his early twenties, Garvey left Jamaica. He worked and traveled through Central and South America. Wherever he went, he saw

blacks living in poverty. In 1914, he founded the Universal Negro Improvement Association (UNIA) in Jamaica. The goal of UNIA was political, economic, and cultural independence for black people. Garvey believed that blacks would gain equality only through their own efforts. He also called on blacks to take pride in their African heritage. UNIA was the beginning of black nationalism.

Garvey brought UNIA to Harlem in 1916. Soon, there were UNIA branches in cities across the country. Thousands of African Americans became members. Garvey began businesses to help African Americans gain economic independence. One business was the Black Star Line, a steamship company. By 1920, Garvey decided that African Americans would never gain equality in the United States. He began to talk about creating a nation in Africa. The Black Star Line was part of Garvey's Back-to-Africa plan. However, Garvey was not a businessman. Nor were the people he chose to run UNIA's finances. In 1922, Garvey was charged with mail fraud. He was convicted in 1925. Two years later he was deported to Jamaica.

Marcus Garvey gave ordinary African Americans hope, confidence, and pride. His message of black nationalism lives on.

The Crash

Thinking on Your Own

People who own stock in companies may receive dividends. These are cash payments based on how much profit the companies make. In what companies would you invest? List two in your notebook. Then use the vocabulary words to explain why you think each is a good investment.

The stock market **crash** that ended the prosperity of the 1920s had its beginnings in that same prosperity. *Crash* is the term given to the end of the long rise in the value of stocks. Many Americans lost money in the Crash of 1929, and this caused businesses to suffer.

focus your reading

How did buying stocks on margin lead to the stock market crash?

What factors contributed to "Black Tuesday"?

What caused the Great Depression?

vocabulary

crash	stock exchange
stocks	depression
margin	overproduction

The Stock Market

Much of the wealth of the 1920s was on paper. It was not actual money that people had in the bank. Instead they invested their savings in **stocks**, or shares, in corporations. Shares were bought and sold on the stock market.

By the end of the 1920s, more and more investors were buying stocks on **margin**. They did not pay the full price of the stocks. Instead, they paid 10 percent of the price and borrowed the rest. The idea was that when the value of the stock went up, they would sell the stock. There would be enough money to make a profit and repay the loan. This worked as long as the value of stocks kept going up.

Investors watch the ticker as stock prices fall.

But during the summer of 1929, stock prices started to fall. By September, there were serious problems. More and more investors began to sell. Some were afraid that they would not be able to pay off the margin loans. Other Americans were afraid they would lose all their savings.

Wall Street filled with people after the crash of the stock market.

stop and think

Imagine you had invested your life savings in the stock market. How would you have felt on October 29? What would you do? Talk over your ideas with a partner. In your notebook, write a paragraph about your feelings as you watched the stock market fall.

The Crash

The sell-off of stocks began on October 21, 1929. As more investors saw the value of stocks fall, more investors sold their stocks. The stock market dropped sharply and kept dropping. October 29, 1929, came to be known as "Black Tuesday." Sixteen million shares of stock were sold off on that day. This was two to four times as many as usual. Americans lost between $10 and $15 billion on that single day.

The **stock exchanges**, where stocks are actually bought and sold, closed for two days. The closing was supposed to give investors time to cool off. It did not work. By November 13, 1929, the value of stocks had fallen by $30 billion.

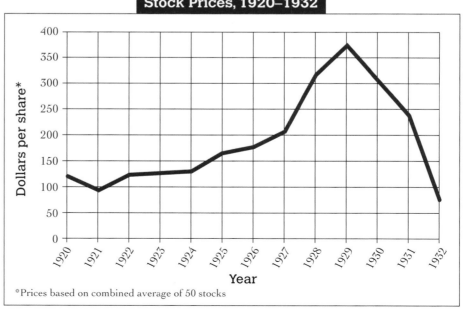

Stock Prices, 1920–1932

*Prices based on combined average of 50 stocks

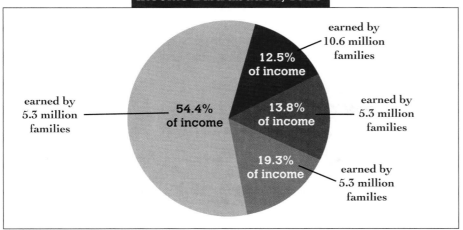

Income Distrubution, 1929

earned by 10.6 million families — 12.5% of income

earned by 5.3 million families — 54.4% of income

13.8% of income — earned by 5.3 million families

19.3% of income — earned by 5.3 million families

Causes of the Great Depression

The stock market crash did not cause the Great **Depression**. A depression is a period of very little business activity, very high unemployment, and falling wages and prices. The problems with the economy were far greater than the stock market.

All Americans did not share in the wealth of the 1920s. By 1929, about 19 million families, or 71 percent, earned less than $2,500 per year. Most families had no savings. Most workers could not afford the goods that factories turned out. They also had no money to live on if they lost their jobs. This uneven distribution of wealth was one cause of the Great Depression.

Overproduction was another cause. By the end of the 1920s, businesses were producing more goods than people could buy. Factories began to close. People lost their jobs.

Farmers had borrowed money to buy new equipment and more land. When the price for crops fell, farmers could not repay their loans. Many farmers lost their farms and joined the growing number of unemployed workers. When loans went unpaid, banks closed. The shaky banking system was another cause of the Great Depression.

Other nations were suffering through their own economic hard times. They could not afford to buy U.S. crops and manufactured goods. This also hurt the U.S. economy.

Putting It All Together

Create a concept map about the causes of the Great Depression. Draw and label a large circle "Causes of the Great Depression." Then add lines and smaller circles for the causes. Include as many details as you can.

Read a Primary Source

The Crash

The following newspaper article appeared the morning after Black Tuesday. It describes some stockholders on Black Tuesday. Stockbrokers' offices had rooms where their customers could watch the ticker—the machine that printed the changing prices of stocks. The term *quotations* refers to various stock prices.

reading for understanding

What was the ticker telling investors about the value of their stocks?

Whom do you think "the butcher, the baker, the candlestick maker" are supposed to represent?

The reporter says that crowding around the ticker was similar to standing around what?

Why do you think no one wanted to listen to someone else's story of lost money?

October 30, 1929

"Groups of men, with here and there a woman, stood about . . . all over the city yesterday watching spools of ticker tape unwind and as the . . . paper. . . grew longer at their feet, their fortunes shrunk. Others sat . . . on tilted chairs in the customers' rooms of brokerage houses and watched a motion picture of waning wealth as the day's quotations moved silently across a screen.

"It was among groups such as these . . . that drama and perhaps tragedy were to be found. On the floor of the Exchange itself there was little to indicate that the butcher, the baker, and the candlestick maker, all were dumping holdings upon a market whose buying appetite was sated.

"But the crowds about the ticker tapes, like friends about the bedside of a stricken friend, reflected in their faces the story the tape was telling. There were no smiles. There were no tears either. Just . . . fellow-sufferers. Everybody wanted to tell his neighbor how much he had lost. Nobody wanted to listen. . . ."

Abridgement of "Crowds at Tickers See Fortunes Wane" *The New York Times,* October 30, 1929. Copyright 1929 by The New York Times Co. Reprinted with permission.

The Great Depression

Thinking on Your Own

Examine the illustrations in this lesson. Think about what they tell you about the lesson. Choose one photo to write about. In your notebook, describe what it shows and what can be learned about the Great Depression.

The economy continued to worsen throughout 1930. Some investors saw their savings wiped out in the crash. Others lost their savings when banks failed. Some people were heavily in debt with no way out. More banks failed as farmers and business owners could not repay their loans. Companies that were still doing business lost confidence in the economy. They stopped buying equipment and began laying off workers. More businesses closed, and more workers lost their jobs. More farmers lost their farms. More banks failed. The Great Depression was growing worse.

focus your reading

How did the Great Depression affect people?

What did President Hoover do about the Depression?

How did his handling of the Bonus Army affect President Hoover?

vocabulary

foreclosed   relief

shantytowns   bonus army

public works

A plumber advertises his services on a sandwich board during the Depression.

Deepening Unemployment

Joblessness increased steadily after 1929. By the end of 1932, 12 million workers—25 percent of the workforce—were unemployed. Some 30,000 businesses failed in 1932 alone. African Americans and women were especially hard hit by unemployment. Often a woman was fired from a job so a man with a family could keep his job. Employers ignored the fact that women headed families or that their husbands might be out of work.

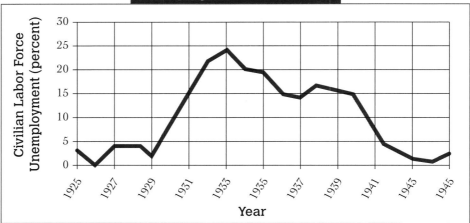

Unemployment, 1925–1945

Some unemployed workers tried selling apples or pencils on street corners. Some families piled suitcases and all the family members into a car. They drove off in search of jobs. Families with mortgages could also find themselves on the sidewalk. Banks **foreclosed** when people fell behind in their loan payments.

Many families had nowhere to go. They joined other people already living in **shantytowns**. These were like villages but the shelters were cars or were constructed out of cardboard and wood. Shantytowns grew up around cities and towns. Some people called them Hoovervilles. Herbert Hoover was elected president in 1928. People blamed him for not doing more to end the Depression.

State and local governments and charities set up bread lines and soup kitchens to feed the hungry. By 1932, they too were running out of money. There were too many people to feed. President Hoover seemed to be doing little to help, and the Depression was tightening its hold on the nation.

stop and think

In your notebook, write a two-line headline for each of the following: (1) the problems African Americans faced in the Depression, (2) the loss of homes because of bank foreclosures. Share your headlines with a partner.

Voluntary Action

President Hoover did not believe that the federal government should step in to help people. As a Republican, he believed this was the role of state and local governments. He did believe in voluntary action. He asked companies to remain open and not to reduce wages. Little came of Hoover's requests.

Construction of Hoover Dam began in 1931.

By 1931, Hoover realized that the federal government had to do something. He supported federal government spending on **public works** projects. These projects created new jobs and provided **relief**, or aid, for the unemployed. Among the projects were highways, dams, and public buildings like libraries.

In 1932, Hoover asked Congress to pass the Reconstruction Finance Corporation. It lent money to banks, railroads, and insurance companies. Hoover then agreed to the Emergency Relief and Construction Act that provided money to state governments for relief and for public works. Farmers, in an effort to raise prices, destroyed their crops. At the same time, some Americans were starving. Hoover's time was running out.

Bonus Army

The final blow to Hoover's hope of reelection was the **bonus army**. In 1924, Congress voted a $1,000 bonus to all veterans of World War I. The bonus was to be paid in 1945. Jobless veterans wanted the bonus to be paid immediately. They needed the money to support themselves.

A group of about 20,000 unemployed veterans gathered in Washington, D.C., in June 1932. Called the Bonus Army, they camped in Hoovervilles in the city. The veterans came to urge Congress to pass a bill to pay the bonus early. The House approved the bill. The Senate rejected it.

By the end of July, there were still about 2,000 veterans and their families in Washington, D.C. Hoover sent the army to clear them from empty buildings, not from the shantytowns. His order was ignored. Newspapers showed soldiers with bayonets chasing veterans and their families. These photos seemed to prove that Hoover did not care about the average person.

Soldiers use tear gas to disperse members of the bonus army in 1932.

Putting It All Together

Imagine you are an unemployed worker in 1932. What should President Hoover do to help you? In your notebook, write a letter to President Hoover asking him for this help.

Chapter Summary

Immediately after World War I, Americans worried about **anarchists** and **communists** taking over the country. This period is known as the Red Scare. Immigration laws were tightened and a **quota** system added.

For some Americans the 1920s were a time of prosperity. **Mass production**, often using an **assembly line**, produced great quantities of goods. **Consumers** were only too willing to use **installment credit** to buy goods.

The Harlem Renaissance celebrated pride in African and African-American heritage and brought up the issue of **racism**. The 1920s were also called the Jazz Age.

The 1920s ended with the stock market **crash**. Many people had been buying stock on **margin**. As the price of **stocks** on the **stock exchanges** fell, investors lost their money. **Overproduction** of crops forced many farmers into ruin. The nation plunged into the Great **Depression**.

President Hoover believed that providing **relief** to people was the job of state and local governments. He did support federal money for **public works**. Many Americans, however, believed the federal government should do more. **Shantytowns** emerged as banks **foreclosed** on unpaid mortgages. The **bonus army** protested veterans' rights in Washington, D.C.

Chapter Review

1 The immigration laws of the 1920s favored immigrants from northern and western Europe. Why do you think this happened? In your notebook, write a paragraph to explain your ideas.

2 Imagine you work for an advertising agency in 1925. With a partner, write a one-minute radio commercial to sell the Model T. Research more about this car in the library or on the Internet.

3 Use a T-chart to list the causes and effects of the Great Depression. On the left side, list the events that contributed to the stock market crash. On the right side, list the changes to people's lives.

Skill Builder

Analyzing Maps

Maps are very useful tools. Follow these steps when you have to answer questions about a map:

- Read the title of the map. What is it about?
- Read the map key. What do the symbols stand for?
- Examine the map.
- Look at the placement of the symbols on the map.
- Reread the explanation for each symbol to be sure you understand what it shows.

The following is an historical map. It shows a particular event, in a particular place, at a particular time. The Dust Bowl occurred because of severe windstorms in the Great Plains. The rich topsoil blew away. Farmers left their farms because it was useless to try to plant crops. These farm families joined all other people looking for work.

1 Which states lost people because of the loss of topsoil?

2 Which six states suffered the greatest losses of topsoil?

3 Choose one route people took out of the Dust Bowl. List the states they traveled through and where they ended.

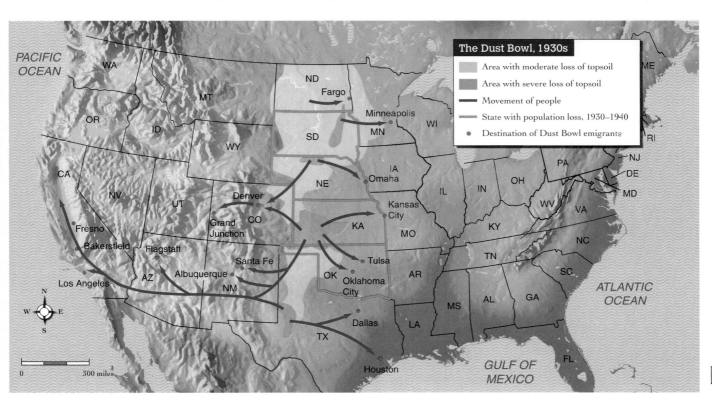

The Dust Bowl, 1930s

- Area with moderate loss of topsoil
- Area with severe loss of topsoil
- Movement of people
- State with population loss, 1930–1940
- Destination of Dust Bowl emigrants

5

UNIT

THE NEW DEAL AND WORLD WAR II

In the election of 1932, President Herbert Hoover faced Franklin Roosevelt. Roosevelt was the Democratic governor of New York. His campaign promised a New Deal for Americans. He won in a landslide. Once in office, Roosevelt set to work to solve the problems of the Great Depression.

At the same time, Roosevelt and the nation faced another serious problem. Dictators had come to power in Germany and Italy. By the end of the 1930s, they were taking over other nations. How long would it be before Europe was at war? Would the United States enter the war if it came?

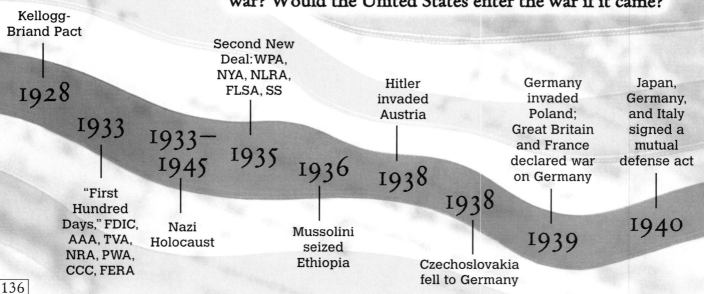

Kellogg-Briand Pact

1928

1933

"First Hundred Days," FDIC, AAA, TVA, NRA, PWA, CCC, FERA

1933–1945

Nazi Holocaust

Second New Deal: WPA, NYA, NLRA, FLSA, SS

1935

1936

Mussolini seized Ethiopia

Hitler invaded Austria

1938

1938

Czechoslovakia fell to Germany

Germany invaded Poland; Great Britain and France declared war on Germany

1939

Japan, Germany, and Italy signed a mutual defense act

1940

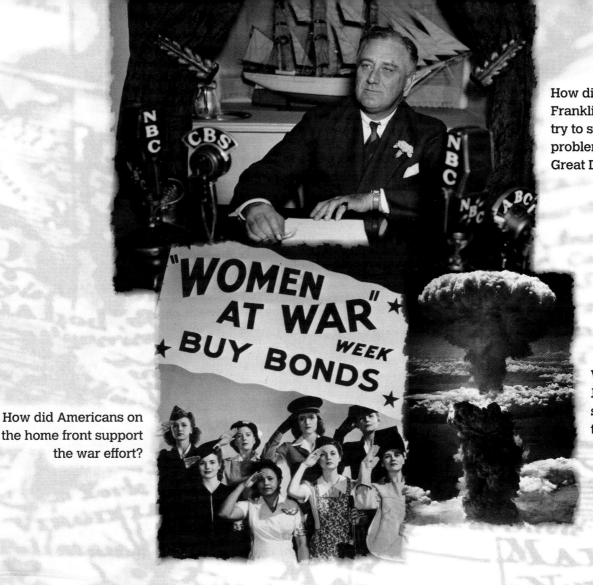

How did President Franklin Roosevelt try to solve the problems of the Great Depression?

"WOMEN AT WAR" WEEK BUY BONDS

How did Americans on the home front support the war effort?

Why did Japan finally surrender to the Allies?

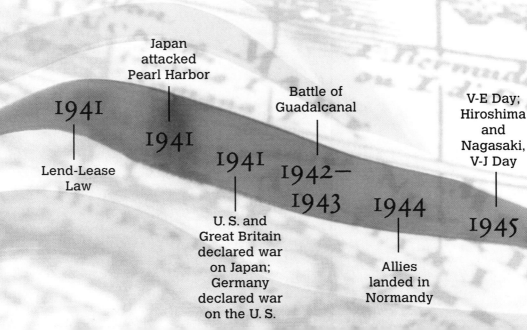

Lend-Lease Law
1941

Japan attacked Pearl Harbor
1941

U. S. and Great Britain declared war on Japan; Germany declared war on the U. S.
1941

Battle of Guadalcanal
1942–1943

Allies landed in Normandy
1944

V-E Day; Hiroshima and Nagasaki, V-J Day
1945

Chapter 9
FRANKLIN D. ROOSEVELT AND THE NEW DEAL

Getting Focused

Skim this chapter to predict what you will be learning.

- Read the lesson titles and subheadings.
- Look at the illustrations and read the captions.
- Examine the maps.
- Review the vocabulary words and terms.

The New Deal provided jobs and food, but it did not end the Great Depression. The economy did recover during World War II. Think about why this may have happened. Talk over your ideas with a partner. In your notebook, write a paragraph that explains why you think the nation's economy improved so much after the nation went to war.

The First Hundred Days

Thinking on Your Own

If you were Franklin D. Roosevelt on your first day in office, what would you do? Think about what you already know about the Great Depression. Then make a list of people you would want to help and how you would help them. As you read the lesson, create a list of what President Roosevelt actually did.

"I pledge you, I pledge myself, to a new deal for the American people," declared President Roosevelt in his 1933 inaugural address. In his "First Hundred Days" in office, President Roosevelt sent 15 bills to Congress. He wanted relief money for workers, and business reforms. He believed that banks and corporations had to change the way they operated. Not all his ideas worked, but Americans were relieved that the government was acting.

focus your reading

What was Roosevelt's first action as president?

How did the New Deal help the jobless and farmers?

What was the National Recovery Administration?

vocabulary

run on the banks

sound

President Roosevelt was inaugurated on March 4, 1933.

People waiting to withdraw money during the run on banks.

The Banking Crisis

The day after he took office, Roosevelt declared a bank holiday. This closed all banks for four days. There had been a **run on the banks**. Many banks had failed because people took out all their money. The bank holiday would stop this.

The president then sent Congress the Emergency Banking Relief Act. Congress passed it with little debate. Under this law, federal examiners reviewed the accounts of all banks that were still operating. The examiners found that about 75 percent were **sound**. These banks had the financial resources to reopen at the end of the bank holiday. The findings reassured the public. The run on banks was over.

Later in 1933, Congress set up the Federal Deposit Insurance Corporation (FDIC). This agency insures the money people deposit in banks. The FDIC still operates today.

stop and think

President Hoover did not believe that government should tell private businesses what to do. Do you think he would have agreed with the Emergency Banking Relief Act? Discuss the question with a partner. Then write a paragraph in your notebook to explain your answer.

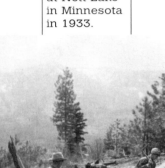

The CCC planted trees at Nett Lake in Minnesota in 1933.

Relief Programs

In May 1933, the president sent a series of bills to Congress to provide people with immediate help. Congress set up the Civilian Conservation Corps (CCC), the Federal Emergency Relief Agency (FERA), and the Public Works Administration (PWA). These agencies put people to work to give them money for food and shelter. They replanted forests, built schools, and fixed roads. In May, Roosevelt also turned to the problems of farmers, who made up approximately 20 percent of the population. He asked Congress to set up the Agricultural Adjustment Administration (AAA) to pay farmers to produce fewer crops. Sending fewer crops to market would raise crop prices. That would provide farmers with more income.

In California, the Central Valley Project built canals.

Also in May, Congress approved the Tennessee Valley Authority (TVA). It built dams and power plants along the Tennessee River. The plants provided people in the South with cheap electricity.

In June, the National Recovery Administration (NRA) was set up to work with businesses. The purpose of the NRA was to help businesses regulate themselves.

First Hundred Days of the New Deal

AGENCY	GOALS
Civilian Conservation Corps (CCC)	• Provided paid jobs, housing, and food to about 3 million single men, ages 18 to 25 • Replanted forests, built up sand on beaches, and did maintenance work in parks • Added a few camps for women at the urging of Eleanor Roosevelt • Separated African Americans into segregated camps and paid them less
Tennessee Valley Authority (TVA)	• Built 20 dams on the Tennessee River and its tributaries in 7 Southern states • Provided cheap electricity • Helped keep rivers from flooding
Agricultural Adjustment Administration (AAA)*	• Paid farmers to destroy crops in order to reduce crop surpluses • Made payments called subsidies to farmers to stop planting land • Did not help tenant farmers, most of whom were African Americans
Federal Emergency Relief Agency (FERA)	• Gave federal money to state and local governments for work relief projects • Included projects to build sewers, schools, playgrounds, parks, and airports
National Recovery Administration (NRA)*	• Helped businesses develop codes of fair competition within industries • Regulated how much businesses could produce and how much they could charge • Included codes on minimum wage, maximum work hours, right to join unions
Public Works Administration (PWA)	• Provided jobs building dams, highways, bridges, schools, sewer systems, and public buildings

* Later declared unconstitutional

Putting It All Together

In your notebook create a timeline for the First Hundred Days of the New Deal. Write a sentence next to each entry to explain what each law or agency did.

Biography

Eleanor Roosevelt (1884–1962)

Eleanor Roosevelt, the first activist first lady, came from a wealthy and well-known family. President Theodore Roosevelt was her uncle. In 1905, she married Franklin Roosevelt who was a distant cousin. In 1932, she became first lady when her husband took office as president. However, Eleanor Roosevelt was already well known in New York State politics. After 1932, she became world famous.

In the early 1900s, Eleanor Roosevelt was active in the Progressive movement. By 1921, she was assisting her husband in Democratic politics in New York. In 1928, he was elected governor of New York State, and in 1932, president of the United States.

As first lady, Eleanor Roosevelt had a great deal of influence. No first lady had ever held press conferences. Eleanor Roosevelt had regularly scheduled press conferences. She discussed politics on her radio program. She wrote a daily newspaper column called "My Day" and a monthly magazine column called "If You Ask Me."

Eleanor Roosevelt was also the "eyes and ears" of the president. In 1921, Franklin contracted polio and was never again able to walk without crutches. Because of his difficulty in getting around, she traveled the country in his place. She reported to the president what she saw and what she heard from ordinary Americans. Throughout her life, Eleanor Roosevelt worked for equal rights for women and African Americans. Young people were a special concern to her.

After Franklin's death in 1945, Eleanor Roosevelt was asked to be the U.S. representative to the United Nations. She chaired the UN's Commission on Human Rights and co-wrote the Universal Declaration of Human Rights. After 1952, she traveled worldwide in support of the UN and social issues. In 1961, President John Kennedy reappointed her to the UN. In that year he also created the Presidential Commission on the Status of Women as a result of her urging. Eleanor Roosevelt remains one of the most admired women in world history.

The Second New Deal

Thinking on Your Own

Read the vocabulary list. Find each word in the text. Read a sentence or two before and after the sentence with the vocabulary word. Try to figure out what each word means. Write the meaning for each word in your notebook. When you have worked through the list, check your ideas with the Glossary definitions.

By 1935, the worst of the Great Depression was over. Unemployment was decreasing, but the economy had not picked up very much. People on both the political **right** and **left** were criticizing the New Deal. The president was forced to rethink the government's efforts to lead the country toward **recovery**.

The right had two arguments. First, they did not want government interfering in business. Second, they were worried about the way the federal government was paying for relief projects. They wanted a **balanced budget**,

This 1938 cartoon is critical of President Roosevelt's spending policies.

THIS IS ONE RABBIT THAT NEVER FAILED ME!

SPENDING

OLD RELIABLE!

> **focus your reading**
>
> What were some Second New Deal programs?
>
> Why did the president attempt his court-packing plan?
>
> What were the successes and failures of the New Deal?
>
> **vocabulary**
>
> the right
>
> the left
>
> recovery
>
> balanced budget
>
> deficit
>
> unconstitutional
>
> landslide

but Roosevelt was creating a **deficit**, or shortage. People on the right thought that the government should not pay out more than it took in through taxes. Roosevelt, however, was borrowing money instead.

The political left wanted more reforms. They wanted more government limits on business. They wanted more social programs to help the poor. Senator Huey P. Long called for each

American family to receive $5,000. Long's *Share Our Wealth Society* had 27,000 local clubs by 1935, but the movement ended with Long's assassination.

The president reacted to his critics. Instead of trying to please everyone, Roosevelt decided to form an alliance with the working class, organized labor, and the poor. To raise more money, he proposed an increase in tax rates on the incomes of wealthy people and on large corporations. These changes formed the basis of the Second New Deal.

This family in Nipomo, California, was forced to sell their tent in order to buy food.

Relief and Reform

In January 1935, Roosevelt proposed the Works Progress Administration (WPA). In addition to construction projects, the agency oversaw a number of programs for artists. Among the projects were painting murals in government buildings, photographing conditions of tenant farmers and migrant workers, writing histories of former slaves, and publishing state guide books.

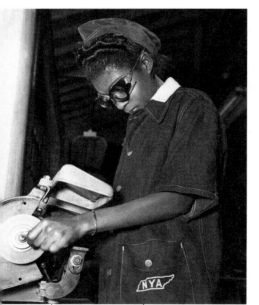

An African-American student in the NYA program.

The National Youth Administration (NYA) helped high school and college students stay in school. The National Labor Relations Act (NLRA) helped workers and labor unions. Between 1933 and 1943, union membership rose from just over 2 million workers to almost 14 million. The Fair Labor Standards Act (FLSA) replaced some of the NRA codes. In 1935, the Supreme Court had declared the act authorizing the NRA **unconstitutional**.

Another program of long-term importance to the country was Social Security (SS). For the first time, American workers would have old-age pensions so they could retire. The NLRA, FLSA, and SS are still in operation today.

Second New Deal

AGENCY/ACT	PURPOSE
Works Progress Administration (WPA), 1935	• Provided jobs building highways, roads, streets, public buildings, parks, bridges, and airports • Created work for artists, writers, photographers, actors, and musicians • Included an emphasis on jobs for women
National Labor Relations Act (NLRA), also known as the Wagner Act, 1935	• Allowed collective bargaining (negotiating between an employer and a union for wages, hours, and benefits) • Set up the National Labor Relations Board (NLRB) to supervise elections for workers to decide whether to organize a union
National Youth Administration (NYA), 1935	• Provided part-time work for young people, 16 to 25 • Enabled high school and college students to remain in school and to learn skills
Social Security Administration (SS), 1935	• Provided monthly payments to retired, older workers • Provided monthly payments to those with disabilities and to poor families with children • Included unemployment insurance, which provided monthly payments to the unemployed for a short period of time
Fair Labor Standards Act (FLSA)	• Set maximum 40-hour work week • Set the minimum wage at $0.25 an hour • Ended employment of children under 16

Court Packing

President Roosevelt won reelection in 1936 in a **landslide**. His vote total was so huge that he decided he could take on the Supreme Court. The Court had declared the AAA as well as the NRA unconstitutional. The Court was about to decide several other cases involving New Deal laws.

Roosevelt proposed to Congress that the number of judges on the Supreme Court be raised from seven to nine. This would give him the opportunity to add judges who would be more likely to support the New Deal programs. The newspapers and his critics accused Roosevelt of trying to pack the court. His proposal became known as the court-packing plan. Although nothing came of the plan, the Court began upholding the constitutionality of New Deal laws.

This cartoon represents the Democratic response to President Roosevelt's Supreme Court Reform Plan.

ALL I SAID WAS "GIMME SIX MORE JUSTICES!"

The Successes and Failures of the New Deal

The New Deal was far from perfect. Many Americans were left out. For example, in the beginning Social Security did not cover tenant farmers, farm workers, or household workers. Many of these workers were African American. The NLRA and the Wagner Act did not cover farm workers either—most of whom were Latino.

Eleanor Roosevelt worked hard to get women and African Americans included in New Deal programs. African Americans also started to protest their treatment. As a result, the president began to appoint African Americans to important government posts. Those who became his informal advisors were known as the Black Cabinet.

By the late 1930s, the economic recovery was still uncertain. Unemployment remained high, and programs such as the WPA were still needed. However, people felt more confident about the future.

stop and think

President Roosevelt's three goals for the New Deal were relief, reform, and recovery. The relief and reform programs were supposed to cause the economic recovery. In your notebook, make a T-chart. Label the columns "Relief Programs" and "Reform Programs." With a partner, list programs in this lesson in the correct column.

The Black Cabinet in 1939

Putting It All Together

Think about the Great Depression and the New Deal. Do you think President Roosevelt was right about what government should do for its citizens? Write your ideas in your notebook. Discuss them with a partner. Then write a paragraph explaining what you think the role of government should be.

Read a Primary Source

Letter to Mrs. Roosevelt

As first lady, Eleanor Roosevelt received hundreds of thousands of letters a year from Americans. Some writers complained about her or about the president's policies. Some writers suggested actions that the government should take. Others asked for help. Many of the letters came from children and young people. Their requests were simple: a bicycle to ride to school, money to make payments on a new refrigerator, help with college tuition, and clothes to wear.

reading for understanding

Why can't Miss E.B. afford to buy a dress?

Do you think that she is hinting that she wants shoes, too? Explain your answer.

What do you think of Miss E.B.'s reason for wanting a graduation dress? Explain your answer.

Bangor, Mich.,
April 27, 1935

Dear Mrs. Roosevelt:

I am appealing to you because I know you might be able to help me. I graduate this year and I haven't enough money to buy a dress. I give all I earn for food for the family.

I have been worried and this is the only solution I could come to. I need a light dress and as I am quite little I would need about (a girl's) size 14 or 15 in dresses. . . .

I'll have to do without white shoes although I've always craved a pair of pumps size $5\frac{1}{2}$ or 5's that I never will get until I get a job which I will work very hard to get.

If I had a lot of money I would take up a nurses course and work for charity. Just to get the pleasure of healing people.

Graduate May 28, "35"

P.S. It's only because I hate to go on the stage with the other girls in my shabby dress. My father works when he is able.

Your Pleaing Friend
Miss E.B.
Bangor, Michigan

(www.newdeal.feri.org)

147

Foreign Policy of the New Deal

Thinking on Your Own

Think about what it would have been like to live in the 1930s when dictators were taking over Europe. Would you have been an isolationist or an internationalist? Look up the words in the Glossary. Then as you read, defend your position in a paragraph.

Although the United States did not join the League of Nations, Americans did not want another war. Throughout the 1920s, the United States worked to keep peace. In 1928, the United States proposed the Kellogg-Briand Pact. This agreement outlawed war. More than 60 nations signed it. In reality, there was no way to keep one nation from attacking another.

Adolf Hitler met with Benito Mussolini in Germany in 1937.

focus your reading

What was happening in Europe in the 1930s?

How did the United States react to the possibility of war?

What did President Roosevelt do to prepare for war?

vocabulary

dictator

totalitarian government

isolationist

internationalist

Lend-Lease Law

Europe in the 1930s

The United States had reason to worry about another war. **Dictators** had come to power in Germany, Italy, and Russia. A dictator rules with absolute power and authority. Adolph Hitler came to power in Germany, Benito Mussolini in Italy, and Joseph Stalin in Russia. All three ruled **totalitarian governments**. A totalitarian government is a government in which one political party controls all political power.

In 1935, Mussolini seized Ethiopia. The following year, Hitler sent soldiers into the Rhineland, between Germany and France. In March 1938, Hitler took Austria. In March 1939, all of Czechoslovakia fell to the Germans. In August, Hitler and Stalin agreed not to attack each other. This meant that Hitler did not have to worry about defending his eastern border. On September 1, 1939, Germany attacked Poland. Within two days, Great Britain and France declared war on Germany.

Charles Lindbergh addressed the America First Committee in 1941.

United States Neutrality

Although Germany and Italy were seizing parts of the world, many Americans wanted the United States to remain neutral. **Isolationists** believed the United States should not get involved in another war in Europe. From 1935 to 1937, Congress passed a series of Neutrality Acts. U.S. companies could not sell weapons to nations at war. Nations also had to pay cash for any nonmilitary goods.

Internationalists wanted the United States to intervene on behalf of the Allies. The key Allies consisted of Great Britain and France. As Hitler's goals became clearer, President Roosevelt became more alarmed.

stop and think

Create a concept map. Label the large center circle "U.S. Neutrality." Label three smaller circles with the names of groups that were concerned with U.S. neutrality. As you read, fill in more information.

Steps to War

In 1940, Roosevelt asked for a series of laws to prepare the nation for possible war. These included additional funding to enlarge the navy, a new draft law, and the **Lend-Lease Law**.

The Lend-Lease Law of 1941 allowed the United States to sell, lend, or lease war materials to Great Britain. Many of the isolationists were angered at these proposals. The America First Committee was formed to suggest, and sometimes demand, ways to keep the United States neutral.

Putting It All Together

A number of steps led to World War II. In your notebook create a flowchart that shows the multiple causes, or steps, to World War II.

Chapter Summary

President Franklin Roosevelt's policies were called the New Deal. He wanted relief for workers, reform of business and government, and **recovery** for the economy. One of his first acts in office was to stop the **run on the banks**. Not all banks were **sound**.

The New Deal had critics on both the political **right** and the political **left**. The right wanted a **balanced budget** for the federal government.

The Great Depression had eased by 1935. But unemployment was still high and the government had a large **deficit**. The president launched a Second New Deal.

Roosevelt won the 1936 election in a **landslide**. The Supreme Court had declared **unconstitutional** the Agricultural Adjustment Administration (AAA) and the National Recovery Administration (NRA). To save new programs, Roosevelt proposed adding to the number of Supreme Court justices. Critics called it court-packing and the idea died.

During the 1930s, **dictators** came to power in Germany, Italy, and Russia. They ran **totalitarian governments**. When war began in Europe, the United States was divided. **Isolationists** wanted the United States to stay out of the war. **Internationalists** wanted the United States to support the allies. The **Lend-Lease Law** increased U.S. aid to the Allies.

Chapter Review

1 Write 2-line headlines to describe each of the following: the bank holiday, the CCC, the TVA, the FERA, the WPA, and the NLRB.

2 Imagine you are living in a CCC camp and building a road through a forest. Write a letter home describing what your day is like.

3 Decide if you would approve of Lend-Lease or not. Write a paragraph to defend your stance.

Skill Builder

Analyzing Political Cartoons

A political cartoon uses symbols and sometimes words to express an opinion, or point of view. The point of view belongs to the cartoonist. But the cartoonist is also expressing the opinion of other people, for example, as in the political cartoon on page 145.

To analyze a political cartoon, follow these steps:

- Identify the **characters** and **symbols**. What is going on in the cartoon? What are the figures (people, animals, or things) doing? What are the words? What do the symbols represent?
- Decide the **topic** of the cartoon. Decide what issue the cartoonist is addressing. Often, cartoons represent an issue that is in the news or was of importance in history.
- Determine the **opinion**. Interpret what message the cartoonist is trying to give. State in your own words the message of the cartoon. Use the characters and the meaning of the symbols and what they are doing.

1 What does the figure of Uncle Sam represent?

2 What is Uncle Sam doing?

3 What does the banging on the ceiling represent?

4 Do you think the cartoonist agreed or disagreed with isolationists?

IT WAS A NICE FIRESIDE ONCE

Chapter 10

THE UNITED STATES IN WORLD WAR II

Getting Focused

Skim this chapter to predict what you will be learning.

- Read the lesson titles and subheadings.
- Look at the illustrations and read the captions.
- Examine the maps.
- Review the vocabulary words and terms.

What do you already know about World War II? List this information in your notebook. Skim the chapter again and add to your list. Then discuss your list with a partner.

Pearl Harbor and the War in Europe

Thinking on Your Own

Create a T-chart to help you remember the importance of different events described in this lesson. Label the columns "Events" and "Importance." As you read, fill in the T-chart.

In mid-September 1939, Soviet troops marched into Poland. Hitler and Stalin divided the country. By September 1940, German soldiers had overrun and seized every nation in western Europe except Great Britain, Sweden, and Switzerland. Great Britain stood alone in Europe to fight Germany. President Roosevelt worked to aid Great Britain.

focus your reading

What caused the United States to go to war in 1941?

Why did the war in Europe end before the war in the Pacific?

What was the Holocaust?

vocabulary

Allies	genocide
Axis	ghetto
Holocaust	Kristallnacht
anti-Semitism	

The New York Times.

LATE CITY EDITION
Increasing cloudiness with rising temperature today. Tomorrow cloudy, somewhat colder.
Temperatures Yesterday—Max .34; Min .25

VOL. XCI...No. 30,634.   Entered as Second-Class Matter, Postoffice, New York, N. Y.   NEW YORK, MONDAY, DECEMBER 8, 1941.   THREE CENTS NEW YORK CITY and Vicinity

JAPAN WARS ON U. S. AND BRITAIN; MAKES SUDDEN ATTACK ON HAWAII; HEAVY FIGHTING AT SEA REPORTED

CONGRESS DECIDED

Roosevelt Will Address It Today and Find It Ready to Vote War

CONFERENCE IS HELD

Legislative Leaders and Cabinet in Sober White House Talk

By C. P. TRUSSELL
Special to The New York Times.
WASHINGTON, Dec. 7—President Roosevelt will address a joint session of Congress tomorrow and will find the membership in a mood to vote any steps he asks in connection with the developments in the Pacific.
The President will appear personally at 12:30 P. M. Whether he would call for a flat declaration of war against Japan was left unannounced tonight. But leaders of

TOKYO ACTS FIRST

Declaration Follows Air and Sea Attacks on U. S. and Britain

TOGO CALLS ENVOYS

After Fighting Is On, Grew Gets Japan's Reply to Hull Note of Nov. 26

By The Associated Press.
TOKYO, Monday, Dec. 8—Japan went to war against the United States and Britain today with air and sea attacks against Hawaii followed by a formal declaration of hostilities.
Japanese Imperial headquarters announced at 4 A. M. (4 P. M. Sunday, Eastern standard time) that a state of war existed among these nations in the Western Pacific, as of dawn.
Soon afterward came the Jap-

PACIFIC OCEAN: THEATRE OF WAR INVOLVING UNITED STATES AND ITS ALLIES

Shortly after the outbreak of hostilities an American ship in the Philippines was raided from the air. At Shanghai (5) a

★ U.S. Bases
□ Japanese Bases

GUAM BOMBED; ARMY SHIP IS SUNK

U. S. Fliers Head North From Manila— Battleship Oklahoma Set Afire by Torpedo Planes at Honolulu

104 SOLDIERS KILLED AT FIELD IN HAWAII

Japanese Envoys, at Moment of Attack, Deliver Reply to U. S. Note—President Sees Cabinet and Drafts Message to Congress

By FRANK L. KLUCKHOHN
Special to The New York Times.
WASHINGTON, Monday, Dec. 8—Sudden and unexpected attacks on Pearl Harbor, Honolulu, and other United States possessions in the Pacific early yesterday by the Japanese air force and navy plunged the United States and Japan into active war.
The initial attack in Hawaii, apparently launched by torpedo-carrying bombers and submarines, caused widespread damage and death. It was quickly followed by others. There were unconfirmed reports that German raiders participated in the attacks.

On December 7, 1941, the United States faced the greatest threat ever to its national security. Japanese aircraft bombed its battleship fleet into twisted wreckage at Pearl Harbor. In the North Atlantic, German submarines searched for American destroyers.

stop and think

Imagine you were alive on December 7, 1941. What would you have thought and felt when you heard the news? Write a paragraph describing your thoughts and feelings. Share it with a partner to see how alike or different your ideas are.

Pearl Harbor

"Yesterday, December 7, 1941—a date which will live in infamy—the United States of America was suddenly and deliberately attacked by naval and air forces of the Empire of

The USS *Arizona* sank on December 7, 1941.

Japan." President Roosevelt spoke these words when asking Congress for a declaration of war against Japan. A large part of the U.S. Pacific fleet was destroyed. More than 3,400 military personnel were killed or wounded.

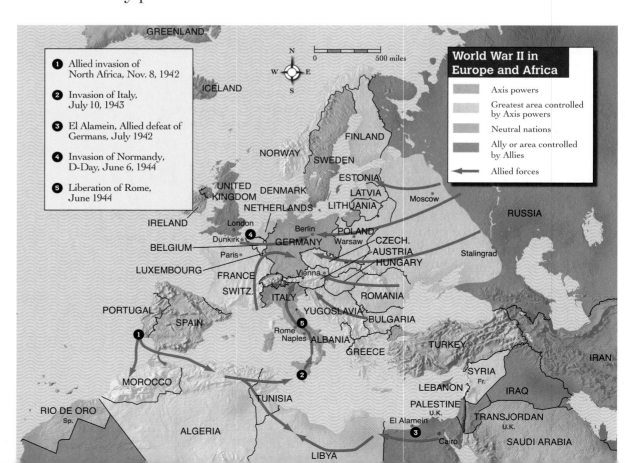

World War II in Europe and Africa

① Allied invasion of North Africa, Nov. 8, 1942

② Invasion of Italy, July 10, 1943

③ El Alamein, Allied defeat of Germans, July 1942

④ Invasion of Normandy, D-Day, June 6, 1944

⑤ Liberation of Rome, June 1944

Axis powers

Greatest area controlled by Axis powers

Neutral nations

Ally or area controlled by Allies

Allied forces

On December 8, the United States, joined by Great Britain, declared war on Japan. They became known as the **Allies**. Germany and Italy declared war on the United States the next week. In September 1940, Germany, Italy, and Japan had signed a mutual defense agreement. They were known as the **Axis**.

Europe and North Africa

The Allies first decided to stop the Axis in Europe and North Africa before turning the full force of their armies and navies against Japan. In October 1942, the British defeated the Germans at the battle of El Alamein, Egypt. In November, the Allies invaded Algeria and Morocco. Under the command of General George Patton, they fought their way east. In May 1943, the Germans surrendered.

In June 1941, Hitler chose to ignore the Non-Aggression Pact and invaded the Soviet Union. In February 1943, Soviet troops defeated German forces at the Battle of Stalingrad. The Soviet army then began the long fight to push the German army west.

In September, Italians removed Mussolini from power. Hitler refused to accept this defeat. He ordered his soldiers to return Mussolini to power and to hold Italy. During the winter of 1943–1944, the Allies fought their way north on the Italian peninsula. In June 1944, they took Rome. However, fighting continued in Italy until the end of the war in 1945.

Allied troops land on the beaches of Normandy on D-Day.

The final push against Germany began with the invasion of France on D-Day, June 6, 1944. General Dwight D. Eisenhower, the commander of Allied forces in Europe, ordered the invasion of France, known as Operation Overlord. More than 2 million Allied troops landed on the beaches of Normandy. Whole cities were destroyed, and the number of casualties continued to grow.

At the same time, Germany was being surrounded by Allied troops. Hitler committed suicide the last week in April, and

Germany surrendered on May 7, 1945. The Allies declared May 8, 1945, V-E Day for "Victory in Europe." Germany had been defeated, but at an enormous cost to human life and materials.

The Holocaust

As the Allies moved east, they found Nazi death camps and the survivors of the **Holocaust**. Hitler hated Jews simply because they were Jewish. He used this **anti-Semitism** as a way to gain power. He focused the anger of the Germans over their defeat in World War I on the Jewish people.

His campaign of **genocide**—the wiping out of an entire racial or cultural group— began when Hitler came to power in 1933. New laws required Jewish citizens to live in **ghettoes**—areas of cities that kept Jews separated from the non-Jews.

On the night of November 9–10, 1938, violence against Jews broke out across Germany. Gangs of Nazi youth attacked Jews, burned 101 synagogues, destroyed nearly 7,500 Jewish businesses, and sent nearly 26,000 Jews to the death camps. This became known as **Kristallnacht**, the night of broken glass.

Buchenwald was liberated by the Allies on April 16, 1945.

In January 1942, German leaders decided on a "final solution." They would rid Europe of Jews, Slavs, Gypsies, and those with mental illness and disabilities. Jews and the others were sent to concentration camps like Auschwitz in Poland and Dachau in Germany. Millions died in the gas chambers of Auschwitz.

Approximately 12 million people died in the Holocaust. About 6 million were Jews. Some countries lost between 83 and 90 percent of all their Jewish citizens.

Putting It All Together

Anti-Semitism and other forms of hatred and discrimination are still a world-wide problem. With a partner think about how education could be used to fight such emotions. Write a paragraph to explain your ideas.

The War in the Pacific

Thinking on Your Own

Add to the T-chart you created in Lesson 1.

In the first few months after Pearl Harbor, the Japanese made some significant gains. They took Burma (now Myanmar) and the Philippines. But the Allies were developing a two-pronged **strategy** to win the war in the Pacific.

The USS *Hancock* was damaged by a Japanese kamikaze attack in 1945.

focus your reading

What was the Allied strategy in the Pacific?

Why did President Truman agree to use the atomic bomb?

What decisions about the future were reached at wartime conferences?

vocabulary

strategy

turning point

surrender

Two-Pronged Strategy in the Pacific

The United States' first objective was to regain islands in the Pacific Ocean lost to the Japanese. General Douglas MacArthur commanded land forces on the Pacific front. He moved his troops from the Solomon Islands to New Guinea and then to the Philippines. These islands became military stepping stones to the Japanese home islands. The U.S. attacked key islands and avoided others.

The second objective was led by Admiral Chester Nimitz who led Allied naval forces through the Central Pacific. This objective was to destroy the Japanese fleet. In May 1942, the Allies turned back a large Japanese fleet at the Battle of the Coral Sea. In

U.S. soldiers go ashore in Toem, New Guinea.

June, the Japanese lost a three-day battle near Midway Island. This was a **turning point** in the Pacific theater, or area of battle.

Between August 1942 and February 1943, the Allies and Japanese fought a series of battles near Guadalcanal in the Solomon Islands. When it was over, the Allies had gained control of their first island on the way to Japan. Between fall 1943 and summer 1944, naval forces fought their way north through the Central Pacific.

Meanwhile, MacArthur was moving toward the Philippines. On October 20, 1944, the invasion of the Philippines began with the Battle of Leyte Gulf. The capital city of Manila did not fall to the Allies until March 1945. However, Japanese forces in the Philippines continued to fight until the end of the war.

<aside>
stop and think

Examine the maps on pages 154 and 158. Make a T-chart of the battles that were taking place simultaneously, that is, at the same time, in Europe and the Pacific. Label one side of the chart "Europe" and the other side "Pacific." Work with a partner to fill in the chart.
</aside>

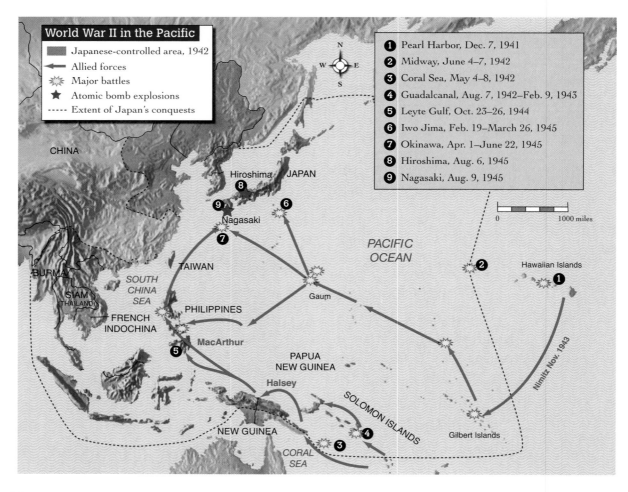

World War II in the Pacific

- Japanese-controlled area, 1942
- ← Allied forces
- ✳ Major battles
- ★ Atomic bomb explosions
- ----- Extent of Japan's conquests

1. Pearl Harbor, Dec. 7, 1941
2. Midway, June 4–7, 1942
3. Coral Sea, May 4–8, 1942
4. Guadalcanal, Aug. 7, 1942–Feb. 9, 1943
5. Leyte Gulf, Oct. 23–26, 1944
6. Iwo Jima, Feb. 19–March 26, 1945
7. Okinawa, Apr. 1–June 22, 1945
8. Hiroshima, Aug. 6, 1945
9. Nagasaki, Aug. 9, 1945

CHINA
Hiroshima
JAPAN
Nagasaki
TAIWAN
SOUTH CHINA SEA
BURMA
SIAM (THAILAND)
FRENCH INDOCHINA
PHILIPPINES
MacArthur
Guam
PACIFIC OCEAN
Hawaiian Islands
PAPUA NEW GUINEA
Halsey
SOLOMON ISLANDS
NEW GUINEA
Gilbert Islands
CORAL SEA
Nimitz Nov. 1943

0   1000 miles

After a fierce battle led by the U.S. Marines, Iwo Jima fell to the Allies in March 1945. Okinawa fell in July after a bloody battle. The intensity of these two battles influenced President Truman's decision to use atomic weapons against the Japanese. The Allies were only 800 miles from Tokyo, the capital of Japan. Allied planes were bombing Japanese cities. The war in Europe had ended, but Japan's military leaders refused to **surrender**.

Dropping the Atomic Bomb

On April 12, 1945, President Franklin Roosevelt died suddenly. Vice President Harry Truman was sworn in as president. Military advisors told Truman that it would take months and cost hundreds of thousands of lives to conquer Japan. The loss of life had been enormous throughout the various battles in the Pacific. Truman knew that defeating the Japanese would involve a massive loss of life.

In 1941, President Roosevelt had established a secret program called the Manhattan Project. Its purpose was to build an atomic bomb. On July 16, 1945, the United States secretly exploded the first atomic bomb. Truman considered the arguments for and against using the bomb on Japan. After listening to many scientists argue against its use, he agreed to use the bomb. The Japanese government was given one last chance to surrender. They refused even to consider it.

The result of the bombing of Hiroshima was complete devastation.

Truman gave the order. On August 6, 1945, the *Enola Gay*—a Boeing B-29 bomber—dropped an atomic bomb named "Little Boy" on the city of Hiroshima. The blast killed between 80,000 and 120,000 people. Burns and radiation poisoning killed thousands more. More than half the city was destroyed. Still, the Japanese refused to surrender. On August 9, a second bomb was dropped on the city of Nagasaki. Between 35,000 and 74,000 were killed. The Japanese government surrendered. August 15, 1945, was proclaimed V-J Day for "Victory over Japan." World War II was over.

Winston Churchill, Franklin Roosevelt, and Joseph Stalin in Yalta, 1945.

Planning for Peace

Planning for peace had gone on at the same time as planning for war. During the war, President Franklin Roosevelt, British Prime Minister Winston Churchill, and Soviet Premier Joseph Stalin met several times to discuss strategy. Russia had joined the Allies after Hitler invaded the Soviet Union in 1941.

The agreements reached at the Yalta Conference in 1945 were particularly important. The three leaders agreed to

- divide Germany into four military zones and to govern them after the war—France would take over the fourth zone
- accept a communist government in Poland until elections could be held
- accept communist-backed governments in countries the Soviet Union had freed from the Nazis

These decisions had global and long-lasting consequences.

Putting It All Together

Examine the photo on page 159 that shows the destruction of Hiroshima. Using the T-charts you made at the beginning of Lessons 1 and 2, describe how the event of Pearl Harbor led to the dropping of the atomic bomb. Use the information to write a paragraph.

Biography

Horacio Rivero (1910–2000)

Horacio Rivero had a long and distinguished career in the service of his country. Rivero was born in Ponce, Puerto Rico. After high school, he was appointed to the U.S. Naval Academy. He graduated in 1931 with a degree in electrical engineering.

Rivero was third in his class of 441 midshipmen. During the 1930s, he continued his education at the Massachusetts Institute of Technology and at Cambridge University in England.

Horacio Rivero is standing fifth from left.

When the United States entered World War II, Rivero was assigned to ships in the Pacific Fleet. Throughout the war he served as a Gunnery Officer and Executive Officer in the Pacific. Rivero saw action at Guadalcanal, the Marshall Islands, Iwo Jima, and Okinawa. He received the Bronze Star and the Legion of Merit for his actions in battle.

In 1954, after several years in command of ships, Rivero was appointed Assistant Chief of Staff for Naval Operations. The following year he was promoted to Rear Admiral. The only other Latino to reach this rank was David Farragut in the Civil War. Over the next few years, Admiral Rivero held a number of positions in the Atlantic Fleet.

By October 1962, Admiral Rivero was Commander of Amphibious Forces, Atlantic Fleet. This post gave him a central role in the Cuban Missile Crisis. To prevent Soviet ships from landing in Cuba, President John Kennedy ordered part of the Atlantic Fleet to the Caribbean.

In 1964, President Lyndon Johnson promoted Rivero to the rank of Four-Star Admiral. He was the first Puerto Rican and first Latino to reach this rank. Admiral Rivero retired from the Navy in 1972. That same year, President Richard Nixon appointed him U.S. Ambassador to Spain. Rivero served in this post until 1975. He died in 2000 at the age of ninety.

War on the Homefront

Thinking on Your Own

As you skim the lesson, discuss with a partner what the illustrations show. Choose one illustration to describe in detail. Write at least one paragraph. Use nouns, vivid adjectives, action verbs, and the vocabulary words to make your paragraph a word picture.

With the declaration of war, the nation was faced with the huge task of **mobilization**. As the country had done in World War I, the United States needed to prepare to fight. This meant increasing the size of the armed forces. It

Ration books were used during the war.

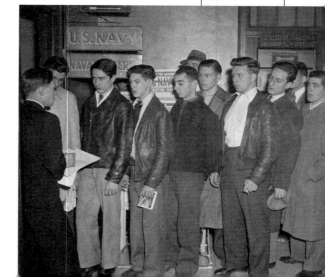

focus your reading

What groups served in the armed forces in World War II?

How did U.S. civilians and industries support the war?

How did the war affect the cause of civil rights for different ethnic groups?

vocabulary

mobilization	inflation
draftee	cost of living
ration	internment

also meant turning out the supplies they needed in order to fight—and paying for them. To achieve these goals, the government took control of the economy in greater ways than ever before. In doing so, the United States spent its way out of the Great Depression.

Young men line up to enlist in the U.S. Navy in Boston on December 8, 1941.

The Armed Forces

All men aged 21 to 35 had registered for the draft beginning in 1940. Draft boards across the nation began calling up **draftees**, all those who had registered. Younger men volunteered for service.

Women also volunteered. Some 350,000 women served in the women's branches of the armed forces. They held noncombatant positions such as nurses, drivers, mechanics, and clerks. Women pilots flew new fighter planes from the United States to the Air Force in Europe.

African Americans, Latinos, and Japanese also served the country. At first African Americans were placed in segregated units and kept out of combat. African-American leaders protested this segregation. President Roosevelt stepped in and ordered that African Americans be trained for combat. By the end of the war, most African-Americans were still serving in segregated units. However, unlike in earlier wars, they were often commanded by African-American officers. Individual African Americans and African-American units were highly decorated for their bravery in combat.

The Tuskegee Airmen, an African-American flying squadron, in 1943

Anne McClellan, a pilot trainee in the Women's Flying Training Detachment

The 100th Battalion

Some 65,000 Puerto Ricans and 400,000 Mexican Americans served in the U.S. armed forces. In addition, Latino-American citizens from other ethnic backgrounds also served.

About 45,000 Native Americans joined the services. A group of 400 Navajo, known as the Navajo Code Talkers, used their skills in an unusual way. Instead of using code to send secret messages, the marines adopted the Navajo language. The Japanese were never able to break the supposed secret code.

Japanese Americans also fought in the war. They made up the 100th Battalion, later 442nd Regimental Combat Team. They fought in Europe and earned the most medals of any combat unit in the war.

Fee Perez inspects bullets for the Remington Arms Company.

War Production

The armed forces needed supplies quickly. The nation's industries had to change from producing washing machines and clothing to airplanes and uniforms. In January 1942, President Roosevelt set up the War Production Board (WPB). Its job was to oversee the production of war goods. It divided raw materials between factories producing war supplies and factories producing consumer goods.

Civilians were asked to make many sacrifices for the war. Food, gasoline, and tires were **rationed**—or given out on a limited basis. By January 1943, people were not allowed to drive their cars except for essential reasons such as a doctor's appointment or going to work.

Victory gardens were popular during the war.

To produce all the materials needed for war, industries needed workers. With 12 million men in the armed forces, factories hired women. In 1942, six million women worked in jobs supporting the war. Workers from Mexico joined the Bracero Program. This project began in 1942 and was sponsored by the United States and Mexico. It provided workers for U.S. farms and railroads.

For the first time in years, people had money in their pockets. Because of rationing, there was little to spend it on. The president was concerned about **inflation**. Inflation is an increase in prices when there is more money available than goods to buy. The president established the Office of Price

stop and think

Reread the headings about the armed forces and war production. Make a list of all the ways Americans supported the war. Check your list with a partner to be sure you included all the ways.

Administration (OPA) to keep prices down for housing, clothes, and food. The OPA set prices on goods to keep the **cost of living** from rising too high or too quickly. To pay for all this, Congress raised taxes, borrowed money, and sold war bonds.

Civil Rights

African Americans still faced discrimination in the workforce. War industries refused to hire African Americans or hired them for the lowest-paying jobs. In 1941, A. Philip Randolph threatened a peaceful march on Washington, D.C., to protest this discrimination. President Roosevelt signed an executive order forbidding discrimination in hiring and promotion in defense industries.

Detroit, Michigan, was a center for industries producing materials for the war. Competition between African Americans and whites was increasing. Jobs and housing were difficult to find. On June 20, 1943, a race riot broke out. That night, 25 African Americans and 9 whites were killed. More than 800 people were injured, and property damage was estimated to be more than $2 million.

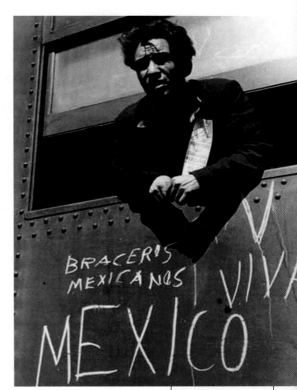

Mexicans came to the United States as part of the Bracero Program.

Latinos also faced discrimination. Although Mexicans found work in the Bracero Program, they earned only 30 cents an hour. They slept in shacks, were overcharged for food, and worked from sunup to sundown. Mexicans were also the target of violence. The anti-Latino zoot-suit riots occurred in Los Angeles, Chicago, Detroit, and other cities.

Japanese Internment

The worst violation of civil rights occurred against Japanese and Japanese Americans. In early 1942, the War Department classified the West Coast as a military zone. The War Department was able to remove anyone considered a threat to national security.

Japanese evacuees at the Tanforan Assembly Center in California in 1942

Many U.S. officials and other Americans feared that Japanese and Japanese Americans would help Japan in the war. As a result, about 120,000 Japanese and Japanese Americans were taken from the West Coast. Some were immigrants, but about two-thirds were born in the United States and were U.S. citizens. They were sent to **internment**, or relocation camps inland. With barbed wire and guard towers, the camps were like prisons.

One Japanese American, Fred Korematsu, refused to leave California. He took his case all the way to the Supreme Court. In 1944, the Court ruled that the government had acted within its rights. According to the president's order, the War Department had the power to remove people from any area termed a military zone.

The interned families spent most of the war in the camps. People were eventually allowed to leave to work in the Midwest or on the East Coast. In 1988, the U.S. government issued an apology to Japanese Americans. Congress awarded $20,000 to each surviving Japanese American.

Putting It All Together

During World War II, President Roosevelt issued many executive orders to help the government manage the war effort. Use the library or the Internet to research one of the orders. Discuss the order with a partner. Then write a paragraph defending why the president should have done this.

Read a Primary Source

Internment of Japanese Americans

Jeanne Wakatsuki was just seven years old when she and her family of twelve were sent to Manzanar. This internment camp in Owens Valley, California, housed 10,000 Japanese internees. The weather was very cold and windy when they arrived. Kiyo and Woody are two of Jeanne's brothers.

"Our pickup point was a Buddhist church in Los Angeles. . . . I remember sitting on a duffel bag. . . . Someone tied a numbered tag to my collar and to the duffel bag. . . .

"We rode all day. . . .

"We had pulled up just in time for dinner. The mess halls weren't completed yet. An outdoor chow line snaked around a half-finished building. . . .

"After dinner we were taken to Block 16, a cluster of fifteen barracks that had just been finished a day or so earlier—although finished was hardly the word for it. The shacks were built of one thickness of pine planking covered with tarpaper. . . . Gaps showed between the planks. . . .

"We woke early, shivering and coated with dust that had blown up. . . . During the night Mama had unpacked all our clothes and heaped them on our beds for warmth. Now our cubicles looked as if a giant laundry bag had exploded and then been sprayed with fine dust. A skin of sand covered the floor. I looked over Mama's shoulder at Kiyo . . . buried under jeans and overcoats and sweaters. His eyebrows were gray, and he was starting to giggle. . . . I looked at Mama's face to see if she thought Kiyo was funny. She lay very still . . . her eyes scanning everything—bare rafters, walls, dusty kids—scanning slowly, and I think the mask of her face would have cracked had not Woody's voice just then come through the wall. . . .

"'Hey!' he yelled. 'You guys fall into the same flour barrel as us?'"

Jeanne Wakatsuki Houston and James D. Houston. *Farewell to Manzanar.* (Bantam: New York 1973)

Chapter Summary

In 1939, Hitler continued his campaign to control Europe. By the end of 1940, Great Britain stood alone in Europe as a free nation. In 1940 Germany, Italy, and Japan joined together as the **Axis**. The nations fighting them were called the **Allies.**

On December 7, 1941, Japan attacked Pearl Harbor. The U.S. and Great Britain declared war on Japan. Germany declared war on the United States. In June 1944, the Allies landed in Normandy. By spring 1945, Soviet forces had driven west and met U.S. troops fighting eastward. On May 8, 1945, Germany **surrendered**.

As U.S. forces moved into the German theater, they found the Nazi concentration camps. Jews had been forced into **ghettos** and suffered through **Kristallnacht**. Hitler acted on his **anti-Semitism** by committing **genocide** against the Jews. This is known as the **Holocaust.**

The Allies developed a two-prong **strategy** for the war in the Pacific. The Battle of Midway was a **turning point**. The war ended on August 15, 1945, after the United States dropped atomic bombs on Hiroshima and Nagasaki.

To win the war, the nation had **mobilized** quickly. **Draftees** were called up for the army. On the home front, there was **rationing**. To combat **inflation**, and help with the **cost of living**, President Roosevelt created the Office of Price Administration.

At home and in the armed forces, African Americans and other groups faced discrimination. The loyalty of Japanese Americans was questioned. Many Japanese were sent to **internment** camps.

Chapter Review

1 Write 2-line headlines for each of the following: the war in Italy, the Normandy invasion, the Holocaust, V-E Day, the war in the Pacific, the bombing of Hiroshima, V-J Day.

2 Imagine you have been sent to an internment camp. Write a letter to President Roosevelt describing how you feel as an American citizen sent to the camp.

Skill Builder

Using Context Clues

Sometimes in reading your textbook, a magazine, or a Web page, you may come across a word you do not know. Using context clues can help you figure out the meaning of the word. Context clues are other words in the paragraph that give you a sense, or an idea, about what the unknown word may mean.

When you come across a word that you do not know, follow these steps:

- Read a sentence or two before and after the sentence with the unknown word.
- Ask yourself, *What are the sentences saying?*
- Ask yourself, *What word would make the most sense as a replacement for the unknown word?*
- Try that word in the sentence. Does the sentence make sense? If so, read on. If not, try again.
- You may be able to figure out what the sentence means even if you do not know every word.

After the bombing of Hiroshima, President Truman said, "We are now prepared to obliterate more rapidly and completely every productive enterprise the Japanese have above ground in any city. . . . If they do not now accept our terms, they may expect a rain of ruin from the air, the likes of which has never been seen on this earth."

1 Write any word or words that you do not know.

2 From the context, or sense, of the paragraph, what do you think the word or words mean?

3 What other words or ideas in the paragraph helped you decide word meaning?

4 Explain what President Truman was threatening would happen to Japan.

6 UNIT

THE COLD WAR

World War II was over, and the United States faced the task of returning to peacetime. Veterans needed jobs. Industries needed to change back to producing consumer goods. Unions wanted raises. African Americans intended to keep the rights they had won during wartime—and to demand more.

But all these issues were overshadowed by the actions of the Soviet Union. The Soviet Union was using its influence to take control of nations in Eastern Europe. Americans came to realize that they had traded a shooting war for a Cold War.

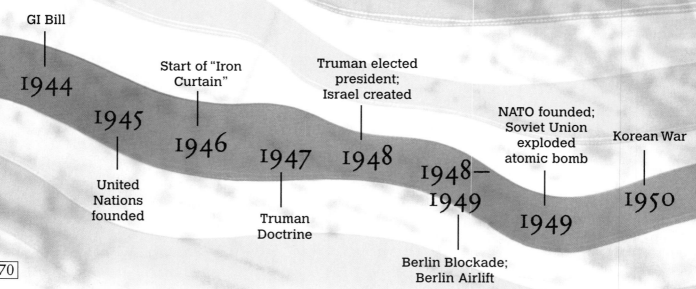

GI Bill

1944

1945

United Nations founded

Start of "Iron Curtain"

1946

1947

Truman Doctrine

Truman elected president; Israel created

1948

1948–1949

Berlin Blockade; Berlin Airlift

NATO founded; Soviet Union exploded atomic bomb

1949

Korean War

1950

What problems did the United States face in the years right after World War II?

How did the Iron Curtain affect the United States?

Why did the United States become involved in the Korean War?

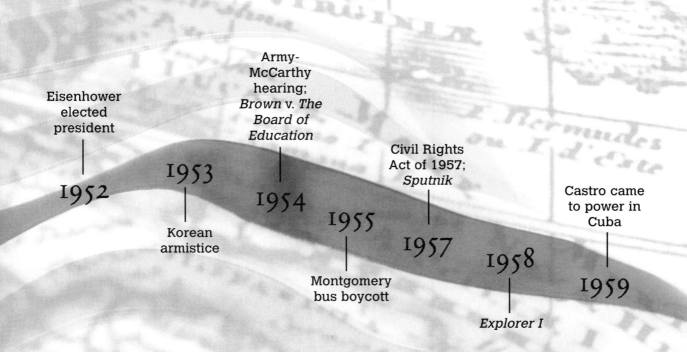

Eisenhower elected president

1952

1953

Korean armistice

Army-McCarthy hearing; *Brown* v. *The Board of Education*

1954

1955

Montgomery bus boycott

Civil Rights Act of 1957; *Sputnik*

1957

1958

Explorer I

Castro came to power in Cuba

1959

Chapter 11

TRUMAN AND THE COLD WAR

Getting Focused

Skim this chapter to predict what you will be learning.

- Read the lesson titles and subheadings.
- Look at the illustrations and read the captions.
- Examine the maps.
- Review the vocabulary words and terms.

What problems do you think the United States faced when World War II ended? Make a list with a partner. As you read this chapter, check your list against what really happened.

The Fair Deal

Thinking on Your Own

Turn each subhead in this lesson into a question. As you read the lesson, answer each question in your notebook. Try to use the vocabulary words.

The president and the nation faced major issues after World War II. More than 12 million men and women had served in the U.S. armed forces. These veterans would be coming home. How would they adjust to being civilians again? Another issue was converting industries from war goods back to producing consumer goods.

focus your reading

How were veterans of World War II helped to readjust to civilian life?

What labor issues occurred in the late 1940s?

Why was President Truman unable to pass all of his Fair Deal proposals?

vocabulary

closed shop

executive order

coalition

Returning Veterans

To help returning servicemen adjust to civilian life, Congress passed the GI Bill of Rights in 1944. The act provided unemployment payments and created an agency to help veterans find a job.

GIs returning home after World War II

Low-interest home mortgages under the GI Bill helped millions of people to buy their first homes. Some veterans took advantage of low-interest loans to start their own businesses. The GI Bill of Rights also paid veterans to go to college. This helped reduce unemployment, as it kept many returning soldiers out of the job market. It also gave the nation a highly skilled future work force.

Labor Issues

Most veterans were men. While men served in the armed forces, six million women took their jobs in war industries. These factories were now refitted to produce cars, washing machines, and similar consumer goods. Although many women either needed to work or wanted to work, most lost their jobs to returning veterans. So did many African Americans.

The GI Bill helped many veterans purchase a home.

During the war, the government had controlled prices and wages. Unions had agreed not to strike. Once the war was over, price controls were lifted and manufacturers raised prices. Employers, however, did not raise wages. In 1945 and 1946, a number of unions went on strike for higher wages. Among the industries hit were railroads, mining, and steel manufacturing. A railroad strike in 1946 halted all trains. Trains were needed to move materials and goods across the country. President Truman threatened to draft the strikers. In the end, the strikers gained some of their demands and returned to work.

Conductors went on strike on May 18, 1946.

In 1947, Congress passed the Taft-Hartley Act. It gave the president the power to stop strikes that threatened the health and safety of the nation. It also banned the **closed shop**. The closed shop required that an employer hire only union members. As a Democrat, the president was pro-labor, and vetoed the bill. Congress had a Republican majority and passed the bill over his veto. The Taft-Hartley Act became law.

stop and think

In your notebook, list at least three postwar problems that affected factory and railroad workers.

Party Politics and the Fair Deal

The fight over the Taft-Hartley Act showed the tension between the president and the Republican Congress. Truman sometimes continued the policies of the New Deal by **executive order**. An executive order is a decision made by the president that does not require approval. He ended discrimination in the armed forces and in federal government jobs this way.

For most of his plans, however, Truman needed Congress to pass laws. He sent Congress proposals to increase the minimum wage, construct public housing, expand Social Security, and develop a system of national health insurance. He also sent a civil rights bill that would protect the voting rights of African Americans. Republicans and conservative Southern Democrats in Congress formed a **coalition**, or alliance. They voted down his proposals.

By the election of 1948, Truman had not achieved very much. Most politicians expected him to lose. Instead he took his campaign to the people. Calling the Congress "Do-Nothing," he blamed the Republicans for not dealing with the nation's problems.

President Truman ran for reelection in 1948.

The support of labor, African Americans, and farmers led to Truman's reelection. He pressed Congress to pass his proposals, which he called the Fair Deal. Congress agreed to raise the minimum wage from 40 cents to 75 cents an hour. It also extended Social Security payments to more workers and provided money to build public housing. Congress refused to pass a civil rights act, provide national health insurance, or give farmers subsidies. These issues became part of the Democrats' agenda for the future.

President Truman's reelection victory was so close, the *Chicago Daily Tribune* printed the wrong headline.

Putting It All Together

Make a two-column chart. On one side, list what President Truman accomplished. On the other, list what he failed to accomplish. In a paragraph, explain whether the Fair Deal was a success or a failure.

The Cold War and McCarthyism

Thinking on Your Own

What do you think the term "Cold War" means? Before you read the lesson, look at the photographs and maps in this lesson. Then write a definition in your notebook. As you read the lesson, decide how accurate your definition is. Revise it if necessary.

While dealing with **domestic policies**, President Truman and the nation were facing a crisis in **foreign policy**. The alliance among the United States, Great Britain, and the Soviet Union had collapsed. The Soviet Union was now the enemy. In 1949, it exploded its first atomic bomb. Now both the United States and the Soviet Union had nuclear weapons.

focus your reading

What was the original purpose of the United Nations?

What was the "Iron Curtain"?

How did the United States respond to the danger posed by the Soviet Union?

What was the Berlin Crisis?

Why was Senator McCarthy successful for a time?

vocabulary

domestic policy	foreign aid
foreign policy	Cold War
Iron Curtain	censure
containment	McCarthyism

The United Nations

At one of the wartime meetings between Roosevelt, Churchill, and Stalin, Roosevelt proposed a United Nations to replace the League of Nations. The UN's purpose would be to negotiate disputes between nations. It would also use force, if necessary, to stop aggressor nations. In 1945, an international conference drew up a charter and the United Nations was founded.

Physicist Leo Szilard, who helped develop the atomic bomb, shows a headline announcing Russia's successful atomic bomb test.

The first meeting of the United Nations on January 1, 1946

A Security Council of 15 nations would be responsible for maintaining world peace. However, the United Kingdom, China, France, the Soviet Union, and the United States would each have a permanent seat and a vote. In order to settle any disputes, these five powers must agree. This proved to be an obstacle to world peace as the Soviet Union expanded.

Soviet Expansion: The Iron Curtain

Soviet troops occupied a large section of Eastern Europe at the end of World War II. Stalin promised to hold free elections in these nations. Instead, he used his troops to ensure that communists came to power in Poland, Czechoslovakia, Albania, Hungary, Bulgaria, Romania, and Yugoslavia. The Soviet Union was also pressuring Turkey for land.

Soviet tanks occupy Hungary in 1956.

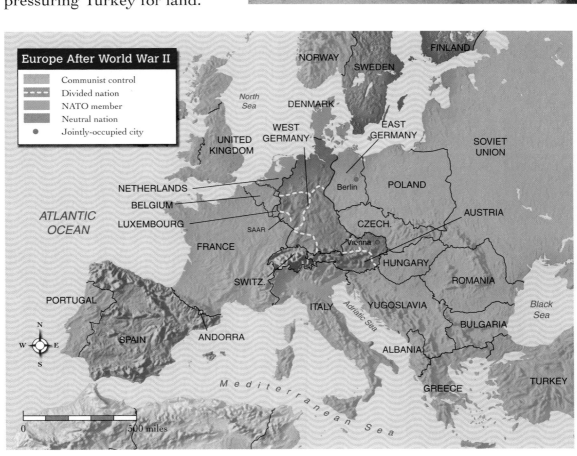

Europe After World War II

- Communist control
- Divided nation
- NATO member
- Neutral nation
- Jointly-occupied city

NORWAY
FINLAND
SWEDEN
North Sea
DENMARK
WEST GERMANY
EAST GERMANY
SOVIET UNION
UNITED KINGDOM
NETHERLANDS
Berlin
POLAND
BELGIUM
LUXEMBOURG
AUSTRIA
ATLANTIC OCEAN
SAAR
CZECH.
Vienna
FRANCE
HUNGARY
SWITZ.
ROMANIA
PORTUGAL
ITALY
YUGOSLAVIA
Black Sea
Adriatic Sea
SPAIN
ANDORRA
BULGARIA
ALBANIA
TURKEY
GREECE
Mediterranean Sea

N W E S

0   500 miles

The world was divided between the free nations of the West and the communist nations of Eastern Europe. Britain's prime minister, Winston Churchill, saw the danger. He said, "an **iron curtain** has descended across the continent" between the two groups of nations. He declared that the Soviet Union would not stop at the borders of Eastern Europe.

Hunger created unrest in Germany in 1953.

The U.S. Response

President Truman was determined to use U.S. resources against the Soviet threat. After World War II, the United States was the most powerful democratic, or free, nation in the world. It had not suffered the bombing of the war. Its economy was strong. To fight communism, Truman adopted the policy of **containment**. That is, the United States would contain the Soviet Union's empire and keep it from expanding its boundaries any farther. The United States would provide **foreign aid**—money, equipment, or military support—to nations in danger of falling to communism.

Containment remained the policy of the United States throughout the **Cold War**. During the Cold War, the United States and the Soviet Union never actually went to war. However, each country supported other nations in their struggle to expand their sphere of influence.

Greek resistance fighters transport communist prisoners in 1948.

The policy of containment was first tested in 1947. President Truman asked Congress for $400 million in aid for Greece and Turkey. In his speech, Truman said that the United States must help free peoples struggling against "armed minorities or outside pressures." Known as the Truman Doctrine, his plan worked. Greece remained free, and Turkey gave up nothing to the Soviet Union.

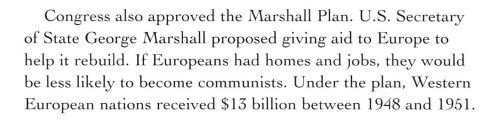

Congress also approved the Marshall Plan. U.S. Secretary of State George Marshall proposed giving aid to Europe to help it rebuild. If Europeans had homes and jobs, they would be less likely to become communists. Under the plan, Western European nations received $13 billion between 1948 and 1951.

Berlin and NATO

The agreement between the Allies was to divide Germany into four zones at the end of World War II. Berlin, Germany's capital, lay within the Soviet zone. It, too, was divided into four zones.

In 1948, Great Britain, France, and the United States united their zones. An angry Stalin responded with the Berlin blockade. He wanted to force the three nations out of Berlin. No car, train, or boat was allowed to enter the West Berlin zones. Truman responded with the Berlin Airlift. For ten months, American and British planes airlifted millions of tons of supplies to two million West Berliners. In May 1949, Stalin finally ended the blockade. The result was the division of Germany into two nations—the Federal Republic of Germany (West Germany) and the German Democratic Republic (East Germany). Berlin was divided into two zones.

stop and think

Create a concept map to help you remember U.S. responses to Soviet actions. In the large central circle write "Containment." Then add smaller circles for each response explained in the three sections you just read. Share your map with a partner to be sure you included every response.

Airplanes delivered food and supplies during the Berlin Airlift.

In 1949, the United States, Canada, and ten nations of Western Europe set up the North Atlantic Treaty Organization (NATO). The purpose was mutual defense. The twelve nations declared that an attack against one nation was an attack against all twelve.

In response, the Soviet Union and seven communist nations formed the Warsaw Pact in 1955. They pledged that an attack against one was an attack against all. The Warsaw Pact ended in 1991 after the collapse of the Soviet Union. NATO still exists.

McCarthyism

From the time the communists came to power in the Soviet Union in 1917, Americans feared that communism would spread to the United States. This fear fueled the Red Scare and anti-immigration policies of the 1920s. After World War II, there was another Red Scare. Senator Joseph McCarthy, Republican of Wisconsin, used this fear for his own purposes.

Senator McCarthy charged that communists and communist sympathizers were everywhere in the federal government. His charges created publicity. Public support for him grew. He seemed so powerful that most members of Congress were afraid to speak out. He accused his critics of being soft on communism or of being communists themselves.

Joseph McCarthy and Joseph Welch in 1954

In 1954, McCarthy said that there were communists in the U.S. Army. The Army-McCarthy hearings were shown on television. It soon became clear to the audience that there was no proof for McCarthy's charges. The Senate **censured**, or condemned, McCarthy for his behavior. McCarthy lost his reelection campaign in 1954. Since then, the term *McCarthyism* is used to describe an attack on a person's loyalty without any proof.

Putting It All Together

McCarthy used Americans' fear to further his own career. He misled millions of well-meaning people. Write a two-line headline about the Senate censure of McCarthy.

Biography

Margaret Chase Smith (1897–1995)

Margaret Chase Smith represented the people of Maine for 32 years, first in the House of Representatives and then in the Senate.

She was the first woman to be elected to both houses of Congress. She served longer than any other female member of Congress. Chase Smith was the first woman to be nominated for president.

Born in Skowhegan, Maine, Margaret Chase taught school for a short time, but soon entered the business world. In 1930, she married Clyde H. Smith, who was active in local Republican politics. After her marriage, Chase Smith joined the Republican state committee. Her husband was elected to the U.S. House of Representatives in 1936. After his death in 1940, Chase Smith won a special election to complete his term. She won reelection to the House in 1942, 1944, and 1946. In 1948, she campaigned for U.S. senator from Maine and won. Chase Smith served four terms as senator. In 1964, her name was among those listed for possible nomination for president at the Republican National Convention.

Chase Smith showed her political courage early in her career. In 1940, she voted for Roosevelt's Selective Service Act although the Republican leadership opposed it. In 1948, Chase Smith worked to get the Women's Armed Services Integration Act passed. The law set up women's branches of the armed forces and gave women equal pay, rank, and privileges with men.

Chase Smith's biggest challenge came in opposing Senator Joseph McCarthy. Many of her fellow Republicans cheered him on. Chase Smith saw him for the dangerous and unprincipled person he turned out to be. She was the first senator to speak out against McCarthy and McCarthyism.

The Fall of China and the Korean War

Thinking on Your Own

What do you know about China? In your notebook, list the information that you already know about this nation. As you read this lesson, add to your list.

The Cold War was not limited to Europe and the Soviet Union. In 1949, Chinese Communists took control of China. A year later, fighting broke out in Korea between the Communist and non-Communist forces.

focus your reading

What happened in China after World War II?

Why did the Korean War occur?

vocabulary

Nationalist China

demilitarized zone

The Fall of China

When World War II was over, two groups—Nationalists and Communists—fought for control of China. In 1949, the Communists, under Mao Zedong, won. They drove the Nationalists from the mainland to Taiwan, a large island in the China Sea. Communist China became the People's Republic of China (PRC). The Nationalists controlled the much smaller **Nationalist China**, or simply, Taiwan.

The communist victory in China stunned the world. China had been one of the Allies during World War II. To see China fall to communism angered and frightened

Tiananmen Square in 1955

stop and think

Imagine you are the editor of a newspaper. With a partner, think about the kind of editorial you would write about the fall of China to the Communists. Would you try to calm people's fears? Or would you increase their fears? Make a list of points you would include in your editorial.

Americans. One reason was the Soviet Union. Americans thought that because China and the Soviet Union were communist nations, they would team up against the free world. However, Stalin and Mao did not agree on communist philosophy. They also disagreed over the boundaries between China and the Soviet Union. By 1960 the two were rivals, not allies.

The Korean War

The first place the Cold War turned hot was in Korea in 1950. After World War II, Korea was freed from Japanese rule.

However, Soviet troops remained in the northern section and U.S. troops remained in the southern part. The UN tried to work out a plan for uniting the two sections.

In 1948, South Koreans held elections and set up a democratic government. U.S. troops withdrew. That same year the Soviet Union installed a communist government in North Korea. The Soviets, too, withdrew their soldiers. The nation was divided at the 38th parallel of latitude.

"Freedom of education depends on liberty" is written on a sign carried by Korean marchers.

Medical corpsman A.J. Wichman Jr. at a M.A.S.H. unit in Korea in 1953

On June 25, 1950, the North Koreans invaded the South in a surprise attack. The UN Security Council voted to send soldiers to help the South Koreans. The Soviet Union had walked out of the Security Council to protest another matter. As a result, it could not block the vote to send aid to the South Koreans. Sixteen nations contributed to the UN "police action." Most of the forces were from the United States and South Korea.

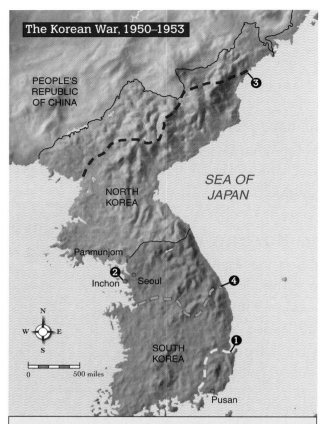

The Korean War, 1950–1953

PEOPLE'S
REPUBLIC
OF CHINA

NORTH
KOREA

SEA OF
JAPAN

Panmunjom

Inchon ○ Seoul

SOUTH
KOREA

Pusan

N
W — E
S

0   500 miles

❶ Farthest advance of the North Koreans, Sept. 1950
❷ U.N. landing, Sept. 1950
❸ Farthest advance of U.N. forces, Nov. 1950
❹ Farthest advance of North Koreans and Chinese, Jan. 1951

By the time the United Nations' forces arrived, North Korea had occupied most of the Korean Peninsula. Fighting had bogged down along the 38th parallel. In July 1951, peace talks began. Finally, in July 1953, an armistice was signed. A **demilitarized zone** (DMZ) was set up between North and South Korea at the 38th parallel. No peace treaty has ever been negotiated. The armistice is still in effect. Korea remains two nations—the communist north and the democratic south.

The DMZ divides North from South Korea.

Putting It All Together

Examine the map of the Korean War. Using the map, write a paragraph to explain what happened during the war. Share your paragraph with a partner to make sure another person can follow your explanation.

Read a Primary Source

Truman Addresses Korean Conflict

In April 1951, President Harry Truman spoke to the nation about the Korean conflict. In the following excerpt, he explains why the United States joined the fight.

reading for understanding

What does President Truman say the United States is doing in Korea?

According to the president, when is the best time to meet danger?

What is the goal of the struggle in Korea?

"I want to talk to you tonight about what we are doing in Korea. . . . In the simplest terms what we are doing in Korea is this: We are trying to prevent a third world war. . . .

"The communists . . . are engaged in a monstrous conspiracy to stamp out freedom all over the world. If they were to succeed, the United States would be numbered among their principal victims. It must be clear to everyone that the United States cannot and will not sit idly by and await foreign conquest. The only question is: When is the best time to meet the threat and how?

"The best time . . . is in the beginning. It is easier to put out a fire in the beginning when it is small than after it has become a roaring blaze. And the best way to meet the threat of aggression is for the peace-loving nations to act together. If they don't . . . they are likely to be picked off, one by one. . . .

"If history has taught us anything, it is that aggression anywhere in the world is a threat to peace everywhere in the world. When that aggression is supported by the cruel and selfish rulers of a powerful nation who are bent on conquest, it becomes a clear and present danger to the security and independence of every free nation. . . . This is the basic reason why we have joined in creating the United Nations. . . .

"The struggle of the United Nations in Korea is a struggle for peace. The free nations have united their strength in an effort to prevent a third world war.
. . . [T]his nation and its allies . . . do not want to widen the conflict. We will use every effort to prevent that disaster. And in so doing, we know that we are following the great principles of peace, freedom, and justice."

from *A Patriot's Handbook.*
Caroline Kennedy, ed. (New York: Hyperion, 2003)

185

Chapter Summary

As World War II ended, millions of veterans returned to civilian life. The federal government passed the Servicemen's Readjustment Act, known as the GI Bill, to help them.

Congress also passed the Taft-Hartley Act to give the president the power to stop strikes that threatened the health and safety of the nation. The act also banned the **closed shop**.

President Truman wanted to continue the policies of the New Deal. He could take some actions by **executive order**. But others required passage of laws by Congress. A **coalition** of conservative Southern Democrats and Republicans blocked many of his proposals. After he won reelection in 1948, he launched the Fair Deal.

While dealing with **domestic policy**, President Truman and the nation faced a crisis in **foreign policy**. To deal with the new Soviet threat, President Truman adopted **containment** towards **Iron Curtain** countries. Containment used **foreign aid** in fighting the **Cold War**. The United Nations was formed in 1945 with the purpose of avoiding further armed conflict.

Senator Joseph McCarthy used the fear of a communist takeover of the United States to further his own career. This became known as **McCarthyism**. When it became clear that he had no proof, he was **censured** by the Senate.

The world was shocked when Communists took control of **Nationalist China** in 1949. Shortly after, troops from communist North Korea invaded democratic South Korea. The United Nations sent troops. An armistice was signed setting up a **demilitarized zone** between the two nations.

Chapter Review

1 Write two-line headlines for each of the following: (1) men and women using the GI Bill, and (2) the Berlin blockade.

2 Design an ad either for or against the reelection of President Truman. Use a picture and text in your ad.

Skill Builder

Making Inferences

An inference is a statement that interprets and explains the meaning of facts. It is not a fact, but it is based on facts. For example, you ask a friend to go to the movies. The friend says, "I can't. I told my little brother I'd help him with his school project." This is not the first time that your friend has helped a younger brother or sister. You put all these times together and decide that your friend is a responsible person. This conclusion is an inference. You make inferences all the time without knowing it.

Making an inference about a reading selection uses the same process. You take information that you read and analyze it in relation to information that you already know. Why do you need to use inference? Sometimes you need to make connections between what you are learning now and what you learned earlier.

To make inferences, follow these steps:

- Identify the stated facts. Ask yourself: What are the facts in this piece of reading?
- Review what you already know about the topic, person, or event.
- Use the new information (the stated facts), what you already know, logic, and common sense to form a conclusion. Logic is clear thinking.

Use inferences to answer the following questions about President Truman's speech on page 185.

1 What is the threat that President Truman refers to in his speech?

2 What does he mean when he talks about the fire and the roaring blaze?

3 When President Truman says "cruel and selfish rulers of a powerful nation," what nation does he mean?

Chapter

12 The Eisenhower Years

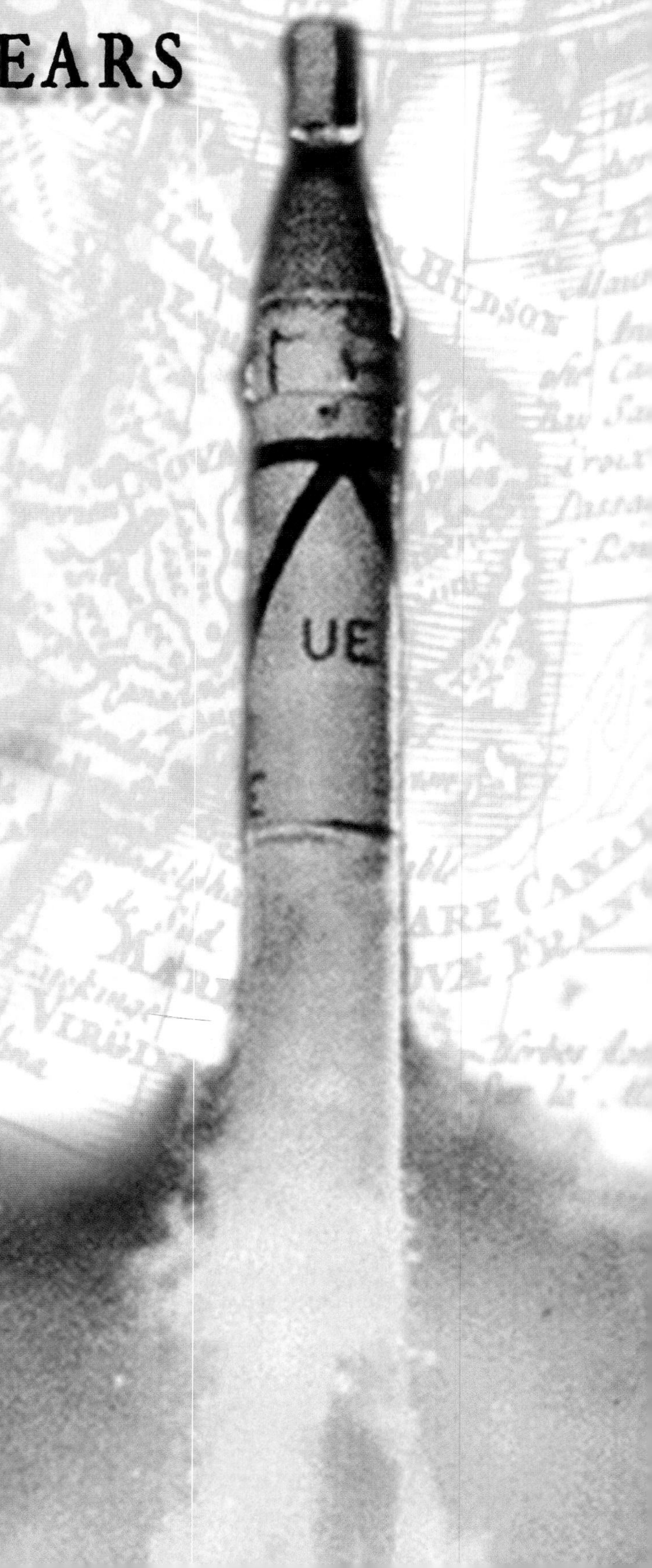

Getting Focused

Skim this chapter to predict what you will be learning.

- **Read the lesson titles and subheadings.**
- **Look at the illustrations and read the captions.**
- **Review the vocabulary words and terms.**

Begin a "Civil Rights" page in your notebook. As you study the rest of this textbook, make a civil rights timeline. Include court cases as well as laws. Begin with President Truman's executive order in 1948 to integrate the armed forces.

Dynamic Conservatism

Thinking on Your Own

Americans often elect war heroes to public office. These heroes include George Washington, Ulysses S. Grant, Theodore Roosevelt, and Dwight D. Eisenhower. Why do you think Americans do this? Explain your ideas in a paragraph in your notebook.

President Truman decided not to run for reelection in 1952. The Democrats nominated Adlai Stevenson, the governor of Illinois. Republicans chose Dwight Eisenhower, a former general and a hero of World War II. He had commanded Allied troops in Europe and led the D-Day invasion of France. Eisenhower easily won the election.

focus your reading

How did President Eisenhower put dynamic conservatism into practice?

Which New Deal programs were expanded during President Eisenhower's administration?

What kinds of government programs did President Eisenhower support?

vocabulary

dynamic conservatism

urban

space race

Political Philosophy

Once in office, President Eisenhower adopted what he called **dynamic conservatism**. He wanted to follow conservative economic policies but was willing to continue some social programs. Balancing the government's budget is an example of a conservative economic policy. So is limiting the role of government, especially in business.

Eisenhower soon put his philosophy into practice. To stimulate the economy, he cut federal taxes. To balance the budget, he cut funding for public housing and school construction. To decrease the role of government in business, the president eliminated the Reconstruction Finance Corporation (RFC), the agency set up during the Great Depression.

1952 campaign button

I LIKE IKE

Social Policies

Some of Eisenhower's supporters had expected him to roll back New Deal social programs. However, President Eisenhower did not even try. While campaigning he had said that if any political party attempted to eliminate Social Security, labor laws, and farm programs, "you would not hear of that party again in our political history."

President Eisenhower and Vice President Nixon in 1960

stop and think

Reread Eisenhower's quote about social programs and political parties. What do you think it means? Discuss it with a partner and then write an explanation in your notebook.

During his administration, some New Deal programs were actually expanded. Another ten million people were covered under Social Security. Many of these were farmers who owned their own farms. The minimum wage was increased from 75 cents to one dollar an hour. The rules for unemployment compensation were expanded to cover additional groups of workers.

New Programs and New Boundaries

President Eisenhower did not believe in "big government." However, he saw the need for government investment in large, important projects.

Alaska became a state in 1959.

President Eisenhower signed the proclamation making Hawaii the 50th state on August 21, 1959.

The interstate highway system that we have today is the result of the Federal Highway Act of 1956. More than 40,000 miles of highway were built. Suburbs spread farther out from cities because it became so easy for people to drive into cities to work. However, public transportation—railroads and buses—lost business. Many **urban** African Americans and Latinos also lost. Highways often were built through their neighborhoods.

The National Interstate Highway System

Explorer I, America's first satellite, was launched on January 31, 1958.

The nation moved into the space age under President Eisenhower. In 1957, the Soviet Union launched the first space satellite, *Sputnik*. Newspaper headlines announced that the Soviets had beaten the United States to space.

In reality, U.S. scientists were working on a similar space program. In January 1958, the United States launched *Explorer I*, the first U.S. space satellite. Later that same year, Congress set up the National Aeronautics and Space Administration (NASA). Its purpose was to win the **space race**.

Putting It All Together

Write a definition of dynamic conservatism. Discuss with a partner what this term means. Write a short paragraph explaining how this term relates to Eisenhower's policies and accomplishments.

Civil Rights and School Desegregation

Thinking on Your Own

What do you know about the efforts of African Americans to gain their civil rights? Who were their leaders? List the people and events in your notebook. Begin to make your civil rights timeline. Be sure you know the meaning of each vocabulary word.

In 1896, *Plessy* v. *Ferguson* legalized second-class citizenship for African Americans. It was another 59 years before anyone in power would rule that "separate but equal" was false. In the meantime, African Americans were actively working to gain their rights.

focus your reading

What court case overturned "separate but equal"?

How did the Montgomery bus boycott begin?

Why was there a crisis over integrating Central High School in Little Rock, Arkansas?

vocabulary

desegregation   integration

segregation   boycott

An End to "Separate but Equal"

Jackie Robinson in 1950

By 1954 the NAACP had argued several **desegregation** cases before the U.S. Supreme Court. In 1954, they filed *Brown* v. *The Board of Education of Topeka, Kansas*. It took on segregation in public elementary and secondary schools.

Every school day, Linda Brown walked past a school for white children. She had to ride a bus to a school for black children. With the help of the NAACP, her father filed a lawsuit against the school district.

Thurgood Marshall presented the case in front of the U.S. Supreme Court. He argued that the psychological effects of **segregation** harmed African-American children. As a result, segregated schools were not "separate but equal." The Supreme Court agreed. It overturned the earlier decision in *Plessy* v. *Ferguson*. All public schools across the nation were to be integrated. However, **integration** would not be achieved that easily—or quickly.

stop and think

Do you agree that segregated schools are not equal to integrated schools? List reasons to support your position. Then discuss your ideas with a partner.

Montgomery Bus Boycott

African Americans in the South faced segregation everywhere. They could not eat in the same restaurants as whites, or drink from the same water fountains. They had to sit upstairs at the movies and ride in the backs of buses.

Rosa Parks

One day in 1955, Rosa Parks took a stand. She was a member of the Montgomery, Alabama, NAACP. Parks was riding home from work and the bus was becoming crowded. When the driver told her to give her seat to a white man, she refused. The driver warned her that she would be arrested. She still would not move.

Parks's arrest launched the **boycott** of Montgomery buses by African Americans. For 381 days, they walked everywhere they went. One of the leaders of the boycott was a young minister, the Rev. Dr. Martin Luther King, Jr. He would become famous for his work in the Civil Rights Movement.

The boycott ended in 1956 with another U.S. Supreme Court ruling. The court declared segregation on Alabama buses unconstitutional. Parks and fellow African Americans could sit wherever they wanted on a bus.

Linda Brown in a 1953 class photo

African-American students are protected as they enter Little Rock Central High School in 1957.

Desegregation and Civil Rights

The Supreme Court ruled that schools were to be desegregated—or open to members of all racial and ethnic groups. However, not everyone obeyed. In 1957, Central High School in Little Rock, Arkansas, planned to admit nine African-American students. The governor stepped in and ordered the Arkansas National Guard to turn the students away. President Eisenhower could not allow the governor to ignore federal law. He sent 1,000 U.S. army soldiers with fixed bayonets to surround the building. The nine students were escorted inside to class. Central High School was officially desegregated.

The events in Little Rock focused the nation's attention on civil rights. In 1957, Congress also passed the first civil rights law since Reconstruction. The act was passed over objections of many Southern lawmakers. It made denial of the right to vote a federal crime. The law set up a civil rights division in the Justice Department and also the Commission on Civil Rights. The commission investigates violations of voting rights.

Chairperson of the U.S. Commission on Civil Rights, Dr. Mary Frances Berry, in 2004

Putting It All Together

Write a letter to the editor about an issue in this lesson. Before you write, list in your notebook the points you want to make. Share your letter with a partner. Discuss how to make the points in your letter stronger.

Biography

Thurgood Marshall (1908–1993)

Thurgood Marshall was the grandson of enslaved Africans. He was born in Baltimore, Maryland, and graduated from Lincoln University in Pennsylvania. He studied law and in 1933 received a law degree from Howard University in Washington, D.C.

After graduation, Marshall opened his own law practice. Marshall also worked with Charles Hamilton Houston at the NAACP in Baltimore. Houston was special counsel to the NAACP. Houston and Marshall determined to use the court system to fight segregation. For several years the two of them worked together. In 1938, Marshall took over the position of special counsel for the NAACP.

Between 1938 and 1961, Marshall argued a number of important civil rights cases before the U.S. Supreme Court. One of the most famous is *Brown* v. *The Board of Education of Topeka, Kansas*. This case overturned the doctrine of "separate but equal" facilities for African Americans. He won other civil rights cases that

- gained admission to law school for African Americans in Missouri and Texas

- gained African Americans the right to vote in primary elections in Texas

- ended segregation on buses and railroads in interstate travel through Virginia

In 1961, President John Kennedy appointed Marshall to a federal district court of appeals. In 1965, President Lyndon Johnson named him Solicitor General of the United States. The person in this position represents the United States in cases before the U.S. Supreme Court. In 1967, Johnson nominated Marshall to the U.S. Supreme Court. He was the first African American named to the Court.

Cold War, Nuclear Weapons, and Dominoes

Thinking on Your Own

Create a concept map for this lesson. Write "Cold War" in the large center circle. As you read, add smaller circles with additional information.

The Korean conflict was an issue in the presidential election of 1952. If elected, Eisenhower promised to end the conflict. In 1953, an armistice was finally signed. The Korean War was just the beginning of President Eisenhower's problems in the Cold War.

focus your reading

What policies did President Eisenhower develop to deal with the Cold War?

What policy was used to deal with issues in Latin America?

What was the Eisenhower Doctrine?

What was the domino theory?

vocabulary

arms race

retaliation

brinkmanship

economic sanctions

domino theory

The Arms Race and Brinkmanship

The Soviet Union exploded its first nuclear weapon in 1949. The **arms race** between the two nations had begun. Each side began stockpiling missiles and nuclear warheads.

Eisenhower believed that the best way to prevent war was to be firm with the Soviet Union. He and his secretary of state, John Foster Dulles, announced a policy of massive **retaliation**. If the Soviets attacked any nation, the United States would retaliate, or strike back, with a nuclear attack.

Dulles said it in another way. He believed that it was necessary at times to get to the brink, or edge, of war.

President Eisenhower in Korea in 1952

Containment was the foreign policy of the U.S. during the Hungarian uprising in 1956.

Only then would the Soviet Union back down. Along with containment, massive retaliation and **brinkmanship** were the basis of U.S. foreign policy during the Cold War.

Latin America

Containing communism was the first defense of the United States during the Cold War. In 1951, Guatemalan communists supported the democratic election of president Jacobo Arbenz Guzman. He began a series of land reforms. As part of them, he seized the property of U.S.-owned companies. President Eisenshower ordered the U.S. Central Intelligence Agency (CIA) into action. Its goal was to keep Guatemala from becoming communist and to get back U.S. property. The CIA armed and trained Guatemalan rebels. The rebels seized the government and overthrew Guzman.

Cuba was even closer to home—90 miles from Florida. In 1959, Fidel Castro seized power in Cuba from a dictator. The new government took over U.S.-owned companies. Castro also limited the rights of Cubans and delayed elections for a new government. Increasingly, he accepted aid from the Soviet Union. The United States placed **economic sanctions** on Cuba to retaliate. The sanctions prevented U.S. companies from buying Cuban sugar. The goal was to create financial hardship in Cuba. The hope was that Cubans would rise up and throw Castro out.

stop and think

What do you think about the policies of massive retaliation, brinkmanship, and containment? Write one sentence for each concept. In your sentence, explain why the concept is right or wrong. Share your sentences with a partner. Talk about your reason for each statement. Did you change your mind during your discussion? Revise your sentences as needed.

Fidel Castro led the Cuban revolution.

The Middle East and the Eisenhower Doctrine

The Cold War reached into the Middle East, too. After World War II, the UN created two nations in the Middle East. Israel was a shelter for Holocaust survivors and any other Jews who wished to settle in a homeland. Palestine was for Arabs who lost their land in the creation of Israel.

Arab nations did not agree with this decision. In 1948, they attacked Israel. Israel fought back and defeated the combined Arab forces. Over the years, the United States took the side of Israel. The Soviet Union supported the Arab nations.

David Ben-Gurion read a declaration of independence for the state of Israel in 1948.

In the 1950s, President Eisenhower was also concerned about keeping communism out of the Middle East. In 1957, he proposed the Eisenhower Doctrine. Under this policy, the United States would use force to help any Middle Eastern nation fight a communist takeover. The president also asked Congress for millions of dollars in economic aid for the region. U.S. support for Israel continues to this day.

U.S. Marines acting under the Eisenhower Doctrine arrive in Beirut, Lebanon, in 1958.

Vietnam and the Domino Theory

The Vietnam War began in the 1950s. After World War II, France tried to regain its former colony of Vietnam. In 1954, communist forces defeated the French in the northern part of Vietnam. The 1954 Geneva Conference produced the Geneva Accords. The Accords stated that Vietnam would be divided into two states at the 17th parallel. The north was ruled by a communist government, and the south was governed by a monarch. The division was supposed to be temporary. Within two years, free and democratic elections were to be held to combine north and south. President Eisenhower did not sign the Accord. He supported the southern regime and helped to create the Southeast Asia Treaty Organization.

President Eisenhower was concerned that the communists would try to take over the south. He developed what is called the **domino theory**. If Vietnam fell to communism, then all of Southeast Asia would fall to communism. To prevent this, he asked for huge amounts of foreign aid for South Vietnam.

Putting It All Together

Use the world map on page 346 as a reference. Write a sentence describing each of the locations mentioned in the lesson: Guatemala, Cuba, Israel, Lebanon, Korea, the former Soviet Union, North Vietnam, South Vietnam, France, Hungary, the Middle East, Latin America. Use the directions north, south, east, and west to explain where these are located.

Read a Primary Source

President Dwight Eisenhower: "The Domino Theory"

President Eisenhower used the game of dominoes to explain the importance of Indochina to U.S. security. *Indochina* was the term used to describe Southeast Asia. The following excerpt is from a press conference on May 12, 1954. The president is answering a reporter's question about why Indochina is important to the free world.

reading for understanding

According to the president, what are the three reasons that Indochina is important to the free world?

Explain the domino theory in your own words.

What are the dominoes that the president names?

What other nations would a communist Indochina threaten?

"THE PRESIDENT. . . . First of all, you have the specific value of a locality in its production of materials that the world needs. Then you have the possibility that many human beings pass under a dictatorship. . . .

"Finally, you have broader considerations that might follow what you would call the 'falling domino' principle. You have a row of dominoes set up, you knock over the first one, and what will happen to the last one is the certainty that it will go over very quickly. So you could have a beginning of a disintegration that would have the most profound influences.

". . . Asia, after all, has already lost some 450 million of its people to the Communist dictatorship, and we simply can't afford greater losses.

"But when we come to the possible sequence of events, the loss of Indochina, of Burma, of Thailand, . . . and Indonesia following, now you begin to talk about areas that not only multiply the disadvantages that you would suffer through loss of materials, sources of materials, but now you are talking really about millions and millions of people.

"Finally, the geographical position [of communism] . . . moves in to threaten Australia and New Zealand.

"It takes away, in its economic aspects, that region that Japan must have as a trading area or Japan, in turn, will have only one place in the world to go— that is, toward the communist areas in order to live.

"So, the possible consequences of the loss are just incalculable to the free world."

from Eisenhower.archives.gov

Chapter Summary

President Dwight D. Eisenhower adopted what he called **dynamic conservatism**. He followed conservative economic policies. He expanded some New Deal social programs. One large government project he proposed was the Federal Highway Act of 1956. Many projects hurt **urban** areas.

African Americans had been working for many years to gain equal rights. In 1954, *Brown* v. *The Board of Education of Topeka, Kansas* ordered an end to **segregation** in all public elementary and high schools. The Montgomery bus **boycott** ended segregated busing in Alabama. Not everyone accepted **integration**. The governor of Arkansas opposed **desegregation**. He refused to allow African-American students to attend a local high school. President Eisenhower sent the U.S. army to escort the students. During the crisis in Little Rock, Congress passed the Civil Rights Act of 1957.

In foreign affairs, Eisenhower adopted the policy of massive **retaliation** toward the Soviet Union. It included the policy of **brinkmanship**. The policy created an **arms race** and also a **space race** with the Soviet Union.

During the 1950s, the United States stepped in to contain communism around the world. President Eisenhower asked Congress for **economic sanctions** against Cuba. The Eisenhower Doctrine was applied in the Middle East to prevent communist takeovers. Concerned about the **domino theory**, President Eisenhower asked Congress for foreign aid for South Vietnam.

Chapter Review

1 Write a paragraph describing the gains of the Civil Rights Movement in the 1950s.

2 Outline Lesson 3. Be sure to follow the outline format you learned in Chapter 4.

3 Create a diagram to illustrate the domino theory. Include the information from the chapter and from the primary source.

Skill Builder

Identifying the Main Idea and Supporting Details

The main idea of a piece of reading material is what the piece is mostly about—the topic. A chapter has a main idea. So does a lesson, a section, and even a paragraph. Sometimes the main idea is stated. Sometimes you have to infer it. You make an inference by connecting information and coming to a conclusion.

Knowing the main idea of what you are reading is useful for several reasons. Any information related to the main idea is important. It is information that you should remember and connect to the main idea. Names, dates, and events will mean more if you can relate them to the main idea. All information connected to the main idea is called supporting details.

To find the main idea in a piece of writing, follow these steps:

- Identify the subject of what you are reading. What or who is it about?
- Look for an idea that all the information (details) relates to. How is this idea connected to the subject?
- Look for a sentence that best states the main idea. This statement is called the topic sentence.
- If there is no topic sentence, then you have to infer the main idea from the details. State your inference in a sentence. This is the main idea.

1 Read the subheading "Political Philosophy" on page 189. (1) What is the main idea of this section? (2) Did you find a topic sentence or did you have to infer the main idea? (3) If you found a topic sentence, write it in your notebook.

2 Read the subheading "Desegregation and Civil Rights" on page 195. Infer the main idea of this section. Write your sentence in your notebook. Explain what details you found to help you infer the main idea.

3 Read paragraph 1 under "Latin America" on page 198. (1) What is the main idea of this paragraph? (2) Write the topic sentence in your notebook.

UNIT 7

THE UNITED STATES AT MID-CENTURY

Overseas the United States was trying to stare down the Soviet Union and prevent World War III. As the 1950s began, the nation faced new challenges from the Soviet Union.

At home, schoolchildren were learning to "duck and cover." In case of a nuclear attack, they were to duck under their desks and cover their heads with their arms. But life went on, and that life was good for many Americans. The population was increasing. The economy was growing. More families owned homes than ever before. For many Americans, the 1950s were a quiet, prosperous time. This would change as the 1960s arrived.

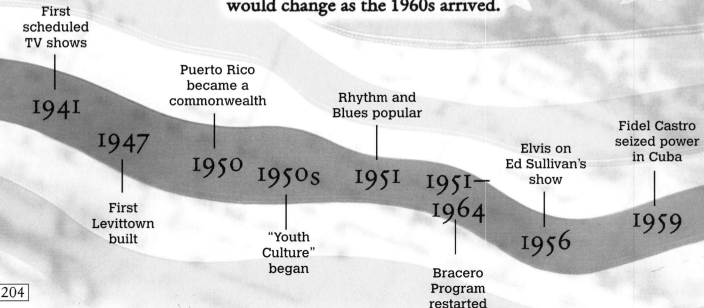

First scheduled TV shows
1941

First Levittown built
1947

Puerto Rico became a commonwealth
1950

"Youth Culture" began
1950s

Rhythm and Blues popular
1951

Bracero Program restarted
1951–1964

Elvis on Ed Sullivan's show
1956

Fidel Castro seized power in Cuba
1959

Why did so many people move to the Sunbelt during the twentieth century?

How did Elvis Presley and rock 'n' roll change U.S. music and popular culture?

What was the Cuban missile crisis? Why did people think that students needed to learn to "duck and cover"?

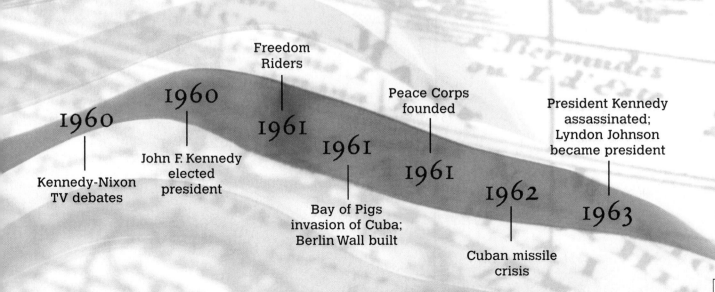

1960
Kennedy-Nixon TV debates

1960
John F. Kennedy elected president

Freedom Riders

1961

1961
Bay of Pigs invasion of Cuba; Berlin Wall built

Peace Corps founded

1961

1962
Cuban missile crisis

President Kennedy assassinated; Lyndon Johnson became president

1963

Chapter 13

THE FIFTIES: THE AFFLUENT SOCIETY

Getting Focused

Skim this chapter to predict what you will be learning.

- Read the lesson titles and subheadings.
- Look at the illustrations and read the captions.
- Examine the maps.
- Review the vocabulary words and terms.

The word *affluent* means wealthy or prosperous. U.S. society in the 1950s was not necessarily rich. But many Americans lived what they considered the good life. What does the phrase "the good life" mean to you? How do the people and things in the pictures in this chapter fit your idea of the good life? Write your ideas in your notebook.

Suburban Living and the Baby Boom

Thinking on Your Own

Look at the pictures that illustrate suburban living. Write a list of words that describe what you see in the pictures. Add to your list as you read.

Dwight Eisenhower took office as president in January 1953. World War II had been over for seven years. The nation had made a remarkable transition from the war effort to peacetime. Even the Korean War did not stop the nation's steady progress. The population was growing and the economy was booming. By 1960, the United States led the world in the production of goods and services.

focus your reading

What caused the growth of suburbs in the 1950s?

How did the growth of suburbs affect cities?

What was the baby boom?

vocabulary

standard of living

suburbia

tract housing

white-collar

baby boom

Americans had the highest **standard of living** in the world. Standard of living measures people's quality of life. Things that had once been luxuries now became commonplace. People eagerly bought washers and dryers, dishwashers, freezers, electric stoves, gasoline-powered lawn mowers, and the new rage: televisions. The ultimate measure of the good life for many Americans, however, was home ownership.

New products made life easier during the 1950s.

"**I'd never go back from Electricity to old-fashioned cooking now!**"

Electric cookers have thermostat control on the oven, quick-heating boiling plates, and new, variable switches which give perfect heat-control from fast boiling to slow simmering—*and lower*, if you want it!

Go round and see one at your Electricity Service Centre. They are friendly, knowledgeable people there, and will be glad to help you. They can also let you have details about easy payments, and the new, free book, full of clever ideas for saving work, ELECTRICITY IN YOUR KITCHEN: or you are welcome to write for a copy to EDA, 2 Savoy Hill, London, W.C.2.

ELECTRICITY
a Power of Good
for cooking!
AND FOR WATER-HEATING TOO!

Suburban Living

Little housing was built during World War II. Building supplies had been used for the war effort. As a result, there was a huge demand for housing after the war. Between 1940 and 1960, the number of Americans who owned their own homes grew from 20 percent to 61 percent.

Various factors made this possible. One was the growth of **suburbia**. About 85 percent of all new homes in the 1950s were built in the suburbs. The GI Bill provided low-interest mortgages. But the bill would have been useless without a supply of homes to buy. Real estate developers and builders bought up large tracts, or pieces, of land near cities. Then they built house after house. William Levitt, who built Levittown, New York, pioneered **tract housing**. Soon tract housing was appearing in suburbs around the country.

Levittown, New York, in 1955

Other factors were the Federal Highway Act and the low price of automobiles. These made the suburbs practical for more people. The Federal Highway Act built 41,000 miles of highway across the nation. Many of these highways put cities within easy driving distance of the new suburbs.

As wages rose, cars became more affordable for workers. Many suburban families became two-car families. Between 1940 and 1960, the number of cars sold in the United States increased from 3.7 million per year to 6.6 million.

People moved from cities to suburbs for several reasons. The first reason was the dream of home ownership. Owning a home meant that the family was successful. Second, for people who grew up in crowded apartments, a house offered privacy. Third, a house in the suburbs also meant an opportunity to live with similar families. These people were white, middle-class, **white-collar** professionals. Most suburban developments had rules against selling homes to African Americans.

Highways increased people's access to the suburbs.

Urban areas such as Baltimore deteriorated during the 1950s.

Cities

Those who were left in cities were often low-income families. Many of these people paid little or no taxes. The tax revenue that cities collected decreased. With lower revenues, the cities had less money for police and fire protection. There was also less money to pay for teachers and to keep up school buildings. The quality of education declined. Services such as fire, police, and sanitation also declined.

To try to solve the problem, cities raised the rates for their sales and property taxes. Some cities began to collect a tax on wages. Stores suffered because people were not buying as much. City dwellers were paying higher taxes, so they had less money. Commuters could shop in the new malls in the suburbs. Businesses moved out of cities because their workers did not want to pay the wage tax.

stop and think

What were the causes of the growth of the suburbs? What were the effects? Create a cause-and-effect flowchart to show the relationship between the causes and effects of the suburbs.

The cities of the Northeast and Midwest suffered the most during the 1950s. Large sections of cities decayed. These sections were home to the poorest city dwellers. Decent, safe, affordable housing was the most pressing problem.

The Baby Boom and the Suburban Family

The population of the United States grew in the 1950s. More babies were born and more people lived longer. **Baby boom** is the term given to the upward trend in births between 1946 and 1961. More than 65 million children were born in those 15 years.

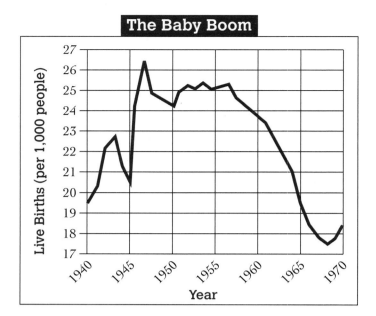

The Baby Boom

Live Births (per 1,000 people) vs. Year

Why was there such a surge in births? World War II and the Korean War kept many men from marrying. Once they returned from duty, they wanted to marry and start families.

Magazines like *Ladies Home Journal* had article after article on keeping house and bringing up children. Along with TV programs like *Father Knows Best*, they created the idea of the happy, suburban family. This family had a father who went to work in an office somewhere. The stay-at-home mom baked cookies and helped the children with their homework.

Few seemed to remember that eight million women had worked in industry during World War II. The ideal was the nonworking wife and mother. In reality, by 1960 about 30 percent of all married women were working outside the home.

Putting It All Together

Write a two-line headline for an article about living in suburbia. Then write a two-line headline for an article about cities in the 1950s. Share your headlines with a partner. Use the terms you listed at the beginning of the lesson.

Biography

William Levitt (1907–1994)

For many Americans, owning their own home is the American Dream. William Levitt made this dream possible for millions of Americans after World War II. He pioneered a type of housing construction that other builders copied.

William (Bill) Levitt was born in Brooklyn, New York. In the late 1920s, he went to work for his father, Abraham. The elder Levitt was a real estate lawyer. He was interested in investing in housing construction.

Levitt & Sons was founded in 1929. By age twenty-two, the younger Levitt was the company president.

One goal of the GI Bill was to help veterans buy homes. Bill Levitt saw an opportunity. Houses were usually built one at a time. Levitt had his crews build houses the way automakers made cars on assembly lines. The crews broke the building process down into individual steps. Crews were assigned to do certain steps on a house. Then they moved on to the next house. At the new house they repeated the same few steps. For example, one crew built the foundation. The next crew put up the frame, a third crew put up the outside walls, a fourth crew put in the windows, and so on. The crews could build 30 houses a day.

Baby-boomer families soon filled block after block of Levitt's two-bedroom houses. The first Levittown was built on Long Island. Levitt carefully chose the site. It was close to New York City and to highways. He built other Levittowns in Pennsylvania and New Jersey.

By 1950, Bill Levitt was famous. He is credited with putting home ownership within the reach of ordinary American workers. In all, Levitt built 46,000 houses between 1947 and the early 1960s.

Immigration and Migrations

Thinking on Your Own

Read the vocabulary words. Use context clues to figure out the meaning of any words you don't understand. Check the Glossary to see how well you did. Remember to use context clues for unfamiliar words whenever you read.

During World War II, most immigration to the United States from outside the Americas was stopped. Mexican workers, however, were brought to the United States to replace U.S. workers on farms and on railroads under the Bracero Program.

focus your reading

What special groups were admitted to the United States after World War II?

What was the Bracero Program?

Why did Puerto Ricans migrate to the mainland?

Why did the Sunbelt states gain political importance?

vocabulary

refugee   seasonal worker

migrate   census

mainland

Immigration

After World War II, immigration began again. In addition to regular immigration, the United States passed an emergency immigration law. Between 1945 and 1951, some 400,000 Europeans were admitted to the United States as displaced persons. They had no homes to return to. Many were Jews who had survived the Nazi concentration camps.

Many Eastern Europeans immigrated to the United States during the 1950s.

Hungarian immigrants arrive in New York City in 1957.

In 1953, Congress passed another **refugee** act. This law allowed people fleeing communism to enter the United States. Some 200,000 immigrants arrived between 1954 and 1959. Many of them were from the Iron Curtain countries of Eastern Europe.

Mexican Workers

In 1951, the Bracero Program was restarted. From 1951 until 1964, some five million Mexicans signed up for the program. They contracted to work on farms and ranches in the Southwest. Their working and living conditions were as bad as they had been during the war. Each year after the harvest, most went back to their families in Mexico.

In addition to legal workers, thousands of other Mexicans came illegally. These undocumented immigrants risked their lives to cross the border between the United States and Mexico. Many came in family groups.

"Braceros" pick strawberries in Salinas, California.

Puerto Rican Migration to the Mainland

In 1917, Puerto Ricans became U.S. citizens. Puerto Rico became a commonwealth in 1950. It has its own constitution and elects its own legislature and governor.

During the 1950s, large numbers of Puerto Ricans **migrated** to the **mainland** United States. They were looking for jobs and better wages than they could get at home. As many as 50,000 Puerto Ricans came each year. By 1970, there were about 800,000 native-born Puerto Ricans on the mainland. More than 470,000 lived in New York City.

Some came with their families to stay. They took jobs in factories and as messengers, cooks, dishwashers, and similar low-paying jobs. Other migrants were **seasonal workers**. They came to work summers on farms in New Jersey, Pennsylvania, and New York. Like the braceros, they worked for low wages and in poor working conditions.

Migrant workers board a plane to Michigan in 1950.

stop and think

Review the push and pull factors for immigration explained in Chapter 4. With a partner, list the immigrant groups mentioned in this lesson, as well as Puerto Ricans. Decide if any of the reasons in Chapter 4 apply to immigrants of the 1950s. Write the reasons next to each group.

Puerto Ricans and Mexicans experienced discrimination from non-Latino Americans. Because of the language differences, people took advantage of them. About 30 percent of Puerto Ricans lived in poverty. Because they earned so little, they could afford housing only in the poorer parts of cities. Schools in these sections offered their children poor quality education. Puerto Ricans, like Mexican Americans, began to protest.

Sun City, Arizona, became a popular location in the Sunbelt.

The Sunbelt

The postwar years also brought a regional shift in population growth. More people moved to the Sunbelt states. The Sunbelt stretches across the southern part of the nation from North Carolina to California. It is made up of the states of the Southeast, Southwest, and West. Beginning with World War II, people began moving from the colder states of the Northeast and Midwest to the Sunbelt. The first migrants followed jobs to the aircraft factories of California and the shipyards of Louisiana and Texas. In the 1950s, retirees went to enjoy the warm, sunny climate.

By the late twentieth century, the Sunbelt was the fastest-growing part of the nation. As the population in the Sunbelt grew, more jobs were created. As a result, more people moved to the area. The mild winters still attracted retirees. The widespread use of air conditioning in homes and offices after World War II also made the hot summers bearable.

Because of the region's growing population, its political importance also grew. A national **census**, or counting of people, is taken every ten years. For several decades, it has shown a shift in population to the Sunbelt. As a result, the states of the Northeast and Midwest lost members of the House of Representatives to states in the Sunbelt. Many of these Sunbelt Congressmen were Republicans. The region's affluent voters tended to vote Republican.

Shift in Members of the House of Representatives, 2000 Census	
States that Gained Representatives	States that Lost Representatives
Arizona +2	Connecticut -1
California +1	Illinois -1
Colorado +1	Indiana -1
Florida +2	Michigan -1
Georgia +2	Mississippi -1
Nevada +1	New York -2
North Carolina +1	Ohio -1
Texas +2	Oklahoma -1
	Pennsylvania -2
	Wisconsin -1

Putting It All Together

Compare the reasons for migration to the Sunbelt with the reasons for Mexican immigration and Puerto Rican migration. Make a table to help sort out the information. Then write a paragraph to compare and contrast the reasons. Include information from your notes on push and pull factors.

Television and Rock 'n' Roll

Thinking on Your Own

Read the vocabulary words. Use each word to describe life today. In your notebook, write your sentences. Then compare them with a partner's sentences.

Mass media are forms of communication and entertainment that reach a large audience. In the 1920s, radio and movies were important mass media. In the 1950s, television, or TV, became the most important form of mass media. Its influence soon overtook radio, movies, newspapers, and magazines. TV helped to spread rock 'n' roll and the **youth culture**.

focus your reading

What kinds of TV programs were Americans watching in the 1950s?

How did rock 'n' roll become popular?

Why did the youth culture develop?

vocabulary

mass media

youth culture

situation comedy

rhythm and blues

generation gap

Television

The first regular TV broadcasts were approved by the Federal Communications Commission in 1941. By 1948, over one million homes had TVs. The sets had small screens, and shows were broadcast only in black and white. By 1957, the nation had 40 million TV sets. Over 80 percent of families owned TVs. Color TV was not broadcast until 1963.

What were most people watching? Many of the shows were family **situation comedies**. The actors were always white. The moms did not work outside the home. The dads wore suits and went to work in offices. The children were well

Father Knows Best was a popular TV show.

dressed and well behaved. Shows revolved around such problems as how to get junior to clean up his room, how to deal with the class bully, or how to ask a girl out on a date. These TV families had little in common with most American families.

stop and think

Read over the types of programming on early TV. How do they compare to current TV shows? With a partner, make a list of shows on TV today. Write a paragraph comparing early TV shows with current programming.

Americans also watched Westerns. These shows glorified the settling of the West by white pioneers. The programs created heroes such as the Lone Ranger, Gene Autry, and Roy Rogers and Dale Evans. Early TV also had talk shows, variety shows, and children's programming. Variety shows had a mix of comedy, music, and acts like jugglers and trained dogs. One of the most popular, longest-running shows was *Howdy Doody*, a children's show. He was a freckled face marionette in cowboy clothes.

Rock 'n' Roll

Some people think that rock 'n' roll began with Elvis Presley in 1956. That was the year he appeared on Ed Sullivan's *Toast of the Town* variety show. But rock 'n' roll began with African-American **rhythm and blues** (R&B) singers. In 1951, white disk jockey Alan Freed in Cleveland began playing African-American R&B records on the radio. White teenagers responded enthusiastically. Up to this point, white stations did not play African-American records.

Soon white singers were recording their own versions of songs by African-American singers. White radio stations played these versions, not the originals. However, white teenagers could tell the difference in sound. They wanted the African Americans' records. By the mid-1950s, white record companies got the message and began signing African-American singers to contracts. Performers like Little Richard, Chuck Berry, and Fats Domino sold millions of records.

Little Richard

Rock 'n' roll is a mix of rhythm and blues, country and western, African-American gospel music, and jazz. Perhaps no performer captured rock 'n' roll better than Elvis Presley.

Teenagers line up outside a New York theater in 1957.

The Youth Culture

The 1950s were the beginning of what is called the youth culture in the United States. Teenagers in the 1950s did not have to work to help support their families. Some teenagers did work, but they used their wages for records, clothes, and entertainment.

Rock 'n' roll with its strong beat and African-American roots was not family entertainment. However, the desire for money got the better of Ed Sullivan's concerns. He signed Elvis Presley for three shows, even though many people thought Presley was not family entertainment. Many other businesses learned the same lesson: Teenagers had money and teenagers knew what they wanted.

Teenagers began to dress alike. Clothing makers saw that they could make money by turning out clothing that teenagers would buy. Movie studios soon followed with movies that appealed to youthful interests. None of the clothes, music, or movies appealed to their parents. As a result, a gap, or separation, appeared between what teenagers liked and what their parents liked. This is called the **generation gap**.

Putting It All Together

Situation comedies showed one view of U.S. life in the 1950s. Rock 'n' roll and the youth culture showed another side of life. Make a Venn diagram that describes each view of life. Review your diagrams with a partner. Add words or remove words that do not seem to fit.

Read a Primary Source

Coming to America, Cesar Rosas

Cesar Rosas came to the United States with his family from a ranch near Hermosillo, Mexico. The time was the late 1950s. Rosas grew up to become the lead guitarist and singer with Los Lobos. In the following piece, he talks about coming to the United States and about rediscovering the music of his native Mexico.

reading for understanding

What does Rosas mean when he says that rock-and-roll songs were "fresh"?

How did Rosas feel about coming to the United States?

Why do you think Rosas laughed after he played Mexican music for the first time in years?

"When I came to the States as a kid I really loved music and rock and roll. . . . This was right at that time the fifties had gone over to the sixties: Ray Charles, Chubby Checker, the Rhythm Tens. . . . Those were my first influences with American rock and roll. It was a big, big influence on me. The songs were fresh. . . .

"But coming to the United States—I'll never forget that! I was really afraid. . . . I was panicked. These people were speaking this other language, they dressed differently, acted differently. It's like going to another planet, you know. What intrigued me though was [my cousins] who also spoke Spanish.

"Although I hadn't really, really been involved in playing the Mexican music, it was always in my blood and in my ears and my heart. See rock-and-roll was, 'Yeh, I want that, I wanna get on with that and absorb it. Everything.' But yeh, this is the stuff I hear at my house, the stuff I grew up with. Mexican music, that was my other world; but I had never . . . played it. So when I started playing, it just all tied in. It was so familiar to me. . . . [B]efore we knew it we had played a couple of songs. Man, I remember that. 'Cause you gotta understand that after playing rock-and-roll for four or five years, to go and play something of your own culture there was something, I can't explain it . . . so rewarding, so easy, and so rich. . . . I mean we'd finish a song and we'd laugh. . . . We'd think, man, this is so silly, but it's such a cool song."

Marilyn P. Davis, *Mexican Voices, American Dreams: An Oral History of Mexican Immigration to the United States,* (New York, 1990).

Chapter Summary

By the end of the 1950s, the United States had the highest **standard of living** in the world. Many returning veterans took advantage of the GI Bill to buy homes in **suburbia**. The homes were in large developments of **tract housing**. Many workers commuted into nearby cities to **white-collar** office jobs. The **baby boom** was one factor that added to the growth of the suburbs. The growing suburbs took people from the cities, which suffered as a result.

After World War II, the United States passed two emergency immigration laws. One allowed **refugees** from Europe to be admitted. The other law allowed people fleeing communism to immigrate to the United States.

Puerto Ricans were U.S. citizens, and many **migrated** to the U.S. **mainland** during the 1950s. Some came as families to stay. Others came as **seasonal workers** to work on farms in the Northeast. The **census** showed that many Americans were migrating to the states of the Sunbelt.

Television became the most important form of **mass media** in the 1950s. Popular shows included **situation comedies**, Westerns, and children's programs. Another influence was rock 'n' roll. It owes much to African-American **rhythm and blues**. Rock 'n' roll music helped to create a **youth culture**. Business people learned to produce goods that appealed to this youth market. The result was a **generation gap** between teenagers and parents.

Chapter Review

1 Design and write an ad for a home in Levittown.

2 This chapter's title is "The Fifties: The Affluent Society." Write a paragraph explaining three reasons why the decade was affluent.

3 Think about the migrants and immigrants who arrived during the 1950s. Write a paragraph explaining what their lives were like in the United States.

Skill Builder

Analyzing Line Graphs

Graphs come in several different types including line, bar, and circle. Each is used to show statistical data in a different way. A line graph is used to show change in the quantity or amount of something over time.

The vertical, or side, of a line graph is the *y*-axis. It shows the quantities or amounts that are shown. The horizontal, or bottom, of a line graph is the *x*-axis. It shows the time period.

Line graphs are good ways to show trends. A *trend* is the general way that something is going. The line shows a trend by going up, down, or remaining the same. By reading trend lines, you can sometimes predict the future.

To analyze a line graph,
- read the title
- read the *y*-axis to see what quantities are used
- read the *x*-axis to see what time period is covered
- read the key to see what the line, or lines, represent

The following line graph shows rural and urban population in the U.S. between 1910 and 1960. Because there are two lines on this graph, there is a key to tell you what each line represents.

1 Where is the time period shown on this line graph?

2 What is the quantity being used to show the population?

3 What color is used to show the rural population?

4 When did urban population outgrow rural population?

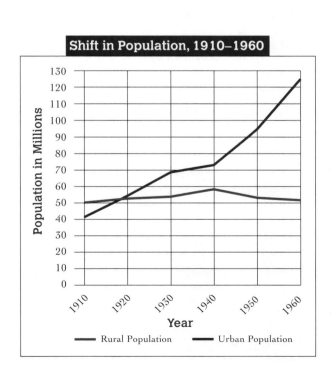

Shift in Population, 1910–1960

Population in Millions / Year

— Rural Population   — Urban Population

Chapter
14 JFK AND THE NEW FRONTIER

Getting Focused

Skim this chapter to predict what you will be learning.

- Read the lesson titles and subheadings.
- Look at the illustrations and read the captions.
- Examine the maps.
- Review the vocabulary words and terms.

In his inaugural address, John F. Kennedy said:

"My fellow Americans, ask not what your country can do for you: Ask what you can do for your country. My fellow citizens of the world: Ask not what America can do for you, but what together we can do for the freedom of man."

President Kennedy has been described as a leader who inspired trust and loyalty. Think of someone who shows good leadership. Write a paragraph to explain why you think this person is a good leader.

The Kennedy Years

Thinking on Your Own

As you read this chapter, create a timeline of events. Be sure to include the programs created, the international events, and other important information.

Because of the Twenty-second Amendment, President Eisenhower could not run for reelection in 1960. The Twenty-second Amendment limits presidents to two terms in office. The Republicans nominated Richard M. Nixon. Nixon had served as vice president under Eisenhower. The Democrats nominated John F. Kennedy.

<table>
<tr><td>focus your reading</td></tr>
<tr><td>How was TV used in the 1960 presidential election?</td></tr>
<tr><td>What problem did President Kennedy have in dealing with Congress?</td></tr>
<tr><td>What was President Kennedy's record on civil rights?</td></tr>
<tr><td>vocabulary</td></tr>
<tr><td>agenda
Medicare
urban renewal</td></tr>
</table>

The Election of 1960

The campaign of 1960 was unusual in two ways. First, John F. Kennedy, a U.S. senator from Massachusetts, was a Roman Catholic. No Catholic had been nominated for president since 1928. There was some concern that a Catholic would have to consult the pope in Rome before making decisions. Kennedy responded that the Constitution set up a strong separation between church and state. As president, he would be sworn to uphold the Constitution.

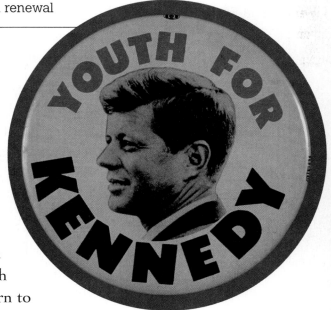

The second unusual factor was the use of television. For the first time, the candidates debated on live TV. Kennedy clearly had the advantage. He was youthful, good looking, and well-prepared. Nixon

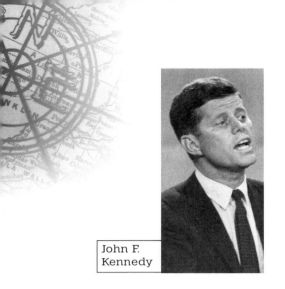

John F. Kennedy

was the better debater. But his face was puffy and he sweated heavily under the hot camera lights. Those who watched on television thought Kennedy had won the debate. Radio listeners thought Nixon had won.

Richard M. Nixon

The two political parties also spent several million dollars on TV ads. The 1960 election marked the beginning of TV's influence on U.S. politics. After his election, Kennedy himself said, "It was TV more than anything else that turned the tide."

The New Frontier

President Kennedy called his **agenda** the New Frontier. However, he found an old problem in dealing with Congress. Like President Truman's, his plans were often blocked by a conservative coalition of Southern Democrats and Republicans. They did not want to increase the power of the federal government in people's lives. They also thought Kennedy's programs cost too much.

For example, President Kennedy proposed **Medicare**, a national health insurance program for older people. It was similar to a program that President Truman had asked Congress to pass. Like Truman's, Kennedy's proposal was voted down. Kennedy's request for more aid to education was also rejected.

Cities, especially in the Midwest and Northeast, were in trouble. Kennedy proposed a new Department of Urban Affairs. Congress voted it down. However, Congress did pass the Area Redevelopment Act and a Housing Act. These provided federal funding for **urban renewal**. The money was used to clear slums and build new housing for poor people in cities.

stop and think

Write two 2-line headlines that might have appeared the day after a Kennedy-Nixon debate. Write one that describes Nixon as the winner. Write the other one as though Kennedy had won. Share them with a partner.

Atlanta, Georgia, underwent urban renewal in the 1960s.

Civil rights activist Robert Moses (center) during a voter registration drive in Mississippi

Civil Rights

The conservative coalition in Congress caused President Kennedy to go slow on civil rights. He had campaigned on a promise to support civil rights. However, he was concerned about Southern Democrats in Congress. If he asked for new civil rights laws, they might block him on other legislation. Instead he used other means to support the efforts of African Americans to gain their civil rights.

President Kennedy appointed his brother Robert as Attorney General. Under Robert Kennedy, the Justice Department aided voter registration drives in the South from 1961 to 1963. The Justice Department also filed lawsuits against segregated bus stations in the South. These suits supported the Freedom Riders in the summer of 1961.

Freedom Riders are protected by Alabama guardsmen in 1961.

The violence against African Americans convinced the president that the nation needed a civil rights law. On June 11, 1963, he spoke to the nation on TV. He announced his plan to ask Congress to pass a civil rights act. The law would (1) end discrimination against voters, (2) ban segregation in public places, and (3) outlaw discrimination in employment. The bill passed the House. But Southern Senators refused to allow the bill to come to a vote. That is where it remained on November 22, 1963.

Putting It All Together

List the ways that Congress blocked Kennedy's agenda. Use these notes to write a paragraph to describe Congress's actions.

Biography

Rachel Carson (1907–1964)

The 1960s was a time of great change. Many social movements began during this period. One was a growing interest in protecting the environment. One of the chief reasons for this was the work of Rachel Carson.

Carson was a biologist and a writer. She enrolled in college with the idea of becoming a writer. However, in her junior year at Pennsylvania College for Women, she switched her major from English to biology.

After college, she went to graduate school at Johns Hopkins University and received a master's degree in zoology in 1932. Carson taught at the University of Maryland from 1931 to 1936. She also taught at Johns Hopkins from 1929 to 1936. Carson did additional graduate work at the Marine Biological Laboratory in Woods Hole, Massachusetts.

Carson was trained as a marine biologist. She studied the oceans, rivers, streams, lakes, and ponds, and the plant and animal life in them. In 1936, Carson went to work for the U.S. Bureau of Fisheries, now the Fish and Wildlife Services. She remained there until 1952.

However, it was not her government work that made Carson famous. It was her books about the sea and the environment. Her four books, *Under the Sea Wind, The Sea Around Us, The Edge of the Sea,* and *Silent Spring,* won high praise for their accuracy, detail, and writing style. All became bestsellers. However, *Silent Spring* did more than provide enjoyment for readers. It helped to launch the environmental movement.

Carson's book described how agriculture was poisoning the environment with harmful chemicals. The use of chemical insecticides and weed killers was polluting the air, land, streams, and rivers. Carson's research alarmed the public. The federal government began a series of investigations into her charges. DDT, one of the major insecticides, was banned. Over time the government passed other laws, such as the Clean Air Act and the Clean Water Act.

Carson did not live to see the changes that her book created. She died two years after *Silent Spring* was published.

The Cold War Heats Up

Thinking on Your Own

To understand an event better, ask and answer questions that tell you the who, what, when, where, why, and how about the event. Create a T-chart in your notebook. On the left, write who, what, when, where, why, and how. As you read, write questions using these words. Then work with a partner to answer the questions.

The Cold War moved into space during the Kennedy years. In 1961, the Soviets were the first to put a human in space. President Kennedy challenged NASA and the nation to be the first to put a human on the moon. His goal was to put an American on the moon by the end of the decade.

focus your reading

Why was the Berlin Wall built?

What was the Bay of Pigs invasion?

Why was the Cuban Missile Crisis so frightening?

vocabulary

tactic

dictator

exile

hot line

The Berlin Wall

On Earth, the Cold War heated up. One crisis was in a familiar trouble spot—Berlin. The four Allies divided Germany and its capital, Berlin, after World War II. In 1948, the Soviets tried to block the other nations from entering West Berlin. Instead President Truman launched the Berlin Airlift. Stalin backed down after 10 months.

In June 1961, Nikita Khrushchev tried another **tactic**. He had become premier, or head, of the Soviet Union in 1958. He insisted that the United States, France, and Great Britain sign a peace treaty with East Germany. The treaty would end the division of Berlin.

The Berlin Wall split the German capital in half.

All four zones would be joined into one city. Berlin would be controlled by communist East Germany. Khrushchev wanted to stop East Germans from escaping through West Berlin. Each week, about 4,000 people fled East Germany through West Berlin.

President Kennedy refused Khrushchev's demands. Instead the president asked Congress for three billion dollars more in defense spending. He sent more troops to West Berlin. He called to active duty some reserve units of the army. He also asked for money to build bomb shelters across the U.S. These were in case of a nuclear attack by the Soviets.

Checkpoint Charlie was an access point between East and West.

The crisis ended in August 1961. Khrushchev had a wall built between East and West Berlin. The wall was made of concrete, steel, and barbed wire. East German soldiers patrolled it 24 hours a day. Still, some East Germans climbed over the wall to freedom. The wall stood until November 9, 1989. The opening of the wall marked the joining of East and West Germany into one democratic nation. It also represented the beginning of the collapse of communism.

stop and think

Look at the picture of the Berlin Wall on page 227. What do you think about it and why it was built? Read the speech by President Kennedy on page 231. Write down all the words that come to mind about the wall and freedom. Share your list with a partner.

The Cuban Revolution

In 1959, Fidel Castro seized power in Cuba. He replaced Fulgencio Battista, a hated **dictator**. At first, the United States aided Castro. But in 1960, Castro and the Soviet Union formed an alliance. Castro adopted a communist government for Cuba. He also began taking over U.S.-owned businesses and property. Thousands of Cubans fled rather than live under communism. Most of the refugees came to the United States. Cuba is only 90 miles from Florida.

Fidel Castro's revolution took control of Cuba in 1959.

Castro's troops captured exiles at the Bay of Pigs.

While President Eisenhower was still in office, the Central Intelligence Agency (CIA) came up with a way to remove Castro. They would use Cuban **exiles** to invade Cuba. Unhappy Cuban citizens would join the exiles. Together, they would overthrow Castro. The plan, however, had to wait for Kennedy to take office.

President Kennedy was unsure of the plan. Military advisers and the CIA, however, were sure it would work. Kennedy agreed to the plan but with one important change. The United States would give the exiles weapons and ships. It would not supply air support. There would be no shelling of Castro's soldiers by U.S. bombers.

The Bay of Pigs invasion was a disaster. About 1,500 exiles landed in Cuba on April 17, 1961. Castro's forces broke up the invasion and killed or captured the invaders. No rebellion against Castro occurred.

The Cuban Missile Crisis

Cuba was again part of a crisis in October 1962. The United States regularly sent spy planes over Cuba. During the summer of 1962, the spy cameras began showing pictures of military construction. By October, it was clear that the Soviets had built secret missile bases in Cuba.

The Cuban Missile Crisis: October 14–28, 1962

Intermediate ballistic missile range = 2,500 miles

Chicago

New York

Washington, D.C.

Los Angeles

MIG jet bomber range = 800 miles

Miami

CUBA

Medium ballistic missile range = 1,500 miles

N W E S

0   1000 miles

On October 22, 1962, President Kennedy announced that the Soviets had placed long-range missiles in Cuba. More missiles were on their way to Cuba on Soviet ships. President Kennedy ordered a military blockade around Cuba. U.S. warships were to keep the Soviet ships from landing. If any missiles were fired from Cuba, the United States would launch a nuclear attack against the Soviet Union.

The nation and the world waited. Was this the beginning of World War III? Americans feared an attack would happen at any time. Secret letters went back and forth between the two leaders. Deals were offered and rejected. Finally, President Kennedy agreed not to invade Cuba. He also agreed to remove U.S. missiles from Turkey, which was on the Soviet border. Khrushchev, in turn, agreed to remove the missiles from Cuba.

President Kennedy led the nation through the Cuban Missile Crisis.

Steps to Cool Down Tensions

The Cuban Missile Crisis scared Americans. Never had the threat of communist attack been so close, or so real. A phone line was set up between the president and the Soviet premier. The phone was called a **hot line**. In case of a future crisis, they could reach each other directly and quickly.

The United States, the Soviet Union, and Great Britain agreed to end above-ground testing of nuclear weapons. The testing was harming the environment. The Limited Test Ban Treaty was signed 18 years after the first atomic bomb. It was the first step toward limiting nuclear weapons in any way.

Putting It All Together

Imagine you are living in October 1962. Write a letter to the president about the Cuban Missile Crisis. Do you agree with his tough stand? Or does it frighten you? Make notes before you begin your letter. Ask a partner to review it. Revise it as needed.

Read a Primary Source

Speech at the Berlin Wall
by John F. Kennedy

In June 1963, President Kennedy visited Europe. On June 26, he stood before the Berlin Wall and delivered the following speech. In it, he called for an end to the wall and a reuniting of the city of Berlin and of Germany. When he uses the phrase "free men," he also means women.

reading for understanding

Why does the president repeat a sentence three times in paragraph one?

What does the president call the wall?

The last sentence means "I am a Berliner." What do you think he means by saying this?

"There are many people in the world who really don't understand, or say they don't, what is the great issue between the free world and the Communist world. Let them come to Berlin. There are some who say that Communism is the wave of the future. Let them come to Berlin. And there are some who say in Europe and elsewhere we can work with Communists. Let them come to Berlin. . . .

"Freedom has many difficulties and democracy is not perfect, but we have never had to put a wall up to keep our people in, to prevent them from leaving us. . . . While the wall is the most obvious and vivid demonstration of the failures of the Communist system, for all the world to see, we take no satisfaction in it, for it is an offense not only against history but an offense against humanity, separating families, dividing husbands and wives and brothers and sisters, and dividing a people who wish to be joined together.

"What is true of this city is true of Germany—real, lasting peace in Europe can never be assured as long as one German out of four is denied the elementary right of free men, and that is to make a free choice. . . . Freedom is indivisible, and when one man is enslaved, all are not free. . . .

"All free men, wherever they may live, are citizens of Berlin, and, therefore, as a free man, I take pride in the words, 'Ich bin ein Berliner.'"

from *In our Own Words*, Robert Torricelli and Andrew Carroll, eds. (New York: Pocket Books, 1999).

231

Legacy and Remembrance

Thinking on Your Own

President Kennedy is one of the better-known presidents in American history. Review the Focus Your Reading questions and the vocabulary with a partner. Then write a bulleted list of things you know about President Kennedy.

The Kennedy administration brought new hope and ideals to the American people. The economy was strong. The president's ideas and visions were exciting. However, history was about to be changed forever.

Kennedy's Programs

Several of the programs that were started during President Kennedy's years in office still exist today. The **Peace Corps** was started by Executive Order on March 1, 1961. President Kennedy appointed R. Sargent Shriver to direct the new program. It trained volunteers to work in developing countries

focus your reading

How do President Kennedy's ideas still impact Americans today?

What were some of President Kennedy's most successful programs?

What is the disagreement over the assassination of President Kennedy?

vocabulary

Peace Corps   theory

cosmonaut   conspiracy

succession

President Kennedy greets Peace Corps volunteers in 1962.

that were in need of assistance. The volunteers worked as teachers, nurses, construction workers, farmers, and in many other jobs. Since it was started, more than 170,000 people have volunteered in 137 countries.

Edwin "Buzz" Aldrin on the moon in 1969

In May 1961, the Soviet Union launched Yuri Gagarin, a **cosmonaut**, into space. The Russian space program had become the first to reach this goal. On May 25, 1961, President Kennedy challenged Congress. He said, "Recognizing the head start obtained by the Soviets . . . we nevertheless are required to make new efforts on our own. . . . I believe that this nation should commit itself to achieving the goal, before this decade is out, of landing a man on the Moon and returning him safely to the Earth." The president's challenge became a reality in 1969.

By the 1960s, the amount of mail traveling across the nation was enormous. Sorting the mail was a tremendous task. Different ideas to improve the sorting of mail had been tried, but failed. In 1963, Postmaster General John A. Gronouski announced a new coding system for U.S. mail. It was called the Zoning Improvement Program—or the ZIP Code.

By July 1963, a five-digit code was assigned to every address in the country. The first digit identified one of nine regions in the United States. The next two digits narrowed the location even more. The final two digits identified individual post offices or zones in larger cities.

The presidential motorcade in Dallas, Texas, in 1963

Kennedy's Assassination

On November 22, 1963, President Kennedy and First Lady Jacqueline Kennedy were in Dallas, Texas. The presidential election was the following year and Texas was an important state. They had flown to Texas to do some early campaigning. They were riding through Dallas in an open car. Crowds along the streets were cheering and waving. The president and Mrs. Kennedy were smiling and waving back.

Lyndon Johnson takes the oath of office aboard the presidential plane.

Suddenly shots rang out from a building in Dealey Plaza. The president fell sideways. He was hit twice. The Secret Service rushed him to the closest hospital, but it was too late. The president was dead.

The Constitution provides for an orderly **succession** when a president dies. It worked in 1945 when Franklin Roosevelt died and Vice President Harry Truman became president. It worked again in 1963. Vice President Lyndon Johnson was also in Dallas. He was sworn in as president on the plane back to Washington with the former president's body and his widow.

Lee Harvey Oswald in custody

The Dallas police acted quickly. Within 45 minutes of the shooting, they caught the suspected assassin, Lee Harvey Oswald. Oswald had lived for a time in the Soviet Union and was a known supporter of the communist takeover of Cuba. Witnesses saw him running from the building where the shots were fired. The rifle used to shoot the president was later traced to him. However, Oswald refused to admit to the killing.

On Sunday morning, November 24, Oswald was being taken from one jail to another. Suddenly Jack Ruby, a small-time nightclub owner, shot him. Ruby was known around Dallas as a character. He was part of a crowd of reporters and camera crews that had gathered in the jail. He forced his way to the front of the crowd and shot Oswald. All the while, TV cameras rolled. The national audience watched in shock.

The caisson and the riderless horse lead President Kennedy's funeral procession.

The Conspiracy Theory

There seemed little sense to either the murder of President Kennedy or of Oswald. Within hours, **theories**, or unproven ideas, began to spread. There was a plot to kill the president. Two people shot the president. Ruby had killed Oswald to protect other people in the plot.

On November 29, 1963, President Johnson appointed The President's Commission on the Assassination of President John F. Kennedy, also known as the Warren Commission. Earl Warren, Chief Justice of the U.S. Supreme Court, chaired the commission. The investigation lasted for several months. In the end, the Warren Commission found that no **conspiracy**, or secret plot, had existed. Lee Harvey Oswald had acted alone.

Earl Warren and commission members in 1964

stop and think

A president's death, war, a natural disaster like a flood, or a terrorist attack like 9/11 brings a nation together. Think about how people must have felt when they learned of the president's death. Write a paragraph to describe these emotions. If you can, interview someone who lived through the Kennedy assassination.

Over the years many people have refused to believe the report of the commission. Various theories about a conspiracy continue to spread. However, the Warren Commission findings remain the official view.

Putting It All Together

The lead is the first paragraph in a news story. Write the lead paragraph for a news article on the assassination of President Kennedy. In your paragraph, explain the who, what, when, where, and how of his assassination. Include details about President Kennedy's accomplishments.

Chapter Summary

John F. Kennedy was elected president in 1960. He called his **agenda** the New Frontier. A conservative coalition blocked a number of Kennedy's proposals, including **Medicare**. However, Congress did pass two bills aimed at **urban renewal**. In 1963, President Kennedy asked for a civil rights act. The coalition in the Senate blocked the bill's passage. Kennedy also formed the **Peace Corps** and challenged America to put a man on the moon. The Soviet Union had launched a **cosmonaut** into orbit in 1961.

The president also faced foreign policy crises. Nikita Khrushchev, head of the Soviet Union, tried a **tactic** in 1961 to push the Allies out of West Berlin. Kennedy resisted. Khrushchev built the Berlin Wall between East and West Berlin.

Cuba was another trouble spot. In 1959, Fidel Castro had overthrown Cuba's **dictator**. In 1961, **exiles**, with U.S. support, invaded Cuba at the Bay of Pigs. The invasion failed. In 1962, the U.S. discovered that the Soviets were building missile bases in Cuba. The Cuban Missile Crisis led to a **hotline** between the U.S. and the Soviet Union.

On November 22, 1963, President Kennedy was assassinated. Lyndon Johnson **succeeded** Kennedy as president. The Warren Commission report has not kept people from believing in various **conspiracy theories**.

Chapter Review

1 Write a paragraph describing whether you think President Kennedy was strong in dealing with the Soviet leader. Use evidence to support your view.

2 Why do you think people have not believed the Warren Commission? Talk over your ideas with a partner. Then write a paragraph explaining your opinion.

3 What do you think is the most important thing that President Kennedy accomplished in his short term in office? Write a paragraph to explain your opinion.

Skill Builder

Summarizing What You Read

Do you ever tell anyone what you do in school? Do you talk about each class in great detail? Do you name everybody who was in every class? Do you repeat every word that every teacher said? No, you mention the important details. That is a summary.

A summary tells the most important things that happened and names the most important people. A summary does not include all the ideas or all the details about what happened. A summary is short. It includes just the main ideas and only the most important details to describe or explain the main ideas.

Every time you describe something that happened to you, you are summarizing information. Summarizing is also a good study tool. Usually you do not need to remember everything about a person or an event in history. You only need to remember the most important things about the person or event. Writing a summary after you study a lesson can help you remember the most important ideas and details.

Follow these steps to create a summary:
- Read the information carefully.
- Take bulleted notes in your own words that include the main ideas.
- Include the most important details that describe or explain the main ideas.
- Do not add your own ideas—a summary does not include your opinion.
- Be short. Be complete. Be accurate.

1 Think about an event that happened to you yesterday. What were the two or three most important things that were part of that event? List them. Think of some details that help to describe or explain those events. List them. Now write the ideas and the details together in a paragraph.

2 Write a summary of the Berlin Wall crisis.

3 Write a summary of the assassination of President Kennedy.

UNIT 8

A New Struggle

The last time a president had died in office was in 1945 when Harry Truman replaced Franklin Roosevelt. However, the nation had changed a great deal since 1945. By 1963, the Cold War dominated foreign policy. The gap between middle class and poor was growing wider. Cities were falling into decay while suburbs grew. President Johnson had to deal with these issues immediately.

Great social and cultural changes occurred during President Johnson's years in office. Some of these changes brought about the end of his political career. These changes were tied up in the unpopular Vietnam War.

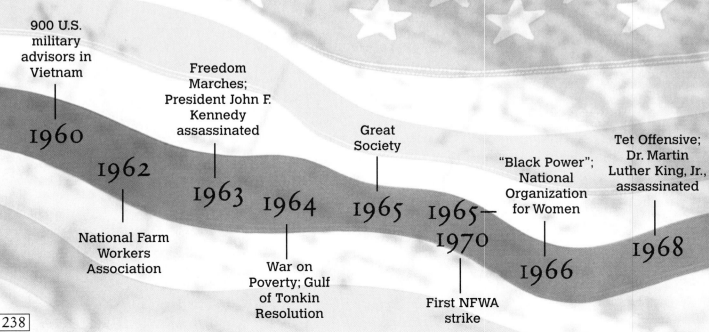

900 U.S. military advisors in Vietnam

1960

National Farm Workers Association

1962

Freedom Marches; President John F. Kennedy assassinated

1963

War on Poverty; Gulf of Tonkin Resolution

1964

Great Society

1965

First NFWA strike

1965–1970

"Black Power"; National Organization for Women

1966

Tet Offensive; Dr. Martin Luther King, Jr., assassinated

1968

How did the civil rights movement affect the nation?

Why did the United States' public turn against the Vietnam War?

What was the goal of Great Society programs?

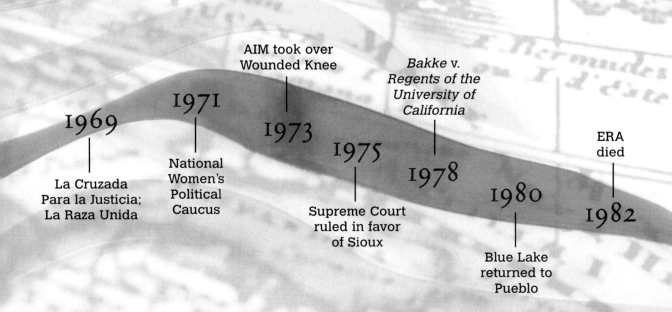

1969
La Cruzada Para la Justicia; La Raza Unida

1971
National Women's Political Caucus

AIM took over Wounded Knee
1973

1975
Supreme Court ruled in favor of Sioux

Bakke v. *Regents of the University of California*
1978

1980
Blue Lake returned to Pueblo

ERA died
1982

Chapter 15

JOHNSON AND THE GREAT SOCIETY

Getting Focused

Skim this chapter to predict what you will be learning.

- Read the lesson titles and subheadings.
- Look at the illustrations and read the captions.
- Examine the maps.
- Review the vocabulary words and terms.

What makes a "Great Society"? Is it good jobs for everyone? Is it the opportunity for anyone to go to college? Is it owning a home? Decide what you think makes a Great Society. Write a paragraph to explain your idea of a Great Society.

Johnson in Command

Thinking on Your Own

Why do you think President Johnson called his anti-poverty program a "war" on poverty? What does declaring a war against something mean? Write a paragraph to explain what a war on poverty today should fight.

President Lyndon Johnson pushed much of President Kennedy's "New Frontier" legislation through Congress. Johnson had entered politics during the New Deal years. He believed the government had a responsibility to help those in need. He also presented these measures to the American people as Kennedy's **legacy**. That made it easier to get the bills through the conservative Congress.

focus your reading

What was the war on poverty?

What did the Civil Rights Act of 1964 do?

What was the main issue in the election of 1964?

vocabulary

legacy

poverty line

conservative

President Lyndon B. Johnson

The War on Poverty

President Johnson's first opportunity came with his State of the Union speech in January 1964. The president declared an "unconditional war on poverty." He asked for funding to help those living at or below the **poverty line**. This is the minimum that the government believes a family of four needs in order to live adequately. President Johnson wanted to attack the causes of poverty. He wanted to help people lift themselves out of poverty.

Flatweeds Job Corps Conservation Center, Jefferson National Forest, Virginia, 1965

Within months, Congress passed the Economic Opportunity Act. The act set up the Office of Economic Opportunity (OEO). This agency managed ten new programs to aid the poor. The goal of all of them was to fight the causes of poverty. Among the programs were Volunteers in Service to America (VISTA), the Job Corps, and the Community Action Program.

VISTA was set up to help poor people improve their lives. VISTA volunteers were sent to cities, rural areas, and Native American reservations. They worked to clean up streams, build roads, and teach nutrition. The Job Corps helped high-school dropouts with job training and counseling. The Community Action Program gave poor people a greater voice in government decisions affecting their neighborhoods.

stop and think

President Johnson said the war on poverty would be fought in the cities, countryside, and classrooms. If the president today declared a war on poverty, what new programs would you recommend?

The Civil Rights Act of 1964

With a great deal of arm-twisting by President Johnson, Congress finally passed a civil rights bill. It was the strongest civil rights law the nation had ever had.

Hank Aaron hit his 500th home run in 1968.

The Civil Rights Act of 1964 banned discrimination on the basis of race, religion, gender, or national origin. Discrimination was now against the law in stores, movie theaters, restaurants, stadiums — anywhere people gather or do business. It also banned the use of different registration requirements for African-American and white voters. The bill had one major weakness—it did not ban the use of "literacy tests" used in the South to keep African Americans from voting. The law did allow the federal government to withhold funds from programs that discriminated. This included schools as well as businesses.

The Civil Rights Act of 1964 brought the vote to more citizens.

The Civil Rights Act also set up the Equal Employment Opportunity Commission (EEOC). Its job was to investigate charges of discrimination in the workplace.

The Election of 1964

The Sunbelt showed its power in the 1964 presidential election. **Conservative** Republicans from the South and West gained enough votes to nominate Barry Goldwater, a senator from Arizona.

The main issue of the campaign involved Vietnam. Goldwater thought the United States should wage all-out war against the communist North Vietnamese. He campaigned on the idea that "Extremism in the defense of liberty is no vice!" President Johnson's message was reassuring. He promised not to send "American boys nine or ten thousand miles from home" to fight a war the South Vietnamese should be fighting.

Voters rejected Goldwater. President Johnson was reelected in a landslide.

Putting It All Together

Think about the war on poverty and the Civil Rights Act of 1964. What did Lyndon Johnson's war on poverty have in common with the New Deal programs of the 1930s? Talk over your ideas with a partner. Then write a paragraph that explains your point of view.

Biography

VISTA Volunteers

In 1961, President John Kennedy proposed the Peace Corps. Its goal was to improve the standard of living in poor countries. In 1964, President Johnson proposed Volunteers in Service to America (VISTA). Its goal was to help people in poor areas in the United States improve their standard of living.

In 1964 the first 20 VISTA volunteers were trained and sent to their assignments. The oldest was eighty-one and the youngest was eighteen. Most were in their early twenties.

Ivy Marshall was sixty when she joined VISTA in 1965. She joined for a specific reason. "When I read in the newspaper and heard of it on the radio and television, I wanted to be a part of this attempt to share our country's opportunities with the less fortunate."

Marshall was sent to a rural mountain area in the Appalachia region of Kentucky. As Marshall recalled, "Several times on my very first day I was tempted to write Washington that there was no way I could manage my life as I would have to live here. With no electricity there can be no TV nor radio. . . . There is no water in the house, so of course, no bathroom."

First Lady "Lady Bird" Johnson speaks to VISTA volunteers.

Marshall worked with women on health care and helped children get library books and clothes to wear to school. She developed a program with the state police so that men who could not read could earn a driver's license. None of the projects were big, but they gave people hope and a sense of importance.

Volunteers signed on for one year. Marshall stayed in her Appalachian community for two years. She wrote in her diary: "I am torn to pieces tonight as I try to decide what to do about staying here. To go or to stay here. . . . I have been staying on month by month so I must soon give notice. I have given my best to this community and now I am torn. . . ."

In the end Marshall left. She had met another volunteer and they decided to marry. Marshall believed she had learned as much as she had taught.

Great Society Agenda

Thinking on Your Own

Create a concept map to help you remember President Johnson's agenda. Draw a large circle in the center. Label it "The Great Society." Draw a line and a smaller circle and label it "The War on Poverty." Add lines and circles to each of these circles with the names of programs that were run under the Great Society and under the war on poverty.

After his landslide victory in the 1964 election, Johnson sent his program for a Great Society to Congress. The Great Society would provide opportunity, equality, and justice for all. As a young man, Johnson had been inspired by President Franklin Roosevelt's New Deal. Johnson used his landslide victory in the 1964 election to set up the Great Society.

The Elementary and Secondary Education Act was signed by President Johnson in 1965.

focus your reading

What kinds of programs made up President Johnson's Great Society agenda?

How did Martin Luther King, Jr., work for civil rights?

Why was the Voting Rights Act of 1965 passed?

vocabulary

standards

resistance

deputize

Great Society Programs

Once elected, President Johnson persuaded, arm-twisted, and convinced Congress to pass his Great Society agenda. The programs fell generally into four areas—health and welfare, housing, education, and consumer and environmental protection. The table on page 246 lists some major programs of the Great Society.

Great Society Programs

Medicare (1965) is a low-cost medical and hospital insurance program for most Americans 65 and over. It was first proposed by President Truman.
Medicaid (1965) provides low-cost health insurance to low-income families and individuals. It is a joint federal and state program.
Department of Housing and Urban Development (1965) oversees housing and the rebuilding of the nation's cities. It also provides money to help with rent.
Head Start (1965) is a preschool program for children in low-income families that prepares them for school. In addition to education, Head Start provides meals and medical and dental services for children, and works with parents and other caregivers to help children at home.
Elementary and Secondary Education Act (1965) provided federal money to schools with large numbers of low-income children. The law was replaced in 2001 with the No Child Left Behind Education Act.
Higher Education Act (1965) offers scholarships, student loans, and work-study programs to students from low- and middle-income families.
Water-Quality Act (1965) and the Clean Air Act (1965) allow the government to set **standards** and goals for clean water and air and to check whether businesses obey.
The National Traffic and Motor Vehicle Safety Act (1966) sets safety standards for all cars, trucks, buses, and other motor vehicles.
The Fair Packaging and Labeling Act (1966) ensures that all consumer products are clearly and accurately labeled.

stop and think

Which programs belong to which categories: health and welfare, housing, education, or consumer and environmental protection? Make a four-column table. Label each column with one of these categories. Write the name of each act in the correct category. Share your table with a partner and quiz each other on the purpose of each act.

Civil Rights

In addition to his other programs, President Johnson pushed through a voting rights act. The Civil Rights Act of 1964 had little impact on voting. African Americans in the South were still being denied their right to vote.

Several civil rights groups formed the Council of Federated Organizations (COFO) to register voters in the summer of 1964. COFO workers spread out across the South. In many places they met **resistance** from whites. In Mississippi, three COFO workers were murdered. Seven members of the Ku Klux Klan were later convicted of the murders.

The COFO worked to register voters in the South.

Dr. Martin Luther King, Jr., decided to stage a march to dramatize the violence and the lack of voting rights. Marchers were to walk the 50 miles from Selma, Alabama, to Montgomery, the state's capital. As they walked peacefully out of Selma on March 7, 1965, they were stopped by the sheriff. He had with him 200 state troopers and other whites whom he had **deputized** as law officers.

The sheriff ordered the marchers to end their protest. Instead, the marchers knelt in prayer. The deputies and the troopers rushed into the kneeling crowd and began beating them. Tear gas darkened the sky. Many marchers were injured. Seventy were hurt badly enough to be hospitalized. All the while, TV cameras broadcast the brutal pictures live into American homes. New marchers from across the country went to Selma to join the march.

Martin Luther King, Jr., and his wife, Coretta Scott King, march from Selma to Montgomery, Alabama, in 1965.

Eight days later, President Johnson addressed a joint session of Congress and the public on television. He proposed a sweeping Voting Rights Act. The law gave federal officials the power to register African Americans in districts where local officials were keeping them from voting. All laws that discriminated against African Americans, such as literacy tests, were banned. The Twenty-fourth Amendment had done away with poll taxes in 1964. Congress acted swiftly and passed the bill. By the end of 1965, some 250,000 African Americans had registered to vote in the South.

Putting It All Together

What do you think about President Johnson's Great Society? Read the Primary Source to find out why he wanted to build a Great Society. Then reread the table "Great Society Programs." Then write a paragraph explaining your view on the Great Society.

Read a Primary Source

The Great Society

In the following speech, President Johnson lays out the reasons for his Great Society program. When he refers to "man," he is also including women.

reading for understanding

What three areas will Great Society programs help?

According to the president, why was it harder to live the good life in American cities?

List three problems in the country that Great Society programs targeted.

"The Great Society rests on abundance and liberty for all. It demands an end to poverty and racial injustice, . . . But that is just the beginning. The Great Society is a place where every child can find knowledge to enrich his mind and to enlarge his talents. . . . It is a place where the city of man services not only the needs of the body and the demands of commerce but the desire for beauty and the hunger for community. . . .

So I want to talk to you today about three places where we begin to build the Great Society: in our cities, in our countryside, and in our classrooms. . . .

It is harder and harder to live the good life in American cities today. The catalog of ills is long: There is the decay of the centers. . . . There is not enough housing for our people or transportation for our traffic. . . . Our society will never be great until our cities are great. . . .

A second place where we begin to build the Great Society is in our countryside. We have always prided ourselves on being not only America the strong and America the free, but America the beautiful. Today that beauty is in danger. The water we drink, the food that we eat, the very air that we breathe, are threatened with pollution. Our parks are overcrowded, our seashores overburdened. Green fields and dense forests are disappearing. . . .

A third place to build the Great Society is in the classrooms of America. There your children's lives will be shaped. . . . "

From President Lyndon B. Johnson's commencement speech at the University of Michigan, May 1964; in Robert Torricelli and Andrew Carrol, eds., *In Our Own Words* (New York: Pocket Books, 1999).

Vietnam War and Antiwar Protests

Thinking on Your Own

Read the Focus Your Reading questions and the vocabulary. Create a two-column chart in your notebook. Label the first column "Pro" and the second column "Con." As you read, note reasons that support the United States' cause in Vietnam and reasons against involvement in Vietnam.

After World War II, the Vietnamese fought for and won their independence from France. However, Vietnam became caught in the Cold War. They could not agree on the type of government to set up, communist or noncommunist. In 1954, they compromised. Two Vietnams would be set up temporarily. Within two years, each would hold elections to decide whether to unite. The elections were never held. Slowly at first, and then quickly, the conflict between the two Vietnams **escalated**—or became more intense.

Ho Chi Minh was the leader of North Vietnam.

focus your reading

How did the Vietnam conflict escalate?

What was the constitutional issue involved in the Gulf of Tonkin Resolution?

Why did the antiwar movement grow?

How did the Vietnam War affect the 1968 election?

vocabulary

escalate

guerrilla

resolution

Vietnam Heats Up

Throughout the 1950s, the United States supported the South Vietnamese. The conflict in Vietnam was the basis of President Eisenhower's domino theory. He believed that if Vietnam fell to communism, all of Southeast Asia would also fall. As a result, President Eisenhower sent foreign aid and military advisors to South Vietnam.

Military advisors trained South Vietnamese troops in 1962.

By 1960, when John Kennedy became president, there were 900 U.S. advisors in South Vietnam. The Viet Cong were well established in South Vietnam. The Viet Cong were South Vietnamese communist **guerrillas**, or rebel soldiers. They were openly fighting to make South Vietnam communist. Between 1961 and 1963, President Kennedy increased the number of advisors in South Vietnam. By the time of Kennedy's death in 1963, there were 16,300 U.S. military personnel working with the South Vietnamese army.

Gulf of Tonkin Resolution

In early August 1964, U.S. destroyers off the coast of Vietnam in the Gulf of Tonkin reported that North Vietnamese patrol boats had attacked them. However, the commander of the destroyer task force questioned whether the reports were accurate. No one actually saw the patrol boats. He advised against the U.S. taking action until he had more information. President Johnson ignored that advice.

The president used these attacks to ask Congress for unusual power. According to the Constitution, only Congress can declare war. The president asked Congress to allow him "to take all necessary measures to repel any armed attack against the forces of the United States and to prevent further aggression." All but two members of Congress voted in favor of the Gulf of Tonkin **Resolution** on August 7, 1964. Congress gave the president the authority to go to war.

Agent Orange was used in Vietnam as a defoliant.

Escalation

President Johnson took full advantage of his new power. He ordered bombing raids on North Vietnam. He also ordered U.S. troops into combat independent of the South Vietnamese army. They were no longer so-called advisors.

stop and think

To keep track of what was happening, create a cause-and-effect flowchart of the escalating conflict in Vietnam. Share it with a partner to make sure you included everything important.

The president's goal was to force the North Vietnamese to withdraw its support from the Viet Cong. His plan did not work. The Viet Cong went on fighting, and the North Vietnamese continued to supply them. In January 1968, the Viet Cong and North Vietnamese launched the Tet offensive. They attacked every major city and military base in South Vietnam.

The president ordered more U.S. soldiers to South Vietnam. By the end of 1969, the number of U.S. soldiers had grown to 536,000. The war was costing $2 billion a month. American and South Vietnamese troops put down the Tet offensive. Still, Americans were shocked that the communist forces were strong enough to mount such an attack.

The Tet Offensive, 1968

✺ Places attacked during the Tet offensive

← Ho Chi Minh Trail

0   500 miles

CHINA
NORTH VIETNAM
Hanoi
GULF OF TONKIN
LAOS
SOUTH CHINA SEA
Demilitarized Zone
Hue
Da Nang
Khe Sanh
Hoi An
Chu Lai
THAILAND
Quang Ngai
Kontum
Qui Nhon
Ban Me Thout
Tuy An
Tuy Hoa
CAMBODIA
Nha Trang
Da Lat
Bien Hoa
Phan Thiet
GULF OF THAILAND
Xuan Loc
Saigon
Tan An
My Tho
Ben Tre
Can Tho
Vinh Long
SOUTH VIETNAM
N W E S

Mekong R.

Walter Cronkite brought the war into the living rooms of America.

Americans Turn Against the War

The antiwar movement in the United States had been growing slowly. The ability of the Viet Cong to continue fighting wherever and whenever they wanted stunned Americans. U.S. troops were not trained to fight a guerrilla war.

The nightly TV news showed high-level U.S. officials describing how well the war was going. The reports from troops and officials on the ground in South Vietnam were vastly

Dr. King spoke out against the Vietnam War.

different. The same news programs showed more and more body bags coming home. Many in the nation stopped believing what the government said.

In time, the public became bitterly divided. Many antiwar activists were young people, especially white, middle-class college students. They took to the streets in large, loud antiwar demonstrations.

African Americans and Latinos also became opposed to the war. Dr. Martin Luther King, Jr., and other civil rights leaders saw that the war was draining money from Great Society programs. They also saw the number of soldiers in Vietnam who were African-American. In the mid-1960s, African Americans made up 10 percent of the population. But they made up 20 percent of those drafted. By 1968, 70 percent of African Americans opposed the war. The story was similar for Latinos.

Vietnam's Effect on the 1968 Election

The presidential election campaign had already begun when the Tet offensive took place. It changed the election. Soon several challengers entered the race for the Democratic nomination. The president narrowly won the New Hampshire Democratic primary. As a result, president Johnson announced he would not run for reelection. He also called for peace talks to end the war.

The Democrats nominated then vice-president Hubert H. Humphrey of Minnesota for president. During the national convention in Chicago, antiwar protesters staged peaceful demonstrations. However, on the third night of the convention,

Antiwar protests became violent at the 1968 Democratic National Convention.

they were met by police with swinging nightsticks and tear gas. TV cameras once again captured scenes of the police beating unarmed young people. A later investigation accused police of a "police riot."

The Republicans nominated Richard Nixon. He ran on a promise of "peace with honor." He said he would get the nation out of Vietnam without letting the communists win. He never clearly stated how he intended to do that. To add to the turmoil, George Wallace, the former governor of Alabama, also ran for president. He was the candidate of the American Independent Party. He promised an end to forced school integration and an all-out fight to win the Vietnam War.

Richard Nixon and his family at the 1968 Republican National Convention

In November, Nixon edged out Humphrey by 500,000 votes. Nixon won with less than half the votes cast.

Putting It All Together

Add information about the antiwar movement and the 1968 election to your two-column chart. Review it with a partner to make sure that you have all the important events. Then write a paragraph that either supports or argues against the U.S. involvement in the Vietnam War.

Chapter Summary

Vice President Lyndon Johnson became president when John Kennedy was assassinated. President Johnson knew it would be easier to get bills passed if they were presented as part of President Kennedy's **legacy**.

President Johnson wanted to help people living at or below the **poverty line**. President Johnson also called for passage of the Civil Rights Act of 1964. In the election of 1964, President Johnson ran against **conservative** senator Barry Goldwater. The president won reelection in a landslide.

President Johnson had shared his vision of the nation as a Great Society. Opportunity, equality, and justice would be available for everyone. His Great Society programs fell into four categories: health and welfare, housing, education, and consumer and environmental protection. He wanted the government to set **standards**.

Civil rights workers were met by **resistance** and even violence on the part of newly **deputized** police officers. In response, President Johnson proposed the Voting Rights Act of 1965.

In the meantime, the conflict in Vietnam was **escalating**. Communist North Vietnam was supplying the Viet Cong, **guerrilla** fighters in South Vietnam. When North Vietnamese ships supposedly attacked U.S. destroyers, President Johnson asked for the Gulf of Tonkin **Resolution**. It gave him power to send troops and supplies to fight without a formal declaration of war by Congress.

By the 1968 Tet offensive, many Americans had lost faith in the government and the war. In March 1968, President Johnson said he would not run for reelection. The Democratic candidate, Hubert H. Humphrey, narrowly lost to Richard Nixon.

Chapter Review

1 Design an ad to promote working for VISTA.

2 Think about the goals of the Great Society programs. Choose one and write a letter to the editor either supporting or objecting to it. Be sure to use reasons to support your opinion.

Skill Builder

Identifying Facts and Opinions

Before 2004 people would say, "The Red Sox have not won a World Series since 1918. I think Babe Ruth put a curse on the Sox when they traded him to the New York Yankees." The first sentence is a fact, while the second sentence is an opinion.

Knowing the difference between facts and opinions is important. This skill can keep you from taking someone's opinion as fact.

To know the difference between fact and opinion, ask yourself the following questions:

- Does the statement include the names of people or places, dates, events, times, or amounts? (probably a fact)

- Can the information be checked in sources like record books and encyclopedias? (probably a fact)

- Does the statement use signal words and phrases like *I think, I believe, probably, perhaps, might, should*? (opinion)

- Does the statement use emotional words like *greedy, lazy, narrow-minded*? (probably an opinion)

- Does the statement use words like *greatest, most, excellent, least, good, bad, poor, satisfactory*? (possible opinion)

- Does the statement use generalizations like *all, none, every, never*? (opinion)

Are the following facts or opinions? In your notebook write a sentence to explain why you know each is a fact or an opinion.

1 Lyndon B. Johnson had spent his life in government service.

2 No one on either side of the debate over the Vietnam War was willing to listen to the other side.

3 Nixon won the election with less than 50 percent of the votes cast.

4 The Vietnam War was an unnecessary drain on the U.S. economy.

Chapter 16

THE SIXTIES: POLITICAL AND SOCIAL CHANGE

Getting Focused

Skim this chapter to predict what you will be learning.

- Read the lesson titles and subheadings.
- Look at the illustrations and read the captions.
- Examine the maps.
- Review the vocabulary words and terms.

The 1960s were a time of great political and social change. Sometimes political change leads to social change. Think about the civil rights movement. How would giving African Americans the right to vote lead to social change? How would school integration lead to social change? Write a paragraph to explain how greater political rights can lead to social change.

The Civil Rights Movement

Thinking on Your Own

Create a timeline of events in the history of the civil rights movement. If you have already started a timeline, add to it.

The year 1963 marked more than the death of a president. It also marked a **turning point** in the civil rights movement. The violence against peaceful demonstrators and the murders of civil rights workers forced the nation to take action.

focus your reading

What sequence of events led to the passage of the Civil Rights Act of 1964?

How did the civil rights movement change in the late 1960s?

What is affirmative action?

vocabulary

turning point

harmony

confrontation

heritage

affirmative action

quota

Taking It to the Streets

In April 1963, Dr. Martin Luther King, Jr., began a series of Freedom Marches through Birmingham, Alabama. It was one of the most segregated cities in the South. In the beginning, the marches were peaceful.

Fire hoses were used against civil rights demonstrators in Birmingham, Alabama.

On May 2, one month into the marches, children joined them. On that day, Sheriff Bull Connor and his men arrested 900 children. From then on, the marches turned violent. Marchers

found themselves facing police and troopers with nightsticks, dogs, and fire hoses. Again, TV cameras showed police out of control. As the nation watched the news each night, the violence escalated. The motel where Dr. King was staying was bombed. His brother's house was also bombed.

President Kennedy sent federal troops to Birmingham. He went on TV to ask for a civil rights law. Segregationists in Congress blocked the law.

To put pressure on Congress, Dr. King organized another march. On August 28, 1963, a quarter of a million people marched through the streets of Washington, D.C. They were there to tell Congress and the nation that the rights of African Americans could no longer be ignored. Whites as well as African Americans marched together. Dr. King spoke to the crowd about his dream of unity and racial **harmony** for the nation.

Civil rights march in Washington, D.C.

President Johnson asked again for a civil rights law in 1964. This time Congress passed the law. Similar events led to passage of the Voting Rights Act in 1965.

Change in Direction

Dr. King and older members of the civil rights movement were dedicated to nonviolent action. They would not attack their opponents. If attacked and beaten, they would not fight back.

New leaders took a more **confrontational** approach. It began with the phrase "Black Power." Stokely Carmichael, leader of the Student Nonviolent Coordinating Committee (SNCC), wanted African-American organizations like SNCC to stop signing up white members. He thought these organizations should be for African Americans alone.

Malcolm X called on African Americans to think of themselves as part of the larger African world. They drew upon their African as well as American **heritage**. This included converting to Islam. Malcolm X focused on gaining political

The Black Panthers demonstrated in New York City in 1969.

power for African Americans. This power could be gained peacefully or violently. It was up to white Americans.

Around 1966, the phrase "Black is beautiful" became popular. Outward signs of African-American pride in their heritage took the form of wearing African fabrics and clothes. Men and women stopped straightening their hair and began growing Afros. African Americans began demanding a realistic view of themselves in movies and on TV.

Dr. King shifted from political to economic goals. He was convinced that ending poverty would end violence and injustice. He did not have time to put his ideas into practice. He was assassinated on April 4, 1968. At the news of his death, African Americans rioted in 125 cities across the country. Forty-five people died.

The civil rights movement did not die with Dr. King. The struggle for African-American rights continues. But it continues as much in courts and in voting booths as it does on the streets.

stop and think

Think about how Dr. King used marches to focus attention on the civil rights movement. Review the Selma march described in Chapter 15 and the marches in this lesson. How did the marches promote the cause of civil rights? Write a paragraph to answer this question.

Taking It to the Courts

In 1964, President Johnson signed an executive order to increase job opportunities for African Americans, women, and minority groups. The order was aimed at the construction industry. It applied to contractors working on building projects funded with federal money. These contractors were to "take **affirmative action**" to make sure that they did not discriminate in the hiring and promotion of minorities. Later, President Richard Nixon set **quotas** for workers on federally funded construction projects. A quota is a number of people that represents a proportional part of the whole.

In time, colleges and universities adopted affirmation action. They used it as the basis for admitting students. These institutions wanted to make sure that their students represented the diversity of American society. As a result, the schools set quotas for male and female students, whites, African Americans, Latinos, Asians, and so on.

Affirmative action changed the hiring process for many programs and industries.

Not everyone agreed with affirmative action. Opponents called it reverse discrimination. They said it discriminated against white men to make up for past discrimination against minorities. Some said the policy assumed that minorities could not earn jobs or be admitted to college without help.

The first test of the case was *Bakke* v. *Regents of the University of California* in 1978. Alan Bakke sued the university when he was turned down for admission to its medical school. He claimed that a less qualified African-American man had been admitted instead. The U.S. Supreme Court ruled that the university's affirmative action policy discriminated against white men. However, the Court said that a policy without fixed quotas could be used.

Since then a number of such cases have been heard in federal courts. In 2003, the Supreme Court upheld the admissions plan of the University of Michigan's law school. It used race as one factor in reviewing applications. Justice Sandra Day O'Connor said the Court hoped that in 25 years such affirmative action policies would no longer be needed.

Affirmative action helped integrate the nation's universities.

Putting It All Together

Complete your timeline of the civil rights movement. What surprised you about the movement? Talk about the movement with a partner. Make a list of things that surprised you both about it. Choose an idea and write a paragraph to explain what surprised you and why.

Read a Primary Source

What Is Black Power?

Stokely Carmichael led the Student Nonviolent Coordinating Committee (SNCC). One day at a rally in 1966, he began using the phrase *Black Power*. The audience picked it up and began to chant it. It became the new motto of the civil rights movement. In the following excerpt, Carmichael and Charles V. Hamilton explain what Black Power means to them.

reading for understanding

What is the point that Carmichael and Hamilton are making in this excerpt?

How will African Americans have their daily needs met?

Why should African Americans unite behind black leaders?

Why is it strange to put African Americans in the same category as the Ku Klux Klan?

"The point is obvious: black people must lead and run their own organizations. Only black people can convey the revolutionary idea—and it is a revolutionary idea—that black people are able to do things themselves. Only they can help create in the community an aroused and continuing black consciousness that will provide the basis for political strength. . . . Black people must come together and do things for themselves. They must achieve self-identity and self-determination in order to have their daily needs met. . . .

"It does not mean merely putting black faces in office. Black visibility is not Black Power. . . . The power must be that of a community, . . . The black politicians must start from there. . . .

"Black power recognizes—it must recognize—the ethnic basis of American politics as well as the power-oriented nature of American politics. Black power therefore calls for black people to consolidate behind their own, so that they can bargain from a position of strength. . . .

"No other group would submit to being led by others. Italians do not run the Anti-Defamation League of B'nai B'rith. Irish do not chair Christopher Columbus Societies. Yet when black people call for black-run and all-black organizations, they are immediately classed in a category with the Ku Klux Klan. . . . [T]he society does not expect black people to be able to take care of their business, and there are many who prefer it precisely that way. . . ."

Stokely Carmichael and Charles V. Hamilton, *Black Power* (New York, 1967).

261

Rights for Latinos and Native Americans

Thinking on Your Own

As you read, create a concept map for this lesson. In the large circle in the center, write "Gaining Rights." Label one smaller circle "Latino Movement" and label another "Native American Movement." Add lines, circles, and labels as you read the subheadings for each group.

The African-American civil rights movement provided a model for other groups to follow. Latinos and Native Americans were two of the groups fighting for their rights in the 1960s and early 1970s.

focus your reading

Who are Latinos?

How did Latinos work to achieve their goals?

How did Native Americans work to achieve their goals?

vocabulary

culture

migrant worker

descent

stereotype

Latinos in the United States

Latinos in the United States had three goals: to gain equal opportunities in business, education, and housing; to gain respect for Latino **culture**; and to increase the number of Latinos elected to office.

By 1960, some 3 million Latinos lived in the United States. Within ten years there were 9 million. A Latino, Latina, or their ancestors come from any Spanish-speaking nation. The largest group of Latinos in the United States are Mexicans. Some came through the Bracero Program. Most came, however, in the 1960s as farm workers. They were **migrant workers** who went from farm to farm, picking fruits and vegetables.

Cinco de Mayo is a celebration of Latino culture.

There are also large numbers of Puerto Ricans, who are U.S. citizens by birth, Cubans, and Dominicans. Smaller numbers of immigrants have come from other Central American and South American nations. By the 2000 census, the number had risen to 35 million. Latinos have their Spanish language in common, most are Roman Catholics, and they share some, if not many, cultural traditions.

Latino Power

The first effort to win rights for Latinos took place among migrant farm workers in California. The National Farm Workers Association organized Mexican American and Mexican migrant workers in a strike against growers. As a result of the union's activities, California passed a law governing labor contracts in 1975. Growers were required to enter into collective bargaining with farm workers' unions.

Rodolfo "Corky" Gonzales

In 1965, Rodolfo "Corky" Gonzales founded La Cruzada Para la Justicia (The Crusade for Justice). Helping Chicanos and Chicanas help themselves and increasing pride in their culture were the goals of La Cruzada. *Chicano* and *Chicana* are shortened forms of *Mexicano* and *Mexicana*. They were used by Latinos and Latinas in the 1960s and 1970s to identify themselves as being of Mexican **descent**. La Cruzada founded a ballet company, weekly newspaper, bilingual school, and day-care center.

Joseph Montoya was elected to the Senate in New Mexico in 1962.

At the same time, other groups were turning to politics to have their voices heard. In 1969 in Texas, José Angel Gutiérrez founded La Raza Unida (The United People) Party. Its goals were to gain better housing and jobs for Latinos and to elect candidates to public office. Over time La Raza Unida inspired similar groups in Colorado, New Mexico, Arizona, and California. The party elected a number of candidates to office.

One of the most successful lobbying efforts of Latinos involved education. They wanted bilingual education for their children. They wanted their children to be taught in Spanish while they learned English. As a result of their efforts, Congress passed the Bilingual Education Act in 1968.

Latinos also took part in antiwar protests during the Vietnam War. Like African Americans and other concerned people, they saw the cost of the war. The money that could fund programs on the homefront was being used for the war.

An anti-discrimination rally in 1971 in Sacramento, California.

Native American Gains

Inspired by other civil rights movements and the Great Society, Native Americans began to lobby for their rights. They wanted greater economic opportunities on reservations, treaties signed in the 1800s to be honored by the federal government, and an end to the **stereotypes** that other Americans had about them. A stereotype is a generalized idea about a person or group that does not allow for individual differences.

Oscar Bear Runner at Wounded Knee in 1973

As a first step, President Johnson signed the Indian Civil Rights Act in 1968. It extends the Bill of Rights to Native Americans and recognizes local laws on reservations.

Some Native Americans protested instead of lobbying. The American Indian Movement (AIM) took

Update the concept map that you began at the beginning of this lesson. Then look at the photographs in this section of the lesson. Choose one photograph and make notes about what you see. Use these notes as the basis of a paragraph. Share your paragraph with a partner. Do you see the same things in the photos? What do you see differently?

over Wounded Knee, South Dakota, to get its message out. Wounded Knee was where the last bloodshed between Native Americans and the U.S. army occurred in the late 1800s. The army had opened fire on elderly Native Americans, women, and children. In 1973, AIM leaders demanded the return of all lands taken as a result of broken treaties. The standoff between AIM and the FBI lasted for 73 days.

Other Native Americans used the courts. They sued either for the return of lost land or for payment for the land. The Sioux lost their land in the Black Hills of South Dakota when gold was found there in the 1870s. In 1975, the Supreme Court ruled that the federal government had to pay the Sioux $105 million for the lost land. In 1980, Blue Lake was returned to the Pueblo of Taos, New Mexico.

Native Americans also had some success with their third goal. The public came to see that the stereotype of Native Americans shown in movies and on TV was just that—a stereotype. Americans realized that Native Americans had many different cultures. They did not all wear buffalo skins and go hunting on horseback.

AIM leader Russell Means shakes hands with U.S. Assistant Attorney General Kent Frizzell after agreeing to a ten-point pact.

Putting It All Together

Write a short paragraph that explains what the African American, Latino, and Native American movements had in common. Use the concept map that you began at the beginning of this lesson for ideas. Write an outline to help organize your thoughts.

Biography

César Chávez (1927–1993) and Dolores Huerta (1930–)

In 1962, César Chávez and Dolores Huerta founded the National Farm Workers Association (NFWA) in Delano, California. Chávez is better known than Huerta, but both played important roles in *La Causa*. This is the name of the migrant worker movement.

Chávez and Huerta came from different backgrounds but arrived at the same belief. Farm workers needed a union if they were to gain higher wages and better working conditions.

Like Chávez, Huerta was the child of migrant workers. Huerta's ancestors had come from Spain when New Mexico was a Spanish colony. Chávez never went past eighth grade. Huerta was a teacher.

The two met when Huerta joined the Community Service Organization (CSO). Chávez was already a CSO volunteer. During the day he picked fruit to earn a living. At night he registered other migrant workers to vote. In time he became CSO's director. When he asked the CSO to support his effort to form a union, CSO refused. The members did not think a farm workers' union could succeed. Chávez left the CSO in 1962. He, his wife Helen, their eight children, Huerta, and a few others started the NFWA.

In 1965, NFWA began its first strike. The union joined Filipino farm workers on strike near Delano. It took five years to settle the strike. During that time, Chávez went on a hunger strike for 26 days. His goal was to bring national attention to the conditions of farm workers. The union called for a nationwide boycott of California grapes picked by nonunion workers. People across the country—perhaps 17 million— supported the boycott and stopped buying grapes. By the end of the strike, the NFWA was known around the country. In 1972, it joined the AFL-CIO and changed its name to United Farm Workers (UFW).

Chávez was the spokesman for NFWA and then UFW. Huerta was vice president of the organization and political activist. Her job was to lobby for laws to protect migrant workers. She also was a tough negotiator for the union with growers.

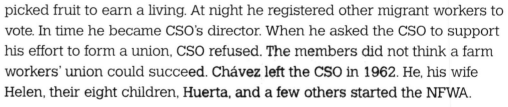

Women's Rights

Thinking on Your Own

Create a concept map to track women's rights. In the large circle in the center write "Women's Rights." Then draw lines and smaller circles for each law that protects women's rights.

Women joined the war effort in World War II in great numbers. When the war was over, they returned to their **traditional** roles as wives and homemakers. In the 1950s, TV programs and women's magazines glorified these roles. By 1960, however, more than 30 percent of U.S. workers were women.

focus your reading

What workplace rights did women gain?

What were some social and political gains women made?

What was the debate over the ERA?

vocabulary

traditional   feminist

Some worked outside the home because they needed to support their families. Others worked because they wanted extras like a second car or a new kitchen. Some women worked because they wanted to use their education. More women were graduating from college than ever before. Others had little to do at home all day while their children were in school.

By 1970, the women's rights movement fought for workplace rights.

Workplace Rights

The move of women into the workplace created change. Women found that they were paid less money than men in similar jobs—if they could get similar jobs. Often women had dead-end jobs as file clerks, secretaries, sales clerks, or cleaning women. Married women discovered they could not get credit cards in their own name, only in their husband's name. Single women also found it difficult to get credit.

Women, however, had learned from the civil rights and antiwar movements. These movements showed women what organized protests could do. Women began to lobby Congress for laws protecting their rights. In 1963, Congress passed the Equal Pay Act. This law made it illegal to pay men and women differently for the same job. Title VII of the Civil Rights Act of 1964 banned job discrimination on the basis of gender. However, by the beginning of the twenty-first century, women still earned less than men on average. The average salary for a man was $51,590 and for a woman, $35,348.

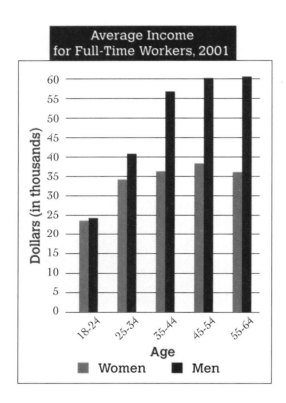

Average Income for Full-Time Workers, 2001

Dollars (in thousands)

Age

■ Women ■ Men

Equal Rights Amendment

The women's, or **feminist**, movement created social and political as well as economic change. The National Organization for Women (NOW) was the major group working for women's rights. It was founded in 1966. Among other efforts, it lobbied for laws against sex discrimination in education.

NOW also lobbied Congress for passage of the Equal Rights Amendment (ERA) to the Constitution. In 1972, Congress passed the ERA. The amendment read: "Equality of rights under law shall not be denied or abridged by the United States or by any State on account of sex." Debate over the law was heated. Supporters believed the ERA would give women the equality in jobs and wages that they had been trying to win for years. Many of those who were against the law were women.

Betty Friedan was an early leader of the feminist movement.

As a result of NOW's work, Congress in 1972 passed a series of laws related to discrimination in education. The most far-reaching was Title IX. It bans discrimination on the basis of gender by any school or college that receives federal

N.O.W. demonstrators at the White House in 1969

funding of any kind. Title IX requires equal treatment of girls and young women from admissions to sports.

By the deadline for ratification, 35 of the needed 38 states had ratified it. Congress extended the deadline for three years. However, opponents waged an intense battle in states that had not ratified the amendment. In the end, the ERA died in 1982.

Social and Political Changes

This time period also saw a great deal of social change. The music of the youth culture began to express issues related to politics and social concerns. A youth counterculture developed around the beat poets of Haight Ashbury, the counterculture center of San Francisco.

U.S. Representative Shirley Chisholm was the first African-American woman to serve in Congress.

In 1967, the Monterey Pop Festival was held in California. The festival brought together members of the hippie movement. This was the first of several large music festivals that continue to this day.

The largest music festival was held during the summer of 1969, in Woodstock, New York. The three days of "peace and music" attracted close to 400,000 people. Woodstock served as a symbol for the peace movement. Performers such as Joan Baez, Jimi Hendrix, Janis Joplin, Santana, The Grateful Dead, The Who, and Crosby, Stills, Nash & Young sang about the unrest of the times.

Jimi Hendrix at Woodstock, 1969

Putting It All Together

Think about the social changes in the United States during the 1960s and early 1970s. Make a T-chart. Label one side "Event" and the other side "Outcome." After you fill in the chart, share your ideas with a partner. As you discuss each other's ideas, add to or cross out ideas. Use facts to support your opinion.

Chapter Summary

The civil rights marches of 1963 marked a **turning point** in the civil rights movement. During the March on Washington, Dr. Martin Luther King, Jr., said he had a dream of a united America living in racial **harmony**. Newer, younger civil rights leaders had a **confrontational** approach to race relations. "Black Power" and "Black is beautiful" awakened in African Americans a pride and an interest in their African **heritage**.

The 1960s saw the passage of the Civil Rights Act of 1964 and the Voting Rights Act of 1965. In 1964, President Johnson also signed an executive order promoting **affirmative action** in the construction industry. Later President Nixon added **quotas** to the policy. Latinos fought to gain equal opportunities in business, education, and housing, and respect for their **culture**. The first effort at gaining economic opportunities occurred among **migrant workers**. People of Mexican **descent** worked for their rights throughout the Southwest.

Native Americans wanted greater economic opportunities on the reservations. They also wanted the federal government to honor broken treaties. A third goal was to end **stereotypes** about Native Americans. Native Americans used lobbying, confrontation, and court cases to gain their rights.

After World War II, women returned to their **traditional** roles. By the end of the 1950s, however, about one-third of women worked outside the home. Faced with discrimination on the job, women, too, began to lobby for laws to protect them. Some became members of the **feminist** movement.

Chapter Review

1 Design and write a flier explaining the boycott of grapes and why people should support the boycott.

2 Many girls still do not have equal athletic opportunities. Imagine your daughter has to carry equipment to a public field to play. The boys' team plays on a school field and the equipment is stored at the field. Write a letter to the school district asking what they will do about this.

Skill Builder

Identifying Point of View

Point of view is how a person feels about, or what a person thinks about, something. That something may be another person, a sports team, or a political issue. If you ask three friends what they think about a movie, you may get three opinions. Each is based on the person's point of view.

Beliefs and values help to shape a person's point of view. Beliefs and values are the result of factors such as age, sex, ethnic background, and religion. Whether a person lives in the city, a suburb, or a rural area also affects point of view.

Knowing someone's point of view helps you to judge the accuracy and objectivity of that person's opinion. *Objectivity* means fairness or lack of prejudice.

To identify someone's point of view:

- identify the author and the author's background. Ask yourself how these might affect what the person thinks.

- identify the author's argument or main idea. Ask yourself if the author has left anything out or is emphasizing just one side.

- look for emotional words or phrases such as *right-wing*, *leftist*, *lovely*, or *delightful*

- look for opinions as well as facts in what the person says

Shirley Chisholm, the first African-American woman elected to Congress, is the author of the following excerpt:

"When a bright young woman graduate starts looking for a job, why is the first question always: 'Can you type?' . . . Why are women thought of as secretaries, not administrators? Librarians and teachers, but not doctors and lawyers? Because they are thought of as different and inferior."

1 What is the topic of this excerpt?

2 What is Chisholm's point of view on the topic?

3 What phrase helps you to identify her point of view?

9 UNIT

YEARS OF CONFLICT

The election of 1968 did not end the division over the Vietnam War. Richard Nixon had promised to end the war. But the war dragged on, and antiwar protests continued. The president was more successful in dealing with the Soviet Union. He brought a new conservatism to the nation's social policies.

President Nixon's desire to be reelected in 1972 resulted in his downfall. Because of the Watergate scandal, he became the only U.S. president ever to resign. In an orderly changeover, vice president Gerald Ford assumed the presidency. Ford lost to Democrat Jimmy Carter in the election of 1976. The nation was ready for a change.

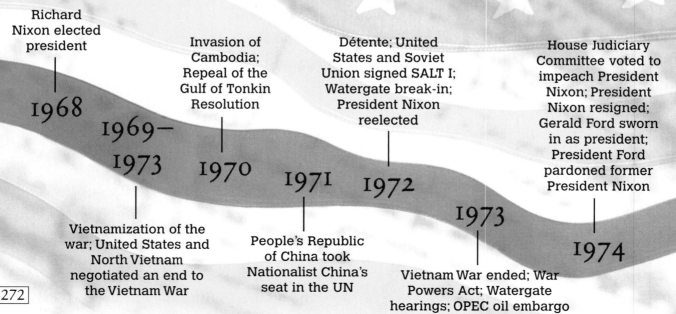

1968
Richard Nixon elected president

1969–1973
Vietnamization of the war; United States and North Vietnam negotiated an end to the Vietnam War

1970
Invasion of Cambodia; Repeal of the Gulf of Tonkin Resolution

1971
People's Republic of China took Nationalist China's seat in the UN

1972
Détente; United States and Soviet Union signed SALT I; Watergate break-in; President Nixon reelected

1973
Vietnam War ended; War Powers Act; Watergate hearings; OPEC oil embargo

1974
House Judiciary Committee voted to impeach President Nixon; President Nixon resigned; Gerald Ford sworn in as president; President Ford pardoned former President Nixon

Why did President Nixon resign in 1974?

How did President Nixon finally end U.S. participation in the Vietnam War?

What does this cartoon say about the need for a Strategic Arms Limitation Treaty?

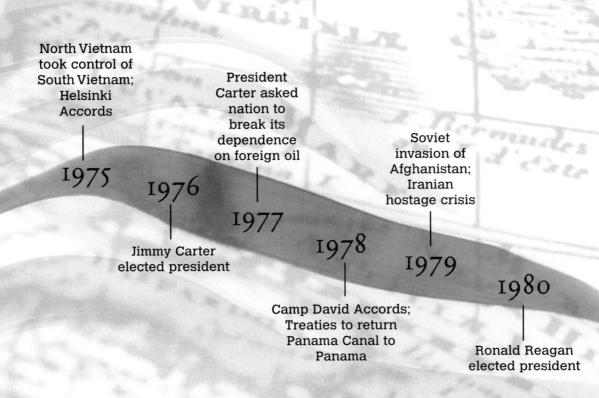

North Vietnam took control of South Vietnam; Helsinki Accords

1975

1976

Jimmy Carter elected president

President Carter asked nation to break its dependence on foreign oil

1977

1978

Camp David Accords; Treaties to return Panama Canal to Panama

Soviet invasion of Afghanistan; Iranian hostage crisis

1979

1980

Ronald Reagan elected president

Chapter 17 THE NIXON YEARS

Getting Focused

Skim this chapter to predict what you will be learning.

- Read the lesson titles and subheadings.
- Look at the illustrations and read the captions.
- Examine the maps.
- Review the vocabulary words and terms.

Create a two-column table in your notebook to organize President Nixon's domestic and foreign policies. Title the table "President Nixon's Policies." Label the left column "Domestic Policy." Label the right column "Foreign Policy." Take notes as you read.

Nixon's Domestic Policies

Thinking on Your Own

As you read the lesson, make an outline to help you remember the important ideas about each subheading.

In his effort to win the 1968 election, Richard Nixon appealed to what he called "Middle America" and the "silent majority." These were hardworking, white middle-class Americans. Many were upset and angered by civil rights gains, antiwar protests, and an increase in crime. Nixon promised the silent majority that he would lower their taxes. He also promised to slow integration and to crack down on crime.

focus your reading

What was Richard Nixon's Southern strategy?

How was New Federalism different from earlier policies?

What was the War Powers Act?

vocabulary

vacancy

block grant

overrode

Nixon's Southern Strategy

As part of the silent majority, Nixon set about capturing the white Southern vote. The South had voted solidly Democratic since Reconstruction. In 1968, Nixon made a number of promises. If elected, he said he would (1) appoint a Southerner to the Supreme Court, (2) name conservatives to federal judgeships, and (3) oppose court-ordered busing to integrate schools. The race was tight, but Nixon won Kentucky, North Carolina, South Carolina, Tennessee, and Virginia.

The *Miranda* case ensured the rights of people under arrest.

stop and think

Do you think President Nixon's campaign was aimed at conservatives or liberals? Talk over your ideas with a partner. You might start by defining *liberal* and *conservative*. Write a paragraph to explain your opinion. Be sure to use facts to support your opinion.

Once in office, Nixon began to fulfill his promises. For example, some parts of the Voting Rights Act of 1965 were to end in 1970. The attorney general tried to keep Congress from extending these parts of the law. He failed, but white Southern voters saw that Nixon had tried. Nixon did end the withholding of federal money to segregated schools.

Beginning with *Brown* v. *The Board of Education* in 1954, the Supreme Court handed down a number of decisions that angered conservatives. The cases included civil rights and the abortion decision in *Roe* v. *Wade*. There were also cases involving criminal rights. In *Miranda* v. *Arizona*, the Court declared that a person suspected of a crime has the right to have an attorney present during questioning.

During President Nixon's time in office, four **vacancies** became open on the Supreme Court. He was able to appoint a new Chief Justice and three other justices. Each time, he filled the openings with a conservative. True to his promise, one of them was a Southerner.

The Warrens, Nixons, and Burgers after the swearing-in ceremony of Chief Justice Burger in 1969

The New Federalism

President Nixon set out to end Presidents Kennedy and Johnson's social programs. He said they were too costly and gave the federal government too much power over people's lives. All of the Great Society's programs to rebuild the cities were stopped. The president called his policies New Federalism. Under New Federalism, President Nixon planned to return more power and more tax money to the states.

Co-op City in New York City was built in 1973.

As part of New Federalism, President Nixon sent a plan for **block grants** to Congress. In the past, the federal government gave state and local governments money for projects. The state or city had to follow federal guidelines in using the money. Under block grants, the federal government would give the state or local government funding for a program. However, the state or city would have more freedom in how to spend it. For example, a city might receive money to build housing. The city could decide the income range for families renting the housing.

War Powers Resolution

The majority of Congress agreed with the president on domestic issues. On a major foreign policy issue, however, they opposed him. According to the U.S. Constitution, only Congress can declare war. However, Congress never declared war in Vietnam. Because of the Gulf of Tonkin Resolution, President Johnson did not have to ask Congress. Congress had given the president the power "to take all necessary measures" to protect U.S. forces.

In 1973, Congress moved to get back its war power. It passed the War Powers Act. The law states that (1) the president must tell Congress within 48 hours if any troops are sent into combat and (2) there is a 60- to 90-day limit on how long the troops may remain without congressional approval. At 90 days, Congress must approve, or the troops must be removed. President Nixon vetoed the bill. Congress **overrode** the veto and the bill became law.

Inductees being sworn into the U.S. Army

Putting It All Together

Imagine you are an editorial writer for a newspaper. Write a two-line headline for an editorial supporting block grants or the War Powers Act. Then write a two-line headline against the grants or act. Exchange your headlines with a partner and discuss the ideas that support your two headlines.

Vietnam, China, the Soviet Union, and Détente

Thinking on Your Own

Make three columns in your notebook. Label the columns "China," "Soviet Union," and "Cold War." Take two minutes and write whatever you remember about each one after World War II. As you read the lesson, check your memory and add new information to each column.

Richard Nixon had promised to end the war in Vietnam if elected. Progress was slow and the war dragged on. At times it seemed that the president was escalating the war, not ending it.

Ending the Vietnam War

After he took office in 1969, President Nixon appointed Henry Kissinger to continue peace talks with North Vietnam. Kissinger was a professor and foreign-policy expert. He spent four years negotiating with the North Vietnamese.

President Nixon also proposed the Vietnamization of the war. His plan was to turn the war over to the South Vietnamese. He began slowly withdrawing U.S. forces from South Vietnam. However, the South Vietnamese were not yet able to defeat North Vietnam without help. As a result, the president

focus your reading

How did the Vietnam War finally end?

How did détente affect U.S. relations with China?

How did détente affect U.S. relations with the Soviet Union?

vocabulary

sanctuary   hard line

détente

Henry Kissinger shaking hands with Le Duc Tho of North Vietnam

Many Cambodian villages were destroyed during the bombing campaigns.

ordered heavier bombing of North Vietnam and targets in South Vietnam. He also ordered air strikes on Vietcong supply routes through neighboring Cambodia.

In 1970, the president sent U.S. and South Vietnamese troops into Cambodia to clear out Vietcong **sanctuaries**, or hideouts. Antiwar protesters took to the campuses and streets again in huge crowds. The president had not told congressional leaders of the invasion before it happened. Congress reacted by repealing the Gulf of Tonkin Resolution.

The major issue in the 1972 election was the continuing war in Vietnam. The Democrats ran antiwar candidate George McGovern. In October, Kissinger announced that peace was at hand. President Nixon was reelected. However, peace talks broke down again in December. The president then ordered more bombing of North Vietnam. Talks resumed in January 1973. The United States agreed to allow North Vietnamese troops to remain in the South. On January 27, 1973, Kissinger announced the Paris Peace Accord. The war was over. All U.S. troops were to withdraw from South Vietnam within 60 days.

stop and think

Create a flowchart to help you remember the steps that finally ended the involvement of the United States in the Vietnam War.

Once U.S. troops were gone, the civil war resumed. In spring 1975, a final large-scale attack by the North Vietnamese defeated the South. On April 30, Saigon, the capital of South Vietnam, fell to the North Vietnamese. The city was renamed Ho Chi Minh City, after the leader of North Vietnam. The two nations were joined under a communist government. Hundreds of thousands of Vietnamese fled the country. Many came to the United States.

Many Americans considered the war a major defeat for the United States. Many also thought it was a war that the nation should not have entered.

Helicopters evacuated the U.S. embassy in Saigon on April 29, 1975.

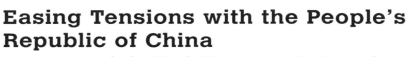

Easing Tensions with the People's Republic of China

While negotiating with the North Vietnamese, Kissinger also made a trip to China. He was on a secret mission to meet with China's leader, Mao Zedong. President Nixon sent Kissinger to find out if China would be interested in opening talks with the United States.

Communist and Nationalist forces fought for control of China after World War II. The Communists won and founded the People's Republic of China. The United States never recognized the People's Republic of China. United States policy recognized the government of the island of Taiwan as the true government of China. Throughout his career, President Nixon had been a strong anti-communist. However, in 1971 he changed his views and the nation's policy.

President and Mrs. Nixon on the Great Wall of China in 1972

President Nixon adopted what became known as **détente**. This means a relaxing of tensions. He realized that it was more important to avoid nuclear war than to take a **hard line** against communists.

As part of détente, the United States in 1971 agreed to allow the People's Republic of China to take the seat reserved for China at the United Nations. The next year, the president visited China. The goal was to begin communication between the two nations. The United States also lifted limits on trade and travel with the People's Republic of China.

President Nixon and Soviet Premier Leonid Brezhnev shake hands at the SALT talks in 1972.

Easing Tensions with the Soviet Union

While President Nixon hoped to improve relations with China, his policy had another goal. By becoming friendly with China, he hoped to force the Soviet Union to be less threatening. After World War II, China and the Soviet Union were allies. However, they soon become rivals for world power. Their shared border also was a trouble spot. President Nixon hoped to play the two nations against each other.

Détente was working with the Soviet Union, too. President Nixon and Leonid Brezhnev, head of the Soviet Union, met at a summit in May 1972. The two men signed the Strategic Arms Limitation Treaty, or SALT I. The treaty froze the production of long-range missiles that could be used for attack. The two nations also agreed to work together on space exploration and health research. They also eased trade barriers. The Cold War seemed to be thawing.

Putting It All Together

Reread the last sentence of the lesson again. Make that your topic sentence. Using information from the lesson, write a paragraph explaining why the Cold War thawed during Nixon's time in office.

Read a Primary Source

What We Achieved with the People's Republic of China

For most of his career, Richard Nixon was fiercely opposed to communism. Yet in 1971, he announced a change in U.S. policy toward China. In 1972, he became the first U.S. president to visit the People's Republic.

reading for understanding

What was President Nixon's goal in going to China?

What process did his trip begin?

What does he say is the basis for peace?

"When I announced this trip last July, I described it as a journey for peace. In the last 30 years, Americans have in three different wars gone off by the hundreds of thousands to fight, and some to die, in Asia and in the Pacific. One of the central motives behind my journey to China was to prevent that from happening a fourth time to another generation of Americans.

"As I have often said, peace means more than the mere absence of war. In a technical sense, we were at peace with the People's Republic of China before this trip, but a gulf of almost 12,000 miles and 22 years of noncommunication and hostility separated the United States of America from the 750 million people who live in the People's Republic of China, and that is one-fourth of all the people in the world.

"As a result of this trip, we have started the long process of building a bridge across that gulf, and even now we have something better than the mere absence of war. . . . We have demonstrated that nations with very deep and fundamental differences can learn to discuss those differences calmly, rationally, and frankly without compromising their principles. This is the basis of a structure of peace, where we can talk about differences rather than fight about them.

"The primary goal of this trip was to reestablish communication with the People's Republic of China after a generation of hostility. . . .

"[P]eace is too urgent to wait for centuries. We must seize the moment to move toward that goal now, and this is what we have done on this journey."

From President Nixon's speech at Andrew's Air Force Base, February 28, 1972; Caroline Kennedy, ed., *A Patriots Handbook* (New York: Hyperion, 2003).

Watergate

Thinking on Your Own

As you read, write a bulleted list of events in the lesson. Then use your list to create a flowchart that tracks the sequence of events.

The year 1972 was a presidential election year. President Nixon had several triumphs that year. The opening of relations with China was viewed by most Americans as a step forward and away from the Cold War. The same was true of the president's summit with Soviet leader Brezhnev. But the Vietnam War still dragged on.

focus your reading

What was the Watergate break-in?

Why were the president's tapes important?

Why did President Nixon resign from office?

vocabulary

operatives   impeach

perjure   articles

transcripts

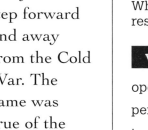

President and Mrs. Nixon campaigning in 1972

The president and his top advisors decided to leave nothing to chance. They wanted to find out as much as they could about Democratic Party plans. They sent spies to Democratic rallies. Their **operatives** spread lies and rumors about opponents. These "dirty tricks," as they were called, were unethical. But the break-in at the Democratic headquarters was illegal.

The Watergate Break-in and Cover-up

The Democratic National Committee headquarters was in the Watergate, a building in downtown Washington, D.C. On June 17, 1972, five men broke into the offices. They were looking for documents that would tell them about the

Democrats' election plans. They also planned to wiretap the phones. A security guard noticed the open door to the offices. He called the police and the five burglars were arrested.

The Watergate building in Washington, D.C.

One of the men was traced to the Committee to Re-elect the President (CREEP). It appeared that the men had been paid from a fund controlled by CREEP. President Nixon declared that no one in the White House had anything to do with the break-in. Voters believed him and returned him to office in November.

Nixon attorney John Dean

The burglars' trial was in January 1973. The judge, John L. Sirica, threatened to sentence them to long terms unless they cooperated with investigators. In March, one burglar broke his silence. He said that the White House had pressured the burglars to lie about the break-in. The burglars had been given $400,000 to remain quiet.

In May 1973, the Senate set up the Select Committee on Presidential Campaign Activities. In June 1973, the president's former personal lawyer, John Dean, testified before the committee. In surprise testimony, he accused former Attorney General John Mitchell of ordering the break-in. He also said the president was involved in the cover-up. The president denied Dean's sworn testimony. More White House and Republican Party officials were called to testify. Rather than **perjure** themselves by lying under oath, they described their roles in Watergate, as the scandal was called.

The Tapes

In July 1973, another White House aide testified that President Nixon secretly taped all conversations in his office. The Senate committee asked the president for the tapes. These would tell them what the president knew and when he knew it. Was he part of the cover-up or an innocent victim of eager advisors? The president refused to hand over the tapes. He claimed executive privilege. According to this principle, executive branch conversations and reports are confidential. Releasing them to others could harm national security.

In an effort to appear cooperative, President Nixon had earlier appointed an independent prosecutor to investigate Watergate. The prosecutor, Archibald Cox, got a court order to force Nixon to hand over the tapes. Nixon refused and ordered Attorney General Elliot Richardson to fire Cox. The attorney general refused and resigned. The deputy attorney general also refused to fire Cox and resigned. Finally, the solicitor general fired Cox. This became known as the "Saturday Night Massacre." It added to the public's view that the president must have known what was going on.

Elliot Richardson

Washington Post reporters Carl Bernstein, left, and Bob Woodward won the Pulitzer Prize for their reports on the Watergate scandal.

Nixon Resigns

Still trying to save himself, President Nixon appointed a new independent prosecutor, Leon Jaworski. He, too, demanded the tapes. Finally, in April 1974, the president released **transcripts**, or written copies, of the tapes. The contents had been heavily edited. In July, the Supreme Court ruled that the president must turn over the actual tapes. Executive privilege could not be used to hide evidence in a criminal case. Nixon obeyed.

In reviewing the tapes, the president's role in the cover-up was apparent. On June 23, 1972, Nixon had ordered the Central Intelligence Agency (CIA) to end its investigation of the break-in. He used national security as the reason. This was six days after the burglary.

President Nixon resigned on August 9, 1974.

The House Judiciary Committee voted to **impeach** the president. They believed there was enough evidence to bring him before the Senate for trial. The committee approved three **articles**, or charges, of impeachment. They found evidence that he had (1) blocked the investigation of the Watergate break-in, (2) misused his power by using federal agencies to violate the rights of citizens, and (3) defied the authority of Congress by refusing to deliver the tapes and other materials requested by the committee. The full House had to vote on the articles. If it voted "yes," the president would stand trial in the Senate.

Former President Nixon leaving the White House after resigning office

Based on what the tapes revealed, it seemed more than likely the president would be impeached. It also seemed likely he would be found guilty. Rather than be further disgraced, Richard Nixon resigned the presidency on August 9, 1974. He was the first and only president to resign. His vice president, Gerald Ford, was sworn in as president.

The attempt to wiretap Democratic headquarters and to spread rumors and lies was an effort to take away from Americans their right to vote. Some Americans felt betrayed by the president. They lost respect for the office of president and for politics in general. Other Americans felt new hope in the American system. The Constitution worked the way it was supposed to.

Putting It All Together

Imagine you are writing a letter to a friend in another country. Explain to your friend why President Nixon resigned. Share your letter with a partner. Discuss whether your information is clearly and accurately stated. Then revise your letter as needed.

Biography

Barbara Jordan (1936–1996)

Barbara Jordan served the voters of Texas and the United States well. She was a member of the House Judiciary Committee that investigated Watergate. She spoke forcefully for the impeachment of President Nixon.

Jordan was born in Houston, Texas, where she went to school. While in high school, and later in college, she developed great skill in debating. In 1952, while still in high school, she won a national debate contest. She graduated from Texas Southern University with a degree in government. Jordan decided to become a lawyer and was admitted to Boston University Law School. After graduation, Jordan decided that she was needed back home in Texas.

In 1960, Jordan campaigned for President Kennedy. She set up a program that sent a Democratic campaign worker into every block in 40 mostly African-American precincts in the county that included Houston. On election day, an amazing 80 percent of registered voters in those precincts went to the polls.

At the time, an African-American woman lawyer was very unusual. Voters were not yet ready to send one to the Texas legislature. In 1962 and again in 1964, Jordan was defeated in her campaign for the Texas House of Representatives. Never one to give up, she won in 1966. Jordan became the first African-American woman elected to the Texas legislature and the first African American to do so since Reconstruction.

In 1972, her district sent Jordan to the U.S. House of Representatives. That was how she came to deliver her speech to impeach President Nixon. Millions saw her on TV. Her years of debating and her law school training paid off. Her speech was well researched, well thought-out, and forcefully spoken.

In 1978, Jordan retired from politics and once again went home to Texas. She joined the Lyndon B. Johnson School of Public Affairs at the University of Texas. Jordan continued to teach and speak for the rights of African Americans, Latinos, and women.

Chapter Summary

In the 1968 election, Richard Nixon promised Southerners that he would fill one **vacancy** on the Supreme Court with a Southerner. President Nixon's domestic program was called New Federalism. **Block grants** under the program gave states more freedom in using grant money than earlier programs had.

Congress passed the War Powers Act in 1973 to limit presidential power. President Nixon vetoed the bill, but Congress **overrode** his veto. While holding peace talks with the North Vietnamese, the president ordered bombing of North Vietnamese **sanctuaries** in Cambodia. Finally, in January 1973, the United States and North Vietnam agreed to end the war.

President Nixon developed a policy known as **détente**. President Nixon had always taken a **hard line** against communism. In early 1972, he became the first U.S. president to visit China.

President Nixon and his top-level supporters decided to leave nothing to chance in the 1972 election. Their **operatives'** plans unraveled when burglars were caught inside Democratic National Committee headquarters. Congress began a series of investigations. Rather than **perjure** themselves, official after official talked. The president eventually handed over **transcripts** of conversations made in his office. The House Judiciary Committee voted to **impeach** the president on three **articles**. Rather than face a probable trial and conviction, President Nixon resigned from office in 1974.

Chapter Review

1 Reread your outline and other notes about President Nixon's policies. Consider the policies you think are important. Write a paragraph explaining why you would or would not vote to reelect President Nixon. Share your paragraph with a partner.

2 Imagine you are President Nixon. Write your resignation speech to the nation. First, with a partner, create a list of the main points you would include.

Skill Builder

Identifying Bias

Bias presents only one point of view or one side of an issue. Bias may be stated or unstated. A person may say that he or she supports a particular point of view. Or you can figure it out using other information. For example, the Sierra Club is a national conservation group. Members of the Sierra Club probably support keeping logging companies out of national forests.

Sometimes a person may appear to be objective. However, when you begin to ask questions, you find the person is giving only one side. For example, a businessman supports building a new sports stadium. He says that it will bring jobs to the city. When you dig a little, you find that his brother-in-law owns the land where the stadium will be built.

To identify bias, ask yourself the following questions:

- Is more than one point of view presented? Is the view of the logging company presented or just the conservationist?

- Can you detect unstated bias? Who is speaking? What does he or she do? To what groups does he or she belong?

- Is there support for the point of view? Are there facts and/or statistics used as evidence? Are they really facts or just opinions?

- Is any emotional language used like *all, never, no one, greedy, corrupt,* or similar words?

Answer the following questions:

1 Would a conservationist speak in support of or against drilling for oil in the Arctic Wildlife Refuge?

2 Would a business group run an ad in support of or against tightening the Clean Air Act?

3 Choose a political issue of interest to you. Write a letter to the editor that is biased in favor of your view. Then write a second letter that is balanced, giving more than just your viewpoint. With a partner, analyze the differences between the two letters.

Chapter 18 BEYOND WATERGATE

Getting Focused

Skim this chapter to predict what you will be learning.

- Read the lesson titles and subheadings.
- Look at the illustrations and read the captions.
- Examine the maps.
- Review the vocabulary words and terms.

The second half of the 1970s focused on energy policy. Presidents asked the U.S. public to conserve, or save, gasoline and home heating fuels. Imagine you work for an advertising agency. You have been asked to design an ad to conserve energy. Decide what you want to say and show. Sketch your idea and write copy—the text—to go with the picture.

Ford's Brief Term

Thinking on Your Own

Read each subheading. Then turn each one into a question. Write them in your notebook. As you read the lesson, answer each question with a full sentence.

Gerald Ford had been a member of the House of Representatives for 25 years. In 1964, he was named house minority leader. Like President Johnson, Ford had spent his career in Congress. But unlike President Johnson, Ford did not have a great vision for the nation.

Gerald Ford being sworn in as president

focus your reading

How did Gerald Ford become vice president and then president?

What were the major issues in foreign policy for the new president?

What was the result of President Ford's economic policy?

vocabulary

pardoned	inflation
recession	conserve
deficit	energy

On September 8, 1974, President Ford **pardoned** Richard Nixon of "any and all crimes" committed while president. The former president had not yet been charged with any crimes. The pardon meant that would never happen. Many Americans thought the pardon was the result of a deal between Nixon and Ford.

Nelson Rockefeller and Gerald Ford

The Twenty-fifth Amendment

The Twenty-fifth Amendment to the U.S. Constitution was passed in 1967. It outlines the process that should be followed if either the president or vice president leaves office. It also explains what to do if either person is not able to fulfill the responsibilities of his job.

In October 1973, Vice President Spiro Agnew resigned. Agnew had taken bribes as the governor of Maryland and as vice president. He also evaded paying income taxes. President Nixon had filled the vacancy by appointing Gerald Ford. Ford was then approved by Congress to be the new vice president. When President Nixon resigned, Vice President Ford became president.

President Ford, in turn, filled the new vacancy for vice president by selecting Nelson Rockefeller, former governor of New York. Congress quickly approved. This meant that for the first time in the history of the United States neither the president nor the vice president had been directly elected by voters.

Foreign Policy

Rudolph Nureyev and Galina Panov, of the Soviet Union, perform in London in 1975 as part of a cultural exchange.

One piece of leftover business for the new president was Vietnam. By the time Nixon resigned, U.S. troops had left Vietnam. By spring 1975, the North Vietnamese and the South Vietnamese were locked in battle. The North Vietnamese had seized control of the South. President Ford asked Congress to send aid to the South Vietnamese, but Congress refused.

The Helsinki Accords, or agreements, were a high point in Ford's term. He continued President Nixon's policy of détente and convinced the Soviet Union to sign the agreements. In all, 33 nations signed the accords in 1975. A major accord made boundaries of nations created after World War II permanent. Other agreements called for more trade and cultural exchanges between Eastern Europe, including the Soviet Union, and western nations. The nations also agreed to guarantee certain human rights.

stop and think

Imagine you are a senator in 1975. President Ford has asked for aid for the South Vietnamese. Would you vote for or against it? Talk over your ideas with a partner. Then write a statement that explains your decision.

The Economy and the 1976 Election

The Great Society and the Vietnam War hurt the U.S. economy. During President Nixon's first term, the nation entered a **recession**. Businesses laid off workers and some businesses even closed. To help the economy, President Nixon cut taxes and increased government spending. The economy began to improve,

In 1976, the United States celebrated its bicentennial.

but the federal **deficit**—money borrowed by the government—rose dramatically. It was soon as high as it had been during World War II.

By the time Ford became president, the economy had slowed again. However, **inflation**, the sharp rise in prices, had become a huge problem. President Ford decided to focus on fighting inflation. He asked U.S. businesses to limit increases in wages and prices. He also asked the public to **conserve**, or save, **energy**. The high price of fuel was feeding inflation. The president then cut government spending. Nothing worked.

The Democrats favored increasing government spending to get the economy growing. This worked during the Great Depression. Unlike President Roosevelt, President Ford disapproved of this economic tool. He vetoed more than 50 spending bills.

In many ways, the election of 1976 was a vote against Watergate. It was also a vote against the failed economic policies of President Ford and the Republicans. The Democrats chose Jimmy Carter, a former governor of Georgia. The race was close, but Carter won.

Source: U.S. Bureau of the Census

Putting It All Together

Write a summary of President Ford's two-year term. Review how to write a summary on page 237 to refresh your memory. Share your summary with a partner to be sure you included all the important points.

Read a Primary Source

Why I Pardoned President Nixon

A month after he took office, President Gerald Ford pardoned Richard Nixon. President Ford went on national TV to explain his reasons for the pardon.

reading for understanding

What hangs over former President Nixon's head like a sword?

What was the biggest concern to President Ford?

What comment of President Ford's was aimed at those who disagreed with him?

Do you agree or disagree with President Ford's decision? Explain your opinion.

"I have come to a decision which I felt I should tell . . . my fellow American citizens, as soon as I was certain in my own mind and in my own conscience that it is the right thing to do. . . .

"As we are a nation under God, so I am sworn to uphold our laws with the help of God. And I have sought such guidance and searched my own conscience with special diligence to determine the right thing for me to do with respect to my predecessor in this place, Richard Nixon, and his loyal wife and family. Theirs is an American tragedy in which we all have played a part.

". . . [I]t is common knowledge that serious allegations and accusations hang like a sword over our former president's head, . . . as he tries to reshape his life, a great part of which was spent in the service of his country. . . .

"But it is not the ultimate fate of Richard Nixon that most concerns me. . . . My concern is the immediate future of this great country. . . . As president, my primary concern must always be the greatest good of all the people of the United States whose servant I am. As a man, my first consideration is to be true to my own convictions and my own conscience. . . .

"I do believe that the buck stops here, that I cannot rely on public opinion polls to tell me what is right. . . . I feel that Richard Nixon and his loved ones have suffered enough and will continue to suffer no matter what I do, no matter what we as a great and good nation can do together to make his goal of peace come true."

From President Ford's address to the nation; Robert Torricelli and Andrew Carroll, eds., *In Our Own Words* (New York: Pocket Books, 1999).

Carter and the Energy Crisis

Thinking on Your Own

What would it be like if there were no more oil? Oil often runs the generators that make your electricity. List all the things you use in a day that are powered by electricity.

Jimmy Carter ran his presidential campaign as a Washington outsider. He had not spent years in national politics. As a result, he said that he did not owe any favors to special interest groups. He could govern with only the good of the public in mind. His lack of experience in government and politics, however, became a problem. It was difficult for him to get Congress to pass his proposals. He did not have close relationships with members of Congress. President Carter also was unable to communicate to the American people his vision for the country. His biggest contribution was his energy policy.

Continuing Economic Problems

The U.S. economy did not improve during President Nixon's months in office in 1974, or through President Ford's two years. Like President Ford, President Jimmy Carter found the economic problems of the nation impossible to solve. Unlike President Ford, President Carter increased government spending to put more money into the economy. The result was rising inflation.

Then the president cut government spending to try to hold down inflation. Funding was cut for social programs like job training and housing. However, having less money in the economy hurt

Unemployment lines were a sign of the poor economy in 1975.

businesses. Businesses failed and more people lost their jobs. The president then asked for an increase in government spending. By then it was 1980, and voters had had enough of his economic policy swings. The economy was a major reason why President Carter served only one term.

OPEC

One of the factors that caused inflation at this time was the rising price of energy like gasoline and heating oil. President Carter said prices would continue to rise as long as the United States depended on foreign oil.

OPEC ministers meet in Abu Dhabi to discuss crude oil prices in 1978.

The major reason for the high price of energy was the Organization of Petroleum Exporting Countries (OPEC). It is an association of oil-producing nations in the Middle East and Venezuela in South America. Member nations agree on how much oil to pump and at what price to sell their oil.

stop and think

Analyze the line graph of inflation on page 293. Write a paragraph to describe the trend of inflation between 1968 and 1980. If you need to review line graphs and trends, reread the Skill Builder on page 221.

OPEC was founded in 1960. In 1973, while President Nixon was still in office, the price of a barrel of oil was $3. Then OPEC decided to raise the price. By 1980, the price had been raised to $30 a barrel. OPEC also decided to use oil as a political weapon. In 1973, OPEC declared an **embargo**, or a ban on trade, against any nation that supported Israel. This included the United States and Western Europe.

OPEC's embargo impacted the U.S. economy.

Israel had been set up in 1948 as the Jewish homeland. As a result, many Palestinians, who are Arabs, were displaced. In 1973, Arabs and Israelis were fighting their fourth war since 1948. The OPEC oil embargo was meant to force Israel's allies to **desert** it.

For the first time since World War II, Americans were faced with a fuel shortage. People waited in long lines to buy a few gallons of gas at a time. **Reserves** of oil for industrial use and for home heating ran low, too. The embargo was called off in March 1974 without achieving its goal. Once the embargo was over, gasoline became plentiful again—but at higher prices. Inflation continued to increase.

The disaster at Three Mile Island in 1979 caused the country to question the safety of nuclear power.

Conserving Energy

Shortly after becoming president, Carter declared a war on energy use. His goal was to cut the nation's dependence on foreign oil. His national energy program called for an increase in coal production. The plan also asked for funding for research on **renewable** energy sources such as solar, or sun, power and wind power. He proposed a Department of Energy to oversee national energy policy and research.

The president also asked the public to do their part to conserve energy. He asked citizens to make fewer car trips and use more public transportation. Homes, offices, and schools should be kept cooler in winter (68°) and warmer in summer (72°).

Automakers began to produce smaller cars with more fuel-efficient engines. A change in regulating the oil industry resulted in some increase in oil production by U.S. companies. The United States greatly reduced its use of foreign oil during the later 1970s.

President Carter

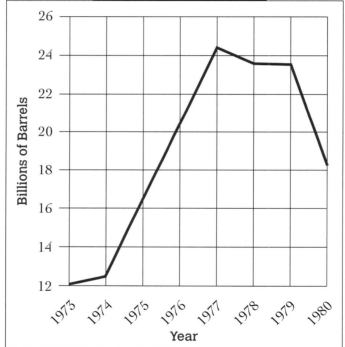

Oil Imports, 1973–1980

Source: U.S. Energy Information Administration

Putting It All Together

Imagine you are President Carter's speechwriter. Write a short speech about the importance of energy conservation. Make some suggestions about how people could save energy. Read your speech to a partner.

LESSON 3

Diplomacy and Camp David

Thinking on Your Own

Create a concept map of President Carter's foreign policy. Draw a large circle in the center of your page and label it "Foreign Policy." Then begin to add lines and smaller circles for each event under his foreign policy.

President Carter was determined to build his foreign policy on what was right and just, or moral. One example is the Panama Canal. You read about the building of the canal in Chapter 5. In 1978, President Carter negotiated that the canal would be returned to the nation of Panama on December 31, 1999.

The central goal of Carter's foreign policy was advancing **human rights**. He criticized earlier U.S. policy, especially toward Latin American dictators. The United States often looked the other way when allies abused the human rights of their people.

focus your reading

Why did détente fall apart?

What was important about the Camp David Accords?

How did the Iranian hostage crisis affect the 1980 election?

vocabulary

human rights

dissidents

decade

fundamentalist

Islamic

U.S.-Soviet Tensions

Former President Carter represented the U.S. at the 1999 handover of the Panama Canal.

President Carter took his human rights campaign to the Soviet Union. He pressured Premier Brezhnev to stop mistreating **dissidents**. These were people who disagreed with communist policies. Relations between the United States and the Soviet Union might have survived if the Soviet Union had not invaded Afghanistan. At the time, Afghanistan was along the southern border of the Soviet Union. In 1978, the Soviet Union removed the Afghan government and set up a government favorable to the Soviets. The Soviets invaded in 1979 when this new government came under attack by other Afghans.

President Carter urged Premier Brezhnev to withdraw Soviet forces. Brezhnev refused. President Carter ordered an embargo on the shipment of grain to the Soviet Union. He also ordered the U.S. Olympic team to boycott the 1980 summer games in Moscow, the

Soviet troops in Afghanistan in 1989

capital of the Soviet Union. Détente had fallen apart. U.S.-Soviet relations were at their lowest point since the 1960s.

During the next **decade**, the United States and Pakistan supported the rebels in Afghanistan against the Soviet forces. In 1989, the Soviet Union admitted defeat and withdrew its troops. Once the Soviets were gone, rival groups within Afghanistan began fighting. In 1996, the Taliban, a group of **fundamentalist** Muslims, took control of the country.

Camp David Accords

President Carter's greatest foreign policy triumph was a peace treaty between Israel and Egypt. On October 6, 1973, Egypt and Syria attacked Israel in what became known as the Yom Kippur War. They wanted to retake land that Israel had seized in 1967 during the Six-Day War. Israel again outfought the Arabs and moved farther into Arab territory. A ceasefire was signed in November 1973, but no peace treaty had been signed.

Arab nations did not recognize the existence of Israel and would not negotiate with it. That changed in 1977. In that year, Anwar Sadat, the president of Egypt, visited Israel. Menachem Begin, the prime minister of Israel, returned the visit. They agreed to begin talks to settle their differences, but nothing was achieved.

The signing of the Camp David Accords

In 1978, President Carter invited Sadat and Begin to Camp David, the presidential compound in Maryland. The two men and their advisors, along with President Carter, talked for 13 days. At the end, President Carter announced that Israel and Egypt had agreed to the Camp David Accords. These agreements were called a "framework for peace." Among the agreements, Egypt recognized Israel, and Israel agreed to give up some of the territory it had captured. The following March, Israel and Egypt signed a formal peace treaty.

stop and think

Make a list of the events you have read about in this lesson that occurred between the United States and other countries. Share your list with a partner to make sure you included everything in the section. Then put the events in sequence.

The hostages in Iran were the focus of the United States in 1979.

Iranian Hostage Crisis

The praise for the Camp David Accords lasted only a few months. At the end of 1979, President Carter suffered a major foreign policy failure in Iran. Iran was a country that ignored human rights. The United States had always backed the shah, or leader, of Iran for two main reasons. First, Iran was a major oil producer. Second, at the time, Iran also bordered the Soviet Union. U.S. officials believed that by supporting the shah, they kept the Soviets out of the Middle East.

In late 1978, Iranians marched in the streets, called strikes, and demanded that the shah step down. In January 1979, the shah finally fled. Ayatollah Ruhollah Khomeini and his fundamentalist supporters proclaimed the new **Islamic** republic of Iran. The ayatollah, or holy one, became the leader of the new government. Later that year, the shah traveled to the United States. Iranians demanded that the United States return him to Iran. President Carter refused. In November 1979, Iranian revolutionaries broke into the U.S embassy in Tehran, Iran. They took 52 Americans as hostages.

The U.S. hostages were freed after 444 days in captivity.

The Carter administration negotiated for the release of the hostages, but without any luck. The hostage crisis had a serious impact on the 1980 election. Combined with the nation's poor economy, the hostage crisis made Carter seem ineffective. He lost the election to a former governor of California, Ronald Reagan. The hostages were finally freed on January 20, 1981. This was the day Ronald Reagan took the oath of office as president. The hostages had been in custody for 444 days.

Putting It All Together

Write a headline about either U.S.-Soviet relations, the Camp David Accords, or the Iranian hostage crisis. Then write a bulleted list of notes about the headline. Use your notes to write one paragraph that explains the *who, when, where, how, what,* and *why* of the headline. Share your paragraph with a partner.

Biography

An Wang (1920–1990)

Today, word processing is just one function of your computer. You can do spreadsheets on your computer. You can design presentations with

color, sound, and action on it. You can listen to music and watch movies on your computer. But computers were not always multimedia entertainment units. Years ago, they were just used as word processors. In 1976, Wang Laboratories brought out the first word processor workstation. It was known as the Wang WPS.

Wang Labs had been founded in 1951 by An Wang. Dr. Wang was born in Shanghai, China, and moved to the United States in 1945. He graduated from Harvard University with a doctorate in physics.

Dr. Wang went into business with $600 and an idea. He set up his business in a garage and produced his first invention, a computer memory device. This was an important contribution to the development of the microprocessor chip. These chips are the basis of today's computers.

In 1964, Wang Labs developed the first electronic typesetting machine. Before then, type for newspapers, magazines, and books was set by hand. The next year, Wang Labs developed desktop calculators powered by transistors. By 1971, Wang's scientists had invented calculators that were programmable. Then came the breakthrough Wang VS in 1976. In 1979, the company introduced the Wang VS minicomputer for businesses.

Wang Labs did much to popularize the use of computers. It was a pioneer in advertising its computers on television. It became the first computer company to advertise during a Superbowl. By 1984, Wang Labs employed 30,000 people.

In 1986, Dr. Wang was awarded the Medal of Liberty by the United States. He was honored as one of the nation's outstanding naturalized citizens.

Chapter Summary

When President Nixon resigned, Vice President Gerald Ford was sworn in as president. After he **pardoned** Nixon, President Ford had to deal with a **recession** and a huge budget **deficit**. These were made worse by rising **inflation**. Because of the high cost of **energy**, the president asked the public to **conserve** energy.

President Ford lost to Jimmy Carter in the 1976 election. One part of Carter's national energy plan called for research on **renewable** energy sources.

In 1973, the Organization of Petroleum Exporting Countries (OPEC) declared an **embargo** against any nation that supported Israel. OPEC hoped to force the U.S. and Europe to **desert** Israel. U.S. oil **reserves** ran low.

President Carter built his foreign policy on moral principles. His major goal was to advance **human rights**. He tried to get the Soviet Union to stop mistreating its **dissidents**. U.S.-Soviet relations soured over the Soviet invasion of Afghanistan. The Soviets gave up and withdrew after a **decade** of fighting rebel Afghans.

President Carter was able to get Israel and Egypt to sign the Camp David Accords. His failure, however, was Iran. **Fundamentalists** set up an **Islamic** republic in Iran after forcing the shah to leave. Iranian revolutionaries held 52 Americans hostage for 444 days. The Iranian hostage crisis helped convince Americans to vote Carter out of office in the 1980 election.

Chapter Review

1 Imagine you are President Carter's campaign manager in 1980. On what policies would you have him campaign? Choose one policy and explain in a paragraph what President Carter could say about it.

2 Write a paragraph to compare and contrast the foreign policies of President Ford and President Carter.

Skill Builder

Analyzing Circle Graphs

In Chapter 3 you read about the shift in population from rural to urban areas. In the Skill Builder on page 221, you read a line graph that showed the number of people who moved between 1910 and 1960. Another way to present this information is on a circle graph. Circle graphs do not show actual numbers, however. They show percentages.

The full circle, or pie, is 100 percent. Each piece is some part, or percentage, of the whole. For example, the total number of people in the United States in 1910 was 91,972,266. This was 100 percent of the population. Of that, 45.6 percent lived in urban areas and 54.4 percent lived in rural areas. The first circle graph shows this information. The second circle graph shows the percentage of population in 1950 who lived in rural areas and in urban areas.

Area of Residence, 1910, 1950, 1980

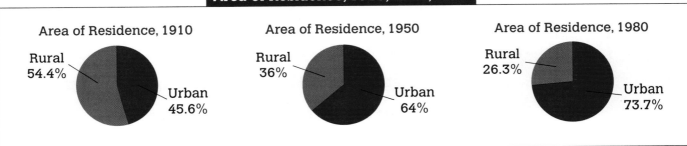

Source: U.S. Bureau of Census, The Statistical Abstract of the U.S.

Use the circle graphs to answer the following questions:

1 Which was greater: the number of people who lived in urban areas or in rural areas in 1980?

2 Compare the urban populations in 1950 and 1910. How much greater is the 1950 population?

3 Write one or two sentences explaining the change in urban and rural population from 1910 to 1980.

4 In 2000, 79 percent of the population lived in urban areas and 21 percent lived in rural areas. Draw a circle graph to show this information.

UNIT 10

Toward a New Millennium

In many ways, the 1980s seemed to mark the end of one stage in U.S. history. In the 1980s the United States shifted from the liberal ideas of the New Deal to more conservative policies. The Cold War ended.

For a time the Clinton presidency slowed the conservative shift at home as the economy bounced back. Americans enjoyed new levels of prosperity. The election of 2000 continued the move to conservativism as the economy entered another recession.

Everything changed at 8:46 A.M. on September 11, 2001, when the first plane flew into the World Trade Center. Terrorists had struck on U.S. soil.

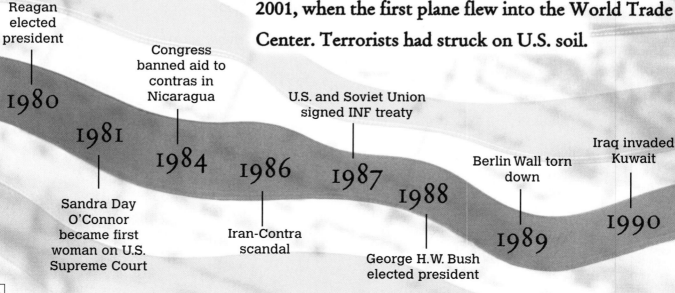

Ronald Reagan elected president

1980

Congress banned aid to contras in Nicaragua

1981

1984

U.S. and Soviet Union signed INF treaty

1986

1987

Berlin Wall torn down

1988

Iraq invaded Kuwait

1989

1990

Sandra Day O'Connor became first woman on U.S. Supreme Court

Iran-Contra scandal

George H.W. Bush elected president

What led to the two U.S. invasions of Iraq?

Why did the Cold War end?

How did computers affect U.S. workers and the economy?

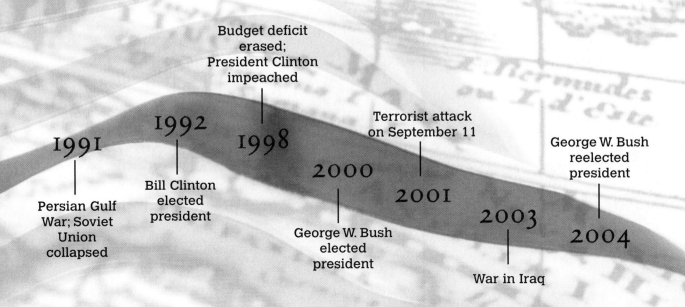

1991
Persian Gulf War; Soviet Union collapsed

1992
Bill Clinton elected president

1998
Budget deficit erased; President Clinton impeached

2000
George W. Bush elected president

2001
Terrorist attack on September 11

2003
War in Iraq

2004
George W. Bush reelected president

Chapter 19

THE REAGAN AND FIRST BUSH YEARS

Getting Focused

Skim this chapter to predict what you will be learning.

- Read the lesson titles and subheadings.
- Look at the illustrations and read the captions.
- Examine the maps.
- Review the vocabulary words and terms.

As you read this chapter, create two concept maps. Label one "Reagan Policies." Then label the second one "George H.W. Bush Policies." Add lines and smaller circles to each as you read the subsections.

Reagan's Conservative Domestic Policies

Thinking on Your Own

The 1980 election is sometimes called the "conservative revolution." No guns were fired. No prisoners were taken. What do you think this phrase means? Do you remember any other bloodless revolution in U.S. history? Write a paragraph to describe how a revolution can occur without fighting.

The 1980 election put a **conservative** in the White House for the first time since the 1920s. Politics is often divided between **liberal** and conservative ideas. Liberal ideas favor a role for government in managing the economy and in funding social programs such as Social Security and Medicare. Conservative ideas favor a limited role for government in the economy and in social programs.

> ### focus your reading
>
> What was Reaganomics?
>
> How did deregulation work?
>
> How did the U.S. Supreme Court change under President Reagan?
>
> ### vocabulary
>
> | | |
> |---|---|
> | conservative | deregulation |
> | liberal | consumer |
> | stagflation | |

In the 1980 election, Ronald Reagan ran on conservative ideas. He represented the more conservative side of the Republican Party. He said that if elected, he would cut taxes. He would also raise spending for the military. Voters were tired of the nation's economic problems. They were also tired of President Carter's lack of leadership. Reagan won easily.

President Reagan stated his agenda clearly in his inaugural speech. He declared that "government is not the solution to our problem. Government is the problem."

Ronald Reagan takes the oath of office.

Reagonomics

Since the Nixon presidency, the economy had suffered on and off from **stagflation**—high unemployment combined with high inflation. Usually, unemployment drops with rising inflation. President Reagan's proposal for fighting inflation and creating jobs was called "Reaganomics." Another term was *supply-side economics*. This theory combines keeping interest rates high with cutting taxes. President Reagan's tax policy gave the biggest tax cuts to wealthy people. The purpose was to create business growth. The theory is that with more money, people will invest in businesses. This creates new jobs. If more people work, there is money to buy goods. If more goods are bought, more goods will be produced and sold.

Tax cuts led President Reagan to cut government programs. The tax cuts created a budget deficit, or shortage. To balance the budget, the president cut funds to social programs. Food stamps, school lunches, student loans for college, and Medicare payments were some of the programs affected. The funding cuts did not produce a balanced budget. However, President Reagan decided to increase funding for the military anyway.

By 1984, Reaganomics appeared to be working. The economy was growing, and voters returned Reagan to a second term. By 1988, 20 million new jobs and 5 million new businesses had been created. However, President Reagan continued to pour money into defense spending. Congress would cut spending on social programs only so much. As a result, the budget deficit grew dramatically.

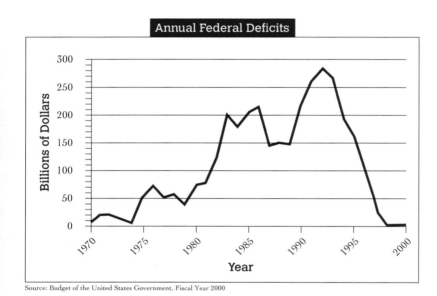

Annual Federal Deficits

Billions of Dollars

Year

Source: Budget of the United States Government, Fiscal Year 2000

stop and think

Analyze the line graph on the national deficit.

(1) In what year did the deficit begin to rise?
(2) When did it begin to decline?
(3) Next to each date, write the name of the president who was in office.
(4) What events added to the deficit? List these events. Check your information with a partner.

Walter Mondale and Geraldine Ferraro ran for president and vice president in 1984.

Deregulation

Decreasing the role of government in business was another goal of President Reagan. Conservatives wanted to do away with large numbers of regulations for businesses. This is called **deregulation**. Beginning in the late 1800s, the federal government had passed many regulations aimed at businesses. The regulations had three goals. One was to protect **consumers** from unsafe products. Another was to ban unfair competition among businesses. The third goal was to protect workers from unsafe working conditions.

President Reagan believed that having to obey regulations cost companies money. This money would be better spent creating jobs. He encouraged deregulation in three major industries—energy, transportation, and banking. He removed the price controls on oil and gasoline. He cut the budgets of federal agencies that regulated businesses. Among the agencies that had their budgets cut were the National Highway Traffic and Safety Administration and the Environmental Protection Agency. Agencies such as the Department of Energy also began to weaken regulations.

Airlines were deregulated during Reagan's administration.

People line up to withdraw savings during the savings and loan crisis.

Banks had been heavily regulated since the New Deal. One type of bank was the savings and loan. Once deregulation occurred, some savings and loan banks made bad investments. These banks failed, and the federal government had to repay depositors. Their deposits were insured by the FDIC, which had been set up during the New Deal for this purpose. In all, the federal government—the U.S. taxpayer—paid $500 billion to savings and loans' depositors.

The Supreme Court

Conservatives believed that the courts were increasing the federal government's power. The courts were also meddling in social issues such as abortion and upholding criminals' rights. Conservatives pointed to the decision in *Miranda* v. *Arizona* as an example. President Reagan wanted to appoint justices who would follow a strict interpretation of the U.S. Constitution. He did not believe that the Constitution was open to broad interpretation.

The
Miranda
Rights

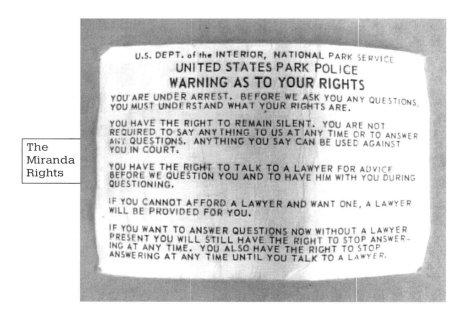

President Reagan had the opportunity to appoint justices to the U.S. Supreme Court. The Chief Justice and three other justices retired while Reagan was president. He named a conservative justice who was already on the Court to be Chief Justice. Then the president nominated conservatives for the other openings.

President Reagan changed the Supreme Court in another way. In 1981, he appointed the first woman justice, Sandra Day O'Connor.

Putting It All Together

What domestic policy goals did President Reagan achieve? List them in your notebook. Discuss with a partner whether the goals made life in the United States easier or harder for ordinary citizens. Write a paragraph to explain your opinion.

Biography

Sandra Day O'Connor (1930–   )

A cowgirl on the Supreme Court? That would be Sandra Day O'Connor. Sandra Day was raised on the Lazy B Ranch in Arizona. Her parents were ranchers. In her autobiography, she wrote about riding horses with her brother.

The ranch was far from town and neighbors. When she was five, Day went to live with her grandmother in El Paso, Texas, during the school year. She graduated from high school in El Paso and entered Stanford University in California. She graduated from college with a degree in economics. Day then enrolled in Stanford's Law School.

When she graduated in 1952, few law firms would hire her, because she was woman. Instead she went to work for the San Mateo, California, district attorney's office. In the meantime she had married John O'Connor. They had met in law school. She moved to Germany during her husband's army service. When his tour of duty was over, they settled in Phoenix, Arizona. Day O'Connor opened her own law office in 1957. In 1960, she closed her practice to care for her two—and then three—sons.

In 1965, Day O'Connor returned to working outside the home. She was appointed assistant attorney general for the state of Arizona. In 1970, she entered the Arizona state senate. In 1972, she became the first female majority leader in any state senate in the nation. In 1974, she won election to the Maricopa County Superior Court. She was appointed to the Arizona Court of Appeals in 1979. In 1981, President Reagan nominated her to become the first woman on the United States Supreme Court.

Sandra Day O'Connor is a conservative but with a moderate view on many issues. She often casts the swing vote, or deciding vote, between liberal and more conservative justices. There are nine justices on the Court. She is often the fifth vote in 5-4 decisions.

Reagan's Foreign Policy

Thinking on Your Own

Make an outline as you read the lesson. If you need to review how to make an outline, reread the Skill Builder on page 69.

President Nixon's decision to open discussions with China angered many conservatives. During President Carter's term, relations with China continued to improve. Relations with the Soviet Union, however, worsened. In the 1970s, nuclear war with the Soviet Union remained a real threat. People also feared that the Soviet Union would impose communism on other nations. This was the situation when Ronald Reagan took office in 1980.

focus your reading

How was the Reagan Doctrine put into effect?

What was Star Wars?

Why did U.S.-Soviet relations improve during Reagan's presidency?

vocabulary

guerrilla

operation

stockpile

controversial

private enterprise

The Reagan Doctrine

President Reagan took an active role in fighting communist threats. He proposed that the United States support **guerrillas** who were fighting communist governments anywhere in the world. Guerrillas are military groups who fight to overthrow an existing government.

The first use of the so-called Reagan Doctrine was in Afghanistan. President Carter had sent $30 million in aid to the Afghan rebels who were fighting Soviet forces. U.S. aid soared to $570 million under President Reagan. In 1988, the Soviets pulled out of Afghanistan. They were unable to defeat the Afghan guerrillas.

U.S. soldiers arrive in Grenada.

President Reagan saw communist threats closer to home as well. In 1983, communist-leaning guerrillas took over the island of Grenada in the Caribbean. Later that year, President Reagan sent U.S. troops to remove them. A new democratic government took over.

The Iran-Contra Scandal

Misuse of the Reagan Doctrine in Nicaragua caused what became known as the Iran-Contra scandal. In 1979, guerrillas called Sandinistas overthrew the pro-U.S. dictator of Nicaragua. The Sandinistas set up a pro-Soviet government. Another group of guerrillas, called contras, wanted to overthrow the Sandinistas. President Reagan ordered the CIA to work with the contras. If the contras succeeded, they would set up a government favorable to the United States.

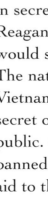

The CIA **operation** took place in secret, because President Reagan did not think people would support U.S. involvement. The nation still remembered Vietnam. However, by 1984 the secret operation had become public. Congress banned any more aid to the contras.

Sandinista troops fighting contras along the Honduras border

Officials in the Reagan administration saw a way around this ban. They used money from the secret sale of weapons to Iran to support the contras. In 1986, this operation also became public. Congressional hearings were held to find out what the president knew and when he knew it. However, nothing was ever discovered linking

stop and think

Why would the Vietnam War have made people careful about involvement in Nicaragua? Talk over ideas with a partner. Then express your opinion in a paragraph.

the president to the scandal. Several people were convicted or ordered to pay fines for their part in the illegal operations. Lieutenant Colonel Oliver North, a National Security Council staff member, and John Poindexter, a National Security Advisor, were both indicted for their roles in the scandal.

Lt. Col. Oliver North

Star Wars

President Reagan continued to increase the nation's **stockpile** of arms. This buildup was at the expense of social programs and a balanced budget.

Model of a Star Wars missile

The most **controversial** part of President Reagan's program was the Strategic Defense Initiative (SDI). It was planned as a defense shield. A network of weapons would be sent into space to guard against a nuclear attack. Critics called it "Star Wars." Nothing ever came of the research for Star Wars. The program was abandoned in the 1990s under President Clinton.

United States–Soviet Relations

President Reagan called the Soviet Union "the evil empire." However, by the early 1980s, the Soviet Union was a mortally wounded empire. Decades of communist control had drained the strength of the Soviet nation. Economic growth was slow. Manufacturing and farming were inefficient. There were shortages of food and basic goods. Things that Americans took for granted, like TVs and cars, were rare. The Soviet people were becoming discontented. Anger and frustration in Eastern Europe ran even higher.

In 1985, Mikhail Gorbachev came to power as head of the Soviet Union. He promised a new openness in government and less government control of the economy. New political parties were allowed to form. The opening of new businesses—**private enterprise**—was encouraged. Spending for new weapons was cut. Gorbachev encouraged the same openness and reforms in Eastern Europe.

President Reagan and Premier Gorbachev

As a result of the change in the Soviet Union, détente was revived. President Reagan and Premier Gorbachev signed the Intermediate-Range Nuclear Forces (INF) Treaty. Both nations agreed to destroy some of their nuclear missiles. This was the first time either nation had agreed to destroy weapons.

Putting It All Together

Create a flowchart of the Cold War. Start with the beginning of the Cold War. Then list each change or event in the Cold War between 1945 and 1988. Review chapters about U.S. foreign policy if necessary. Share your flowchart with a partner to be sure you included everything important.

Read a Primary Source

"Tear Down This Wall"

President Ronald Reagan visited Berlin, Germany, in 1987. It was at the beginning of the change in Soviet policies. In a speech on June 12, he challenged Mikhail Gorbachev, the head of the Soviet Union.

"Twenty-four years ago, President John F. Kennedy visited Berlin, speaking to the people of this city and the world. . . .

"We come to Berlin, we American presidents, because it's our duty to speak, in this place, of freedom. . . .

"Behind me stands a wall that encircles the free sectors of this city, part of a vast system of barriers that divides the entire continent of Europe. . . .

"In the 1950s, Khrushchev predicted: 'We will bury you.' But in the West today, we see a free world that has achieved a level of prosperity and well-being unprecedented in all of human history. In the Communist world, we see failure, technological backwardness, declining standards of health, even want of the most basic kind—too little food. . . . After these four decades, then, there stands before the entire world one great and inescapable conclusion: Freedom leads to prosperity. . . . Freedom is the victor.

"And now the Soviets themselves may, in a limited way, be coming to understand the importance of freedom. . . .

"Are these the beginnings of profound changes in the Soviet state? Or are they token gestures . . . ? There is one sign that Soviets can make that would be unmistakable, that would advance dramatically the cause of freedom and peace.

"General Secretary Gorbachev, if you seek peace, if you seek prosperity for the Soviet Union and Eastern Europe, if you seek liberalization: Come here to this gate! Mr. Gorbachev, open this gate! Mr. Gorbachev, tear down this wall!"

President Ronald Reagan, *Tear Down This Wall*, June 12, 1987. (TheReaganLegacy.com)

---

reading for understanding

What reason does President Reagan give for going to Berlin?

What is President Reagan's challenge to Gorbachev?

Reread President Kennedy's speech on page 231. Compare it to President Reagan's. How are they the same? How are they different?

George H. W. Bush's Four Years

Thinking on Your Own

What do you think this lesson is about? Reread the title of the lesson and the subheadings. Then write three questions you have about this lesson. As you read, answer the questions. Compare your questions and answers with those of a partner.

I n the 1988 election, President Reagan's vice president, George H.W. Bush, became the Republican candidate. The Soviet Union was caught up in its own problems at home and in Eastern Europe. The economy at home was growing. Many Americans were satisfied with the way things were going. Bush won easily over the Democratic candidate.

George H.W. Bush takes the oath of office.

focus your reading

How did the Cold War end?

Why was the Persian Gulf War fought?

What economic problem faced President Bush?

vocabulary

sanctions   superpower

coalition   downsize

End of the Cold War

The long and costly Cold War came to an end during President Bush's term. Gorbachev encouraged economic and political reforms in Eastern Europe as well as in the Soviet Union. Eastern Europeans took him at his word. Their anger at communism boiled over in strikes and protest marches. But the actual revolution took place at the ballot box. In Poland, Hungary, Czechoslovakia, Romania, and Bulgaria, citizens voted to replace communist governments with democratic ones. In Berlin, the hated wall came down. In 1990, East and West Berlin and East and West Germany were reunited in one democratic nation.

Crowds support Lech Walesa, leader of Poland's Solidarity movement and later president of Poland.

Communist officials and high-ranking army officers in the Soviet Union were not happy with the changes in Eastern Europe. They feared a similar overthrow of communism in the Soviet Union. To prevent it, they plotted to take over the government. Faced with opposition from the people, however, the plot failed.

The Berlin Wall came down in 1989.

In December 1991, the Soviet Union dissolved. The 15 Soviet republics declared their independence. Throughout this period, President Bush expressed the support of the American people for freedom and democracy in the former Soviet world.

Saddam Hussein set many oil wells on fire during the Persian Gulf War.

The Persian Gulf War

While communism was unraveling, President Bush was also dealing with Iraq. Its leader, Saddam Hussein, was a brutal dictator. In August 1990, the Iraqi army invaded the neighboring nation of Kuwait. Saddam Hussein was after Kuwait's oil fields and possibly those of Saudi Arabia.

At first President Bush used diplomacy and economic **sanctions**—or restrictions—to try to persuade Saddam Hussein to withdraw. At the same time, the president and the United States put together a **coalition** of 28 nations. The goal was to force Saddam Hussein to remove his troops from Kuwait.

The coalition gave Saddam Hussein a deadline. Iraqi forces ignored the deadline. The coalition launched Operation Desert Storm on January 16, 1991. After six weeks of massive bombing of Iraq, the coalition launched a land assault on Iraqi

Persian Gulf War, 1991

TURKEY
CASPIAN SEA
SYRIA
Tehran
Damascus
Baghdad
IRAN
Amman
IRAQ
KUWAIT
JORDAN
Basra
Kuwait City
PERSIAN GULF
BAHRAIN
Riyadh
QATAR
SAUDI ARABIA
OMAN
UNITED ARAB EMIRATES
RED SEA
YEMEN
INDIAN OCEAN

Iraq and occupied territory
Nations sympathetic to Iraq
Nations contributing forces against Iraq
Oil fields
Allied ground attack
U.S. warship

0   500 miles

stop and think

Analyze the map of the Persian Gulf War. In a paragraph, describe what the map shows. Be sure to use directions such as north and south, not top and bottom, to tell where something is on the map. Share your description with a partner. Ask your partner to follow your description on the map.

forces in Kuwait. After only 100 hours of fighting, the war was over. Iraqi troops withdrew and Kuwait was freed. President Bush and his advisors believed that the coalition did not need to invade Iraq to remove Saddam Hussein.

Domestic Problems

The economy began to slow midway through President Bush's term. The recession had two main causes. First, with the end of the Cold War, the United States was the only **superpower**. It stopped buying as much military equipment as it had during the Cold War. The companies that made these goods began to lay off workers. The armed forces also **downsized**, or shrank in size. The unemployment rate started to rise.

The federal budget deficit also affected the economy. The government was borrowing to pay the interest on the national debt. There was no extra money to spend on programs that could have helped the economy. While campaigning in 1988, President Bush had promised not to raise taxes. However, there seemed no other way to reduce the budget deficit. In a deal with Congress, he agreed to a tax hike in exchange for cuts in spending on social programs.

H. Ross Perot, Bill Clinton, and President Bush debate in 1992.

Voters remembered this when they went to the polls in 1992. In a three-way race, Democratic candidate Bill Clinton defeated President Bush. Clinton had campaigned on promises to cut taxes on the middle class and to reform health care and welfare. Third-party candidate Ross Perot won 19 percent of the vote to President Bush's 37 percent and Clinton's 43 percent.

Putting It All Together

Review your notes from this lesson. Make a two-column chart. Label one side "President Reagan" and the other side "President Bush." Under each column, list the domestic and foreign policy issues faced by each president. Then write a paragraph that compares and contrasts the presidents.

Chapter Summary

The 1980 election began the shift from **liberal** to **conservative** policies in government. Voters elected Republican Ronald Reagan president. One of the first problems the president faced was **stagflation**. To aid economic growth, he cut taxes. This also meant cutting funding for many social programs.

Major industries were **deregulated**. Many government regulations protected **consumers**. As a result of deregulation, many savings and loan banks made bad investments.

The Reagan Doctrine was the basis of his foreign policy. In Nicaragua, it led to a secret CIA **operation** that supported the **guerrillas** and the Iran-Contra scandal. In 1989, the Berlin Wall came down. In 1991, the Soviet Union dissolved and the Cold War ended. The U.S. was the only remaining **superpower**. **Private enterprise** was becoming popular in Eastern Europe. The U.S. and the Soviet Union signed an agreement to lower the **stockpile** of nuclear weapons. One of President Reagan's most **controversial** projects was Star Wars.

President George H.W. Bush pulled together a **coalition** of nations when Iraq invaded Kuwait. Economic **sanctions** did not work. The coalition then launched Operation Desert Storm and drove the Iraqis from Kuwait.

President Bush had less success at home. The economy slid into a recession and companies began to **downsize**. In the 1992 election, voters elected Bill Clinton as president.

Chapter Review

1   Review your notes and outlines. Which president do you think was more successful? Write a paragraph to explain your opinion. Use facts from the chapter as support.

2   Imagine the year is 1989 and you live in East Berlin. Write a letter to a relative in the United States to describe how you feel about the end of the Berlin Wall.

Skill Builder

Analyzing a Bar Graph

A bar graph shows information at a certain time for certain things or groups.

To analyze a bar graph, read

- the title of the graph to learn what the graph is about
- the key, if there is one
- the *y*-axis, or left side, of the graph to learn the range of the numerical information shown
- the *x*-axis, or bottom, of the graph to learn the groups
- the bars, by moving up the columns and across the graph from left to right

Use the bar graph and the chapter to answer the following questions:

1 What is this graph about?

2 What does each color represent on the bars?

3 What is the range of number of employees? the range of years?

4 In what year did federal government employees decline?

5 Who was president during this decline?

6 Which government group has the largest number of employees across all years shown on the graph?

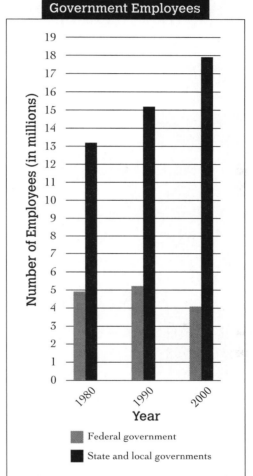

Government Employees

Source: Office of Management and Budget, Budget of the United States Government, FY 2004

Chapter 20

ENTERING THE 21ST CENTURY

Getting Focused

Skim this chapter to predict what you will be learning.

- Read the lesson titles and subheadings.
- Look at the illustrations and read the captions.
- Examine the maps.
- Review the vocabulary words and terms.

You have been alive for many of the events in this chapter. These events are not history. They are the background to your everyday life. Choose a subheading or a photo about something you remember. Write a paragraph describing what you remember about the event or person.

Clinton's Policies at Home and Abroad

Thinking on Your Own

Create a concept map for the Clinton presidency. Draw a large circle and label it "Clinton Presidency." Draw lines and two smaller circles. Label one "Domestic Policy" and the other "Foreign Policy." Complete the map as you read the lesson.

William Jefferson Clinton was the first baby boom president. He came into office with youth and enthusiasm. He was president during the longest expansion of the U.S. economy ever. In addition, the nation was at peace. The only fights were with Congress.

While campaigning, Clinton had promised to improve the health care system. He appointed his wife, Hillary Rodham Clinton, to head a national **task force** for health care reform. The resulting plan was complex. Republicans opposed it. In the end, nothing came of the plan.

President William Jefferson Clinton

The Deficit and Welfare Reform

President Clinton had campaigned on the economy. He believed that the federal deficit needed to be lowered. The federal deficit occurred because the government borrowed money. If the government stopped borrowing, it would not have enough money for all its programs. In order to fund government programs, President Clinton proposed a tax increase on middle- and upper-income people.

Reducing the deficit would lower **interest** rates. If interest rates were lower, consumers would have more money to spend. They would not have to make large interest payments on their loans and credit card debt. The deficit hit zero in 1998. This was five years ahead of schedule. This was due to both the president's

plan and the huge growth in the economy. Computers and Internet businesses powered this growth.

Vice President Gore and President Clinton announce the new federal deficit in 1998.

One of the biggest changes to come about during the Clinton presidency was welfare reform. The president had promised that he would change welfare as we know it. The Welfare Reform Act of 1996 set a limit of five years of aid for any one family. Most adults had to work in order to receive benefits. Money was provided for job training and child care. Tax breaks were available to companies hiring welfare-to-work employees.

Charles Ruff defended President Clinton at the impeachment hearings.

During Clinton's first administration, an investigation into the Whitewater Affair began. The president and his wife were accused of financial wrongdoing in a real estate venture in their home state of Arkansas. A Republican-controlled Congress appointed Kenneth Starr as a special prosecutor to investigate the case. Several members of the president's administration resigned as a result. Despite the ongoing investigation, President Clinton was reelected in 1996.

Impeachment

In December 1998, the House voted to impeach President Clinton for perjury and obstruction of justice. He became only the second president to be impeached. President Andrew Johnson had been impeached in 1868. Clinton was accused of inappropriate behavior with a member of his staff, which he denied. Starr turned his investigation from Whitewater to the president's behavior. In November 1998, Starr presented a report to

Congress. The report charged that the president had lied under oath, **obstructed** justice, and misused the office of the president.

The House began an investigation, and debate was heated. When the vote was taken, it split along party lines. A month-long trial was held in the Senate. Republican senators could not gather enough votes to convict the president. He was acquitted on February 12, 1999.

Foreign Policy

President Clinton tried to achieve peace around the world. Until the collapse of communism, Bosnia had been part of Yugoslavia. Once Bosnia was independent, a civil war broke out. Bosnian Serbs forced Muslim citizens out of the country, killing thousands in the process. President Clinton led the effort to stop this **ethnic cleansing**. He argued that NATO had a **stake**—or serious interest—in ending the conflict. NATO finally agreed to bomb the Serbs' positions. The Serbs agreed to a cease-fire and signed the Dayton Accords in 1996. NATO also sent troops into Bosnia for peacekeeping duty.

U.S. Senator John McCain led a delegation to open ties with Vietnam in 2000.

More trouble broke out in the area in 1998. Kosovo, a province of Serbia, tried to secede. Serbia sent troops into Kosovo. President Clinton again urged NATO to end the violence. NATO bombing resulted in another cease-fire and more peacekeeping duties for NATO member nations.

UN troops in Bosnia

In 1996, President Clinton sent a personal representative to meet with Catholic and Protestant leaders in Northern Ireland. Violence had raged there between the two groups since the 1960s. In 1998, an agreement was reached to share power between Protestant and Catholic members of a new government.

Israeli Prime Minister Rabin, President Clinton, and PLO Chairman Arafat in 1993.

For much of his two terms in office, President Clinton worked to create a lasting peace in the Middle East. He was able to get Israeli and Palestinian leaders to talk. However, he could not get them to agree on a settlement that would lead to lasting peace. In 1993, Prime Minister of Israel Yitzhak Rabin and Palestinian Liberation Organization (PLO) leader Yasir Arafat signed the Declaration of Principles at the White House. Israel agreed to allow Palestinian self-rule in the Gaza Strip. In turn, the PLO recognized the right of Israel to exist. Violence resumed in 2000 between Israelis and Palestinians and lasted for years.

Putting It All Together

Imagine you are President Clinton. You are writing your autobiography. Use the information in this lesson and write titles for five chapters in your autobiography. Share your chapter titles with a partner. Explain why you chose those five events or ideas.

Biography

Pierre Omidyar (1967–   )
Jerry Yang (1968–   )

You may never have heard of Pierre Omidyar or Jerry Yang, but they have influenced people all over the world. Omidyar founded eBay, the online auction site. Jerry Yang cofounded Yahoo!, the Internet search engine.

Pierre Omidyar was born in Paris. His parents were French and Iranian and came to the United States in 1973. While still in high school, Omidyar became interested in computers. He graduated with a degree in computer science from Tufts University. His first job was at Claris, part of the Apple computer company. By 1995, he had held several other jobs and had cofounded a company that he sold to Microsoft.

Omidyar began eBay as a part-time hobby. His fiancée had acquired a large collection of candy dispensers. She wanted an easy way to trade them with other collectors. In 1991, Omidyar put up the site that became eBay. In the beginning, the site was free. As it grew, Omidyar charged a fee for each sale. Within five years, site traffic was doubling, tripling, and more, each year. In 1996, Omidyar sold stock in eBay to the public and became a billionaire. In the meantime, he and his fiancée, Pam, had married. They have become well-known philanthropists, giving away millions of dollars to charity each year.

Jerry Yang, like Omidyar, is an immigrant to the United States. Yang was born in Taipei, Taiwan, and moved to the United States in 1978 with his mother and brother. His father had died eight years before. Yang graduated from Stanford University with a Bachelor of Science and a Master of Science degree in electrical engineering.

Yang and a fellow graduate student, David Filo, often traded information about their favorite Web sites. Yang began putting the list on the Internet as "Jerry's Guide to the World Wide Web." By 1994, his site had become so popular that the two men launched Yahoo! as a business. The following year they incorporated it. By the late 1990s, 40 million people visited the site monthly. In 2004, Yahoo! sold stock and became a public company. By then, Yang was already a billionaire.

George W. Bush's Policies

Thinking on Your Own

The Twenty-sixth Amendment gives eighteen-year-old citizens the right to vote. List at least three reasons why it is important to vote in all elections—for school board, local and state offices, members of Congress, vice president, and president.

In the 2000 election, Vice President Al Gore was the Democratic nominee for president. He faced the Republican nominee, George W. Bush, the son of former President George H.W. Bush. Gore had spent most of his adult life in politics. Bush's political experience included two terms as the governor of Texas. Bush had the support of conservatives in the Republican Party. The campaign was heated and the race was close.

focus your reading

How was the 2000 election decided?

What conservative policies did President Bush propose?

How did President Bush deal with foreign policy?

vocabulary

electoral vote

mandate

nation building

Disputed Election

The election was held on November 7, 2000. The race was so close, however, that the winner was not certain until December 12, 2000. Although Gore won the popular vote by 500,000 votes, **electoral votes** decide the presidential election. The winning candidate must have 270 or more electoral votes. Each state has the same number of electoral votes as the number of its members in Congress.

The electoral vote was so close that the outcome of the election hung on

Vice President Al Gore and George W. Bush debate in 2000.

ballots cast in several districts in Florida. Whoever had the most popular votes would win Florida's electoral votes and the election.

The design of the ballot in one large district was confusing. It had caused some people to vote for the wrong candidate. Other districts used a punch card ballot. If a voter did not press hard enough, the vote was hard to read. Recounts were ordered in those districts.

Hanging chads were a problem in Florida during the 2000 election.

stop and think

"Every vote counts" is a slogan to get people to vote. The 2000 election proved the truth of this slogan. Work with a partner to design two posters to get out the vote in a presidential election. Sketch pictures and write text for your posters.

The U.S. Supreme Court ruled that the recounts could not continue past the date set by law for Florida to cast its electoral votes. The recount could not be completed. Without the recount, Bush was in the lead by 573 votes. He won the presidency by 271 electoral votes to Gore's 267.

The Conservative Agenda

Early in President Bush's first year, it was clear that the economic boom of the Clinton presidency had ended. The nation was in a recession. Unemployment was growing. To boost the economy, the president proposed a tax cut that

President Bush speaks after signing a tax cut in 2001.

Portions of the Arctic National Wildlife Refuge in Alaska were opened to oil drilling.

favored the wealthy. The idea is that the wealthy will invest in businesses and help the economy grow. By 2004, the economy had improved, but growth was still weak. Unemployed people still found it hard to find work.

President Bush's proposals followed conservative ideas in other areas of government as well. Environmental protection laws, such as the Clean Air Act, were weakened. Fewer regulations made it less costly for companies to do business. More federal land was opened to drilling for gas and oil and for logging.

Denver in 2002 as a result of the Clean Air Act.

Weakening of the Clean Air Act could result in Denver returning to a smog-filled city, as it was in 1984.

The president also proposed the No Child Left Behind Education Act. It required student testing and reporting of yearly progress. If schools did not meet the standards for two years in a row, they could be closed. Conservatives and others thought that education was a matter of local control, not federal **mandates**.

Conservatives were not all in agreement about the president's agenda. Some worried about the economy and education. Conservatives were alarmed at the growing federal deficit.

A Foreign Policy of Non-engagement

During the campaign, President Bush said he would not engage in **nation building**. The United States would not play the role of negotiator in other nations' problems. As a result, he did not actively encourage peace efforts in the Middle East. However, by the end of 2002, Israel had become a battleground. Young Palestinians were becoming suicide bombers, and Israel was striking back at their families. World opinion pressured the United States to step in. The president supported a road map to peace. The Palestinians and Israelis made attempts to follow it, but the violence on both sides continued.

Terrorism became a part of life in Israel.

President Bush also changed the course of foreign policy with North Korea. President Clinton had begun talks with communist North Korea. He had hoped to keep the North Koreans from developing nuclear weapons. Toward the beginning of President Bush's term, North Korea seemed to restart its nuclear program. President Bush refused to talk with North Korea unless Japan, South Korea, China, and Russia were present. He hoped to isolate North Korea. Little, if any, progress was made. North Korea continued to make threatening statements about its nuclear program.

Putting It All Together

In a paragraph, compare and contrast the foreign policy of Presidents Clinton and Bush. Talk over your ideas with a partner first. Then write your paragraph.

Terrorism, War, and Foreign Policy

Thinking on Your Own

As you read, create a flowchart to show the sequence of events from September 11, 2001, to the war in Iraq. Compare your chart with that of a partner.

Terrorism against the United States did not begin on September 11, 2001. Nor was it the first time the World Trade Center in New York City was the target. In 1993, six people died when terrorists set off a truck bomb in the garage of the World Trade Center. In 1998, terrorists bombed U.S. embassies in Kenya and Tanzania. More than 200 people died. Two years later, the USS *Cole* was bombed in the port of Yemen. Seventeen U.S. sailors were killed and 39 injured.

focus your reading

What did Al Qaeda want?

Why was the war in Iraq fought?

How did the war on terror and the war in Iraq affect the election of 2004?

vocabulary

fundamentalist

militant

intelligence

insurgent

Al Qaeda and Terrorism

Al Qaeda was linked to both the attack on the USS *Cole* and the U.S. embassy bombings. Al Qaeda is a loose network of Islamic **fundamentalists** who practice a very strict form of Islam. They believe that Western ways are corrupting the Islamic way of life. They want Muslims to return to Islam's traditional values and beliefs. A few fundamentalists have become **militant**. They use violence to achieve their goals.

The U.S. embassy bombing in Nairobi, Kenya

The damaged USS *Cole* in 2000

The leader of Al Qaeda, Osama bin Laden, comes from a wealthy family in Saudi Arabia. In the 1980s, he fought in Afghanistan against the Soviets. After the Soviets left Afghanistan, bin Laden organized Al Qaeda. His goal was to force Westerners out of the Middle East. He was particularly angered by U.S. troops stationed in Saudi Arabia. The United States had stationed troops there during the Persian Gulf War. After the war, U.S. forces remained in Saudi Arabia.

9/11/01

The attack of September 11, 2001, was the result of several years of planning. Nineteen members of Al Qaeda hijacked four airplanes filled with passengers. Two planes were flown into the World Trade Center towers in New York City, and one into the Pentagon, U.S. military headquarters in Washington, D.C. Passengers on the fourth plane learned from cell phone calls about the other attacks. They put up strong resistance, and the hijackers flew the plane into the ground in Pennsylvania. Government officials believe it had been headed for either the Capitol or the White House in Washington, D.C. More than 3,000 people died in these attacks.

People run as the World Trade Center collapses in 2001.

President Bush reacted strongly and quickly. Osama bin Laden operated out of Afghanistan. He had found a safe place under the fundamentalist government of the Taliban. The Taliban had come to power after the Soviet Union withdrew from Afghanistan. Within a month, the United States launched a war against Afghanistan. Three months later, the Taliban government was overthrown. A new pro-Western government was set up. The United States and several other nations sent troops to Afghanistan as peacekeepers. By 2004, groups of Taliban leaders had resurfaced. They took back several local governments and attacked the peacekeepers. Free elections were held in 2004, but Afghanistan remained a trouble spot for years.

At home, the president proposed a new Department of Homeland Security. It combined a number of existing agencies and duties. The goal was to better coordinate the nation's security to prevent another terrorist attack.

stop and think

Write a two-line headline for each of the following: (1) the September 11 attacks, (2) the war in Afghanistan, (3) the creation of the Department of Homeland Security. Share them with a partner.

Secretary of State Colin Powell

War in Iraq

By 2002, President Bush had shifted the foreign policy focus to Iraq. After the Persian Gulf War, the UN sent weapons inspectors into Iraq. They searched for nuclear, biological, and chemical weapons—otherwise known as weapons of mass destruction, or WMD. After the war, Iraq had to destroy its chemical and biological weapons. It also had to stop making them and stop any research on making nuclear weapons. In the late 1990s, Saddam Hussein, the dictator of Iraq, refused to allow the UN inspectors back into the country.

Insurgents in
Baghdad in 2004

By 2002, U.S. and British **intelligence** agencies believed
that Iraq still had WMD. In October 2002, Congress voted to
allow the president to use force as needed to end the Iraqi
weapons program and remove Saddam Hussein from power.
At the same time, the UN gave Iraq a deadline to deliver
information on its weapons programs. Saddam Hussein
declared that no such programs existed.

President Bush, however, was convinced by the intelligence
reports. When the UN refused to vote to go to war, President
Bush ordered an attack on Iraq. Within weeks, United States
and British forces had captured Baghdad, the capital of Iraq.
Inspectors were sent to look for the stockpiles of weapons. No
weapons were found.

Although major combat operations ended quickly, the
fighting did not stop. **Insurgents**, or rebels, began to appear.
Some were rival ethnic groups who fought one another as well
as U.S. forces. Others were loyal to the former dictator. They,
too, fought other Iraqis and U.S. forces. Foreign fighters also
entered Iraq to join in the insurgency. More U.S. troops died
during the insurgency than during the brief war. Insurgents
began kidnapping and killing foreign workers. There seemed
to be no end in sight to the fighting.

The 2004 Election

The war on terror and the war in Iraq were important issues in the election of 2004. President Bush faced a strong challenge from Senator John Kerry, a Democrat from Massachusetts. Other issues of importance to the nation were the economy, healthcare, and education.

President Bush promised to use the might of the United States to end the war in Iraq and to fight terrorism around the world. His plans to recharge the economy included educating and training a skilled workforce, making the tax codes simpler, and helping small businesses to grow. He promised to reduce the cost of health care and provide affordable coverage to those who do not get health care through their job. His second administration would follow up the No Child Left Behind Act of his first administration with a plan to reform America's high schools, strengthen Head Start, and promote national literacy.

President George W. Bush

Senator Kerry promised to end the war in Iraq and develop coalitions with other nations. He called his plan Winning the Peace. Like Bush, he promised to strengthen homeland security. His administration would create new jobs, revitalize manufacturing in the U.S., and reduce taxes for anyone earning less than $200,000. On health care, he promised to reduce the cost of health care and increase coverage to all Americans. He also promised to cut the cost of prescription drugs. On education, Kerry's plan promised to provide more resources for K–12 education, offer more after-school programs, and make sure college was affordable for all.

President Bush was reelected in a close vote.

Putting It All Together

Review the flowchart you made for this lesson. Write a paragraph to summarize the sequence of events. Share it with a partner. Ask if your paragraph includes the most important information from the lesson.

Read a Primary Source

President's Address on Terrorism

On September 20, 2001, President George W. Bush addressed a joint session of Congress and the nation. He described who had attacked the United States on September 11, 2001, and how he planned to respond.

reading for understanding

How did the president characterize Al Qaeda's acts on September 11?

When does the president say the war on terror will end?

Whose fight is the war on terror?

"On September 11, enemies of freedom committed an act of war against our country. Americans have known wars. But for the past 136 years they have been wars on foreign soil, except for one Sunday in 1941. Americans have known the casualties of war. But not at the center of a great city on a peaceful morning. Americans have known surprise attacks. But never before on thousands of civilians. All of this was brought upon us in a single day. And night fell on a different world, a world where freedom itself is under attack. . . .

"The evidence we have gathered all points to a collection of loosely affiliated terrorist organizations known as Al Qaeda. . . .

"Our war on terror begins with Al Qaeda, but does not end there. It will not end until every terrorist group of global reach has been found, stopped and defeated. . . .

"We ask every nation to join us. . . .

"The United States is grateful that many nations and many international organizations have already responded with sympathy and with support. Nations from Latin America to Asia to Africa to Europe to the Islamic world. . . .

"The civilized world is rallying to America's side. They understand that if this terror goes unpunished, their own cities, their own citizens, may be next. Terror unanswered can not only bring down buildings, it can threaten the stability of legitimate governments. . . ."

George W. Bush, Address on Terrorism Before a Joint Meeting of Congress, September 20, 2001; Caroline Kennedy, ed., *A Patriot's Handbook* (New York: Hyperion Books, 2003).

Chapter Summary

Bill Clinton was the first baby boom president. Hillary Rodham Clinton headed a **task force** to reform health care. Opposition was great and the plan died. President Clinton wanted to reduce the budget deficit in order to reduce **interest** rates.

In foreign policy, President Clinton adopted an active role as peacemaker. He convinced NATO nations that they had a **stake** in the **ethnic cleansing** that was taking place in Bosnia and Kosovo. The president personally worked with Israeli and Palestinian leaders on peace. President Clinton's eight years in office were marred by his impeachment. The House charged him with perjury and **obstruction** of justice. The Senate acquitted him.

Al Gore and George W. Bush ran for president in 2000. The race was so close that the **electoral votes** in Florida decided the outcome. George W. Bush won the election after a Supreme Court decision.

President Bush cut taxes. Government agencies began to rewrite or do away with regulations affecting businesses. He and some other conservatives disagreed on the ballooning deficit and education **mandates**.

On September 11, 2001, the United States was attacked by members of Al Qaeda, a group of **militant** Islamic **fundamentalists**. President Bush acted quickly. Within a month, U.S. forces were in Afghanistan fighting the Taliban, supporters of Al Qaeda. By 2003, the president had **intelligence** reports stating that Iraq had weapons of mass destruction. In March, U.S. and British forces attacked Iraq. The war was over quickly, but fighting continued. **Insurgents** fought one another and U.S. forces.

Chapter Review

1 Review the paragraph you wrote at the beginning of the chapter. Now that you have read the chapter, revise your paragraph. Make notes about what to change.

2 Choose one of the lessons and create an outline. Use your outline to help you study the lesson.

Skill Builder

Identifying Propaganda

Propaganda tries to get you to think in a certain way about an issue, a product, or a person. There is often some truth in propaganda, but it also has some untruths. Propaganda may also contain personal opinions that are masked as facts.

- **Name Calling**: An attempt to turn others against a person or group by using a name for the person or group that stirs up fear, anger, or dislike. The use of the word *trigger-happy* to describe Barry Goldwater's Vietnam War policy is an example.

- **Testimonial:** The use of a famous person to support a political candidate or to promote a product. In the 2004 presidential campaign, a group of singers, led by Bruce Springsteen, campaigned for John Kerry.

- **Plain Folks**: The use of words, ideas, and pictures to try to convince others that a man or woman is just an ordinary person, "one of us." President George W. Bush used short sentences and everyday words to get his ideas across to voters. He was often shown in jeans, driving his pick-up truck around his Texas ranch.

- **Bandwagon**: Telling you that everyone else is supporting a particular candidate, so you should, too. This is the basic message of all political parties. Party leaders are supporting candidate X. As a good party member, you should, too.

Which form of propaganda is each of the following?

1   When a sports team is winning, everyone becomes a fan.

2   Your favorite singer says that only stupid people smoke.

3   An actor tries to appeal to young fans by using street slang and wearing hip-hop clothes.

4   A basketball star endorses a line of sports clothes.

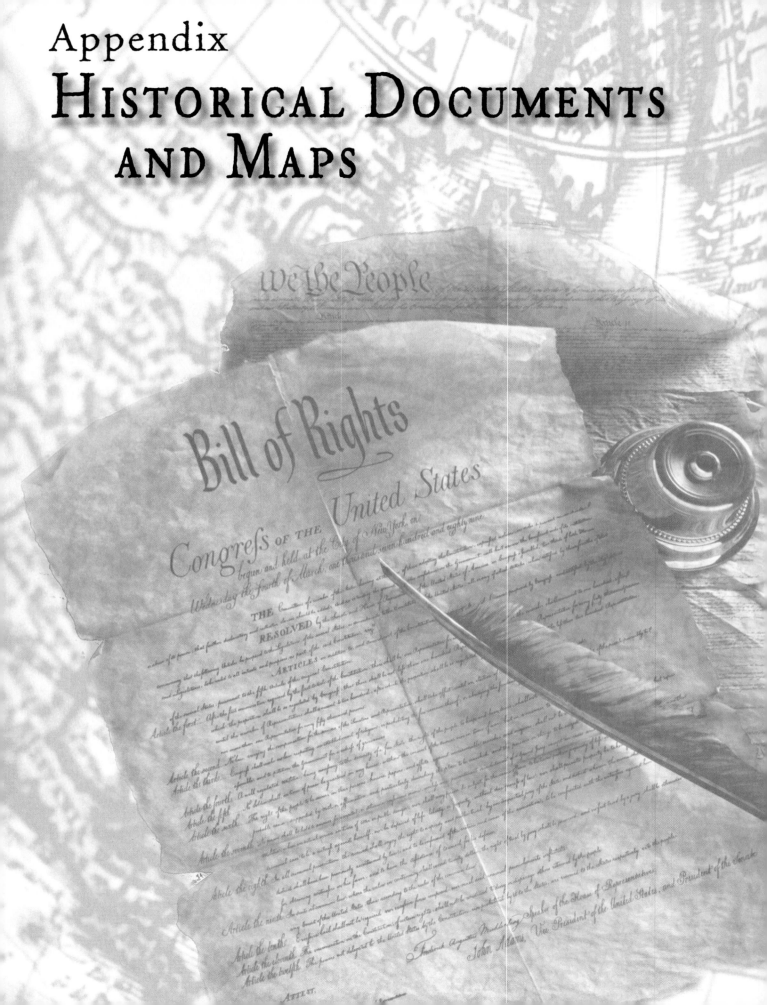

Appendix
HISTORICAL DOCUMENTS
AND MAPS

The Declaration of Independence

Action of Second Continental Congress, July 4, 1776

The unanimous Declaration of the thirteen United States of America

WHEN in the Course of human Events, it becomes necessary for one People to dissolve the Political Bands which have connected them with another, and to assume among the Powers of the Earth, the separate and equal Station to which the Laws of Nature and of Nature's God entitle them, a decent Respect to the Opinions of Mankind requires that they should declare the causes which impel them to the Separation.

WE hold these Truths to be self-evident, that all Men are created equal, that they are endowed by their Creator with certain unalienable Rights, that among these are Life, Liberty and the Pursuit of Happiness — That to secure these Rights, Governments are instituted among Men, deriving their just Powers from the Consent of the Governed, that whenever any Form of Government becomes destructive of these Ends, it is the Right of the People to alter or to abolish it, and to institute new Government, laying its Foundation on such Principles, and organizing its Powers in such Form, as to them shall seem most likely to effect their Safety and Happiness. Prudence, indeed, will dictate that Governments long established should not be changed for light and transient Causes; and accordingly all Experience hath shewn, that Mankind are more disposed to suffer, while Evils are sufferable, than to right themselves by abolishing the Forms to which they are accustomed. But when a long Train of Abuses and Usurpations, pursuing invariably the same Object, evinces a Design to reduce them under absolute Despotism, it is their Right, it is their Duty, to throw off such Government, and to provide new Guards for their future Security. Such has been the patient Sufferance of these Colonies; and such is now the Necessity which constrains them to alter their former Systems of Government. The History of the present King of Great- Britain is a History of repeated Injuries and Usurpations, all having in direct Object the Establishment of an absolute Tyranny over these States. To prove this, let Facts be submitted to a candid World.

HE has refused his Assent to Laws, the most wholesome and necessary for the public Good.

HE has forbidden his Governors to pass Laws of immediate and pressing Importance, unless suspended in their Operation till his Assent should be obtained; and when so suspended, he has utterly neglected to attend to them.

HE has refused to pass other Laws for the Accommodation of large Districts of People, unless those People would relinquish the Right of Representation in the Legislature, a Right inestimable to them, and formidable to Tyrants only.

HE has called together Legislative Bodies at Places unusual, uncomfortable, and distant from the Depository of their public Records, for the sole Purpose of fatiguing them into Compliance with his Measures.

HE has dissolved Representative Houses repeatedly, for opposing with manly Firmness his Invasions on the Rights of the People.

HE has refused for a long Time, after such Dissolutions, to cause others to be elected; whereby the Legislative Powers, incapable of the Annihilation, have returned to the People at large for their exercise; the State remaining in the mean time exposed to all the Dangers of Invasion from without, and the Convulsions within.

HE has endeavoured to prevent the Population of these States; for that Purpose obstructing the Laws for Naturalization of Foreigners; refusing to pass others to encourage their Migrations hither, and raising the Conditions of new Appropriations of Lands.

HE has obstructed the Administration of Justice, by refusing his Assent to Laws for establishing Judiciary Powers.

HE has made Judges dependent on his Will alone, for the Tenure of their Offices, and the Amount and Payment of their Salaries.

HE has erected a Multitude of new Offices, and sent hither Swarms of Officers to harrass our People, and eat out their Substance.

HE has kept among us, in Times of Peace, Standing Armies, without the consent of our Legislatures.

HE has affected to render the Military independent of and superior to the Civil Power.

HE has combined with others to subject us to a Jurisdiction foreign to our Constitution, and unacknowledged by our Laws; giving his Assent to their Acts of pretended Legislation:

FOR quartering large Bodies of Armed Troops among us;

FOR protecting them, by a mock Trial, from Punishment for any Murders which they should commit on the Inhabitants of these States:

FOR cutting off our Trade with all Parts of the World:

FOR imposing Taxes on us without our Consent:

FOR depriving us, in many Cases, of the Benefits of Trial by Jury:

FOR transporting us beyond Seas to be tried for pretended Offences:

FOR abolishing the free System of English Laws in a neighbouring Province, establishing therein an arbitrary Government, and enlarging its Boundaries, so as to render it at once an Example and fit Instrument for introducing the same absolute Rules into these Colonies:

FOR taking away our Charters, abolishing our most valuable Laws, and altering fundamentally the Forms of our Governments:

FOR suspending our own Legislatures, and declaring themselves invested with Power to legislate for us in all Cases whatsoever.

HE has abdicated Government here, by declaring us out of his Protection and waging War against us.

HE has plundered our Seas, ravaged our Coasts, burnt our Towns, and destroyed the Lives of our People.

HE is, at this Time, transporting large Armies of foreign Mercenaries to compleat the Works of Death, Desolation, and Tyranny, already begun with circumstances of Cruelty and Perfidy, scarcely paralleled in the most barbarous Ages, and totally unworthy the Head of a civilized Nation.

HE has constrained our fellow Citizens taken Captive on the high Seas to bear Arms against their Country, to become the Executioners of their Friends and Brethren, or to fall themselves by their Hands.

HE has excited domestic Insurrections amongst us, and has endeavoured to bring on the Inhabitants of our Frontiers, the merciless Indian Savages, whose known Rule of Warfare, is an undistinguished Destruction, of all Ages, Sexes and Conditions.

IN every stage of these Oppressions we have Petitioned for Redress in the most humble Terms: Our repeated Petitions have been answered only by repeated Injury. A Prince, whose Character is thus marked by every act which may define a Tyrant, is unfit to be the Ruler of a free People.

NOR have we been wanting in Attentions to our British Brethren. We have warned them from Time to Time of Attempts by their Legislature to extend an unwarrantable Jurisdiction over us. We have reminded them of the Circumstances of our Emigration and Settlement here. We have appealed to their native Justice and Magnanimity, and we have conjured them by the Ties of our common Kindred to disavow these Usurpations, which, would inevitably interrupt our Connections and Correspondence. They too have been deaf to the Voice of Justice and of Consanguinity. We must, therefore, acquiesce in the Necessity, which denounces our Separation, and hold them, as we hold the rest of Mankind, Enemies in War, in Peace, Friends.

WE, therefore, the Representatives of the UNITED STATES OF AMERICA, in GENERAL CONGRESS, Assembled, appealing to the Supreme Judge of the World for the Rectitude of our Intentions, do, in the Name, and by Authority of the good People of these Colonies, solemnly Publish and Declare, That these United Colonies are, and of Right ought to be, FREE AND INDEPENDENT STATES; that they are absolved from all Allegiance to the British Crown, and that all political Connection between them and the State of Great-Britain, is and ought to be totally dissolved; and that as FREE AND INDEPENDENT STATES, they have full Power to levy War, conclude Peace, contract Alliances, establish Commerce, and to do all other Acts and Things which INDEPENDENT STATES may of right do. And for the support of this Declaration, with a firm Reliance on the Protection of divine Providence, we mutually pledge to each other our Lives, our Fortunes, and our sacred Honor.

John Hancock	Charles Carroll	Geo. Taylor	Josiah Bartlett
Button Gwinnett	Of Carrollton	James Wilson	Wm. Whipple
Lyman Hall	George Wythe	Geo. Ross	Saml Adams
Geo Walton	Richard Henry Lee	Caesar Rodney	John Adams
Wm Hooper	Th Jefferson	Geo Read	Robt Treat Paine
Joseph Hewes	Benja Harrison	Tho M. Kean	Elbridge Gerry
John Penn	Thos Nelson Jr.	Wm Floyd	Step Hopkins
Edward Rutledge	Francis Lightfoot Lee	Phil. Livingston	William Ellery
Thos Heyward Junr.	Carter Braxton	Frans. Lewis	Roger Sherman
Thomas Lynch Junr.	Robt Morris	Lewis Morris	Samel Huntington
Arthur Middleton	Benjamin Rush	Richd. Stockton	Wm. Williams
Samuel Chase	Benja. Franklin	Jno Witherspoon	Oliver Wolcott
Wm. Paca	John Morton	Fras. Hopkinson	Matthew Thornton
Thos. Stone	Geo Clymer	John Hart	
	Jas. Smith	Abra Clark	

The United States Constitution

The pages that follow contain the original text of the United States Constitution. Sections that are no longer enforced have been crossed out. The spelling and punctuation of the document remain in their original format. The headings are not part of the original Constitution.

We the People of the United States, in Order to form a more perfect Union, establish Justice, insure domestic Tranquility, provide for the common defence, promote the general Welfare, and secure the Blessings of Liberty to ourselves and our Posterity, do ordain and establish this Constitution for the United States of America.

Article I
Legislative Branch

Section 1
Congress

All legislative Powers herein granted shall be vested in a Congress of the United States, which shall consist of a Senate and House of Representatives.

Section 2
House of Representatives

Clause 1: The House of Representatives shall be composed of Members chosen every second Year by the People of the several States, and the Electors in each State shall have the Qualifications requisite for Electors of the most numerous Branch of the State Legislature.

Clause 2: No Person shall be a Representative who shall not have attained to the Age of twenty five Years, and been seven Years a Citizen of the United States, and who shall not, when elected, be an Inhabitant of that State in which he shall be chosen.

Clause 3: Representatives and direct Taxes shall be apportioned among the several States which may be included within this Union, according to their respective Numbers, ~~which shall be determined by adding to the whole Number of free Persons, including those bound to Service for a Term of Years, and excluding Indians not taxed, three fifths of all other Persons.~~

The actual Enumeration shall be made within three Years after the first Meeting of the Congress of the United States, and within every subsequent Term of ten Years, in such Manner as they shall by Law direct.

The Number of Representatives shall not exceed one for every thirty Thousand, but each State shall have at Least one Representative; ~~and until such enumeration shall be made, the State of New Hampshire shall be entitled to chuse three, Massachusetts eight, Rhode-Island and Providence Plantations one, Connecticut five, New-York six, New Jersey four, Pennsylvania eight, Delaware one, Maryland six, Virginia ten, North Carolina five, South Carolina five, and Georgia three.~~

Clause 4: When vacancies happen in the Representation from any State, the Executive Authority thereof shall issue Writs of Election to fill such Vacancies.

Clause 5: The House of Representatives shall chuse their Speaker and other Officers; and shall have the sole Power of Impeachment.

Section 3
Senate

Clause 1: The Senate of the United States shall be composed of two Senators from each State, chosen by the Legislature thereof, for six Years; and each Senator shall have one Vote.

Clause 2: Immediately after they shall be assembled in Consequence of the first Election, they shall be divided as equally as may be into three Classes. The Seats of the Senators of the first Class shall be vacated at the Expiration of the second Year, of the second Class at the Expiration of the fourth Year, and of the third Class at the Expiration of the sixth Year, so that one third may be chosen every second Year; and if Vacancies happen by Resignation, or otherwise, during the Recess of the Legislature of any State, the Executive thereof may make temporary Appointments until the next Meeting of the Legislature, which shall then fill such Vacancies.

Clause 3: No Person shall be a Senator who shall not have attained to the Age of thirty Years, and been nine Years a Citizen of the United States, and who shall not, when elected, be an Inhabitant of that State for which he shall be chosen.

Clause 4: The Vice President of the United States shall be President of the Senate, but shall have no Vote, unless they be equally divided.

Clause 5: The Senate shall chuse their other Officers, and also a President pro tempore, in the Absence of the Vice President, or when he shall exercise the Office of President of the United States.

Clause 6: The Senate shall have the sole Power to try all Impeachments. When sitting for that Purpose, they shall be on Oath or Affirmation. When the President of the United States is tried, the Chief Justice shall preside: And no Person shall be convicted without the Concurrence of two thirds of the Members present.

Clause 7: Judgment in Cases of Impeachment shall not extend further than to removal from Office, and disqualification to hold and enjoy any Office of honor, Trust or Profit under the United States: but the Party convicted shall nevertheless be liable and subject to Indictment, Trial, Judgment and Punishment, according to Law.

Section 4
Elections and Meetings

Clause 1: The Times, Places and Manner of holding Elections for Senators and Representatives, shall be prescribed in each State by the Legislature thereof; but the Congress may at any time by Law make or alter such Regulations, except as to the Places of chusing Senators.

Clause 2: The Congress shall assemble at least once in every Year, and such Meeting shall be on the first Monday in December, unless they shall by Law appoint a different Day.

Section 5
Rules of Procedure

Clause 1: Each House shall be the Judge of the Elections, Returns and Qualifications of its own Members, and a Majority of each shall constitute a Quorum to do Business; but a smaller Number may adjourn from day to day, and may be authorized to compel the Attendance of absent Members, in such Manner, and under such Penalties as each House may provide.

Clause 2: Each House may determine the Rules of its Proceedings, punish its Members for disorderly Behaviour, and, with the Concurrence of two thirds, expel a Member.

Clause 3: Each House shall keep a Journal of its Proceedings, and from time to time publish the same, excepting such Parts as may in their Judgment require Secrecy; and the Yeas and

Nays of the Members of either House on any question shall, at the Desire of one fifth of those Present, be entered on the Journal.

Clause 4: Neither House, during the Session of Congress, shall, without the Consent of the other, adjourn for more than three days, nor to any other Place than that in which the two Houses shall be sitting.

Section 6
Privileges and Restrictions

Clause 1: The Senators and Representatives shall receive a Compensation for their Services, to be ascertained by Law, and paid out of the Treasury of the United States. They shall in all Cases, except Treason, Felony and Breach of the Peace, be privileged from Arrest during their Attendance at the Session of their respective Houses, and in going to and returning from the same; and for any Speech or Debate in either House, they shall not be questioned in any other Place.

Clause 2: No Senator or Representative shall, during the Time for which he was elected, be appointed to any civil Office under the Authority of the United States, which shall have been created, or the Emoluments whereof shall have been encreased during such time; and no Person holding any Office under the United States, shall be a Member of either House during his Continuance in Office.

Section 7
How Bills Become Laws

Clause 1: All Bills for raising Revenue shall originate in the House of Representatives; but the Senate may propose or concur with Amendments as on other Bills.

Clause 2: Every Bill which shall have passed the House of Representatives and the Senate, shall, before it become a Law, be presented to the President of the United States; If he approve he shall sign it, but if not he shall return it, with his Objections to that House

in which it shall have originated, who shall enter the Objections at large on their Journal, and proceed to reconsider it. If after such Reconsideration two thirds of that House shall agree to pass the Bill, it shall be sent, together with the Objections, to the other House, by which it shall likewise be reconsidered, and if approved by two thirds of that House, it shall become a Law. But in all such Cases the Votes of both Houses shall be determined by yeas and Nays, and the Names of the Persons voting for and against the Bill shall be entered on the Journal of each House respectively.

If any Bill shall not be returned by the President within ten Days (Sundays excepted) after it shall have been presented to him, the Same shall be a Law, in like Manner as if he had signed it, unless the Congress by their Adjournment prevent its Return, in which Case it shall not be a Law.

Clause 3: Every Order, Resolution, or Vote to which the Concurrence of the Senate and House of Representatives may be necessary (except on a question of Adjournment) shall be presented to the President of the United States; and before the Same shall take Effect, shall be approved by him, or being disapproved by him, shall be repassed by two thirds of the Senate and House of Representatives, according to the Rules and Limitations prescribed in the Case of a Bill.

Section 8
Powers of Congress

Clause 1: The Congress shall have Power To lay and collect Taxes, Duties, Imposts and Excises, to pay the Debts and provide for the common Defence and general Welfare of the United States; but all Duties, Imposts and Excises shall be uniform throughout the United States;

Clause 2: To borrow Money on the credit of the United States;

Clause 3: To regulate Commerce with foreign Nations, and among the several States, and with the Indian Tribes;

Clause 4: To establish an uniform Rule of Naturalization, and uniform Laws on the subject of Bankruptcies throughout the United States;

Clause 5: To coin Money, regulate the Value thereof, and of foreign Coin, and fix the Standard of Weights and Measures;

Clause 6: To provide for the Punishment of counterfeiting the Securities and current Coin of the United States;

Clause 7: To establish Post Offices and post Roads;

Clause 8: To promote the Progress of Science and useful Arts, by securing for limited Times to Authors and Inventors the exclusive Right to their respective Writings and Discoveries;

Clause 9: To constitute Tribunals inferior to the supreme Court;

Clause 10: To define and punish Piracies and Felonies committed on the high Seas, and Offences against the Law of Nations;

Clause 11: To declare War, grant Letters of Marque and Reprisal, and make Rules concerning Captures on Land and Water;

Clause 12: To raise and support Armies, but no Appropriation of Money to that Use shall be for a longer Term than two Years;

Clause 13: To provide and maintain a Navy;

Clause 14: To make Rules for the Government and Regulation of the land and naval Forces;

Clause 15: To provide for calling forth the Militia to execute the Laws of the Union, suppress Insurrections and repel Invasions;

Clause 16: To provide for organizing, arming, and disciplining, the Militia, and for governing such Part of them as may be employed in the Service of the United

States, reserving to the States respectively, the Appointment of the Officers, and the Authority of training the Militia according to the discipline prescribed by Congress;

Clause 17: To exercise exclusive Legislation in all Cases whatsoever, over such District (not exceeding ten Miles square) as may, by Cession of particular States, and the Acceptance of Congress, become the Seat of the Government of the United States, and to exercise like Authority over all Places purchased by the Consent of the Legislature of the State in which the Same shall be, for the Erection of Forts, Magazines, Arsenals, dock-Yards, and other needful Buildings;—And

Clause 18: To make all Laws which shall be necessary and proper for carrying into Execution the foregoing Powers, and all other Powers vested by this Constitution in the Government of the United States, or in any Department or Officer thereof.

Section 9
Powers Denied to the Federal Government

Clause 1: ~~The Migration or Importation of such Persons as any of the States now existing shall think proper to admit, shall not be prohibited by the Congress prior to the Year one thousand eight hundred and eight, but a Tax or duty may be imposed on such Importation, not exceeding ten dollars for each Person.~~

Clause 2: The Privilege of the Writ of Habeas Corpus shall not be suspended, unless when in Cases of Rebellion or Invasion the public Safety may require it.

Clause 3: No Bill of Attainder or ex post facto Law shall be passed.

Clause 4: No Capitation, or other direct, Tax shall be laid, unless in Proportion to the Census or Enumeration herein before directed to be taken.

Clause 5: No Tax or Duty shall be laid on Articles exported from any State.

Clause 6: No Preference shall be given by any Regulation of Commerce or Revenue to the Ports of one State over those of another: nor shall Vessels bound to, or from, one State, be obliged to enter, clear, or pay Duties in another.

Clause 7: No Money shall be drawn from the Treasury, but in Consequence of Appropriations made by Law; and a regular Statement and Account of the Receipts and Expenditures of all public Money shall be published from time to time.

Clause 8: No Title of Nobility shall be granted by the United States: And no Person holding any Office of Profit or Trust under them, shall, without the Consent of the Congress, accept of any present, Emolument, Office, or Title, of any kind whatever, from any King, Prince, or foreign State.

Section 10
Powers Denied to the States

Clause 1: No State shall enter into any Treaty, Alliance, or Confederation; grant Letters of Marque and Reprisal; coin Money; emit Bills of Credit; make any Thing but gold and silver Coin a Tender in Payment of Debts; pass any Bill of Attainder, ex post facto Law, or Law impairing the Obligation of Contracts, or grant any Title of Nobility.

Clause 2: No State shall, without the Consent of the Congress, lay any Imposts or Duties on Imports or Exports, except what may be absolutely necessary for executing it's inspection Laws: and the net Produce of all Duties and Imposts, laid by any State on Imports or Exports, shall be for the Use of the Treasury of the United States; and all such Laws shall be subject to the Revision and Controul of the Congress.

Clause 3: No State shall, without the Consent of Congress, lay any Duty of Tonnage, keep Troops, or Ships of War in time of Peace, enter into any Agreement or Compact with another State, or with a

foreign Power, or engage in War, unless actually invaded, or in such imminent Danger as will not admit of delay.

Article II Executive Branch

Section 1
President and Vice-President

Clause 1: The executive Power shall be vested in a President of the United States of America. He shall hold his Office during the Term of four Years, and, together with the Vice President, chosen for the same Term, be elected, as follows

Clause 2: Each State shall appoint, in such Manner as the Legislature thereof may direct, a Number of Electors, equal to the whole Number of Senators and Representatives to which the State may be entitled in the Congress: but no Senator or Representative, or Person holding an Office of Trust or Profit under the United States, shall be appointed an Elector.

Clause 3: ~~The Electors shall meet in their respective States, and vote by Ballot for two Persons, of whom one at least shall not be an Inhabitant of the same State with themselves. And they shall make a List of all the Persons voted for, and of the Number of Votes for each; which List they shall sign and certify, and transmit sealed to the Seat of the Government of the United States, directed to the President of the Senate. The President of the Senate shall, in the Presence of the Senate and House of Representatives, open all the Certificates, and the Votes shall then be counted. The Person having the greatest Number of Votes shall be the President, if such Number be a Majority of the whole Number of Electors appointed; and if there be more than one who have such Majority, and have an equal Number of Votes, then the House of Representatives shall immediately chuse by Ballot one of them for President; and if no Person have a Majority, then from the five highest on the~~

List the said House shall in like Manner chuse the President. But in chusing the President, the Votes shall be taken by States, the Representation from each State having one Vote; A quorum for this Purpose shall consist of a Member or Members from two thirds of the States, and a Majority of all the States shall be necessary to a Choice. In every Case, after the Choice of the President, the Person having the greatest Number of Votes of the Electors shall be the Vice President. But if there should remain two or more who have equal Votes, the Senate shall chuse from them by Ballot the Vice President.

Clause 4: The Congress may determine the Time of chusing the Electors, and the Day on which they shall give their Votes; which Day shall be the same throughout the United States.

Clause 5: No Person except a natural born Citizen, or a Citizen of the United States, at the time of the Adoption of this Constitution, shall be eligible to the Office of President; neither shall any Person be eligible to that Office who shall not have attained to the Age of thirty five Years, and been fourteen Years a Resident within the United States.

Clause 6: In Case of the Removal of the President from Office, or of his Death, Resignation, or Inability to discharge the Powers and Duties of the said Office, the Same shall devolve on the Vice President, and the Congress may by Law provide for the Case of Removal, Death, Resignation or Inability, both of the President and Vice President, declaring what Officer shall then act as President, and such Officer shall act accordingly, until the Disability be removed, or a President shall be elected.

Clause 7: The President shall, at stated Times, receive for his Services, a Compensation, which shall neither be encreased nor diminished during the Period for which he shall have been elected, and he shall not receive within that Period any other Emolument from the United States, or any of them.

Clause 8: Before he enter on the Execution of his Office, he shall take the following Oath or Affirmation:—"I do solemnly swear (or affirm) that I will faithfully execute the Office of President of the United States, and will to the best of my Ability, preserve, protect and defend the Constitution of the United States."

Section 2
Powers of the President

Clause 1: The President shall be Commander in Chief of the Army and Navy of the United States, and of the Militia of the several States, when called into the actual Service of the United States; he may require the Opinion, in writing, of the principal Officer in each of the executive Departments, upon any Subject relating to the Duties of their respective Offices, and he shall have Power to grant Reprieves and Pardons for Offences against the United States, except in Cases of Impeachment.

Clause 2: He shall have Power, by and with the Advice and Consent of the Senate, to make Treaties, provided two thirds of the Senators present concur; and he shall nominate, and by and with the Advice and Consent of the Senate, shall appoint Ambassadors, other public Ministers and Consuls, Judges of the supreme Court, and all other Officers of the United States, whose Appointments are not herein otherwise provided for, and which shall be established by Law: but the Congress may by Law vest the Appointment of such inferior Officers, as they think proper, in the President alone, in the Courts of Law, or in the Heads of Departments.

Clause 3: The President shall have Power to fill up all Vacancies that may happen during the Recess of the Senate, by granting Commissions which shall expire at the End of their next Session.

Section 3
Duties of the President

He shall from time to time give to the Congress Information of the State of the Union, and recommend to their Consideration such Measures as he shall judge necessary and expedient; he may, on extraordinary Occasions, convene both Houses, or either of them, and in Case of Disagreement between them, with Respect to the Time of Adjournment, he may adjourn them to such Time as he shall think proper; he shall receive Ambassadors and other public Ministers; he shall take Care that the Laws be faithfully executed, and shall Commission all the Officers of the United States.

Section 4
Impeachment

The President, Vice President and all civil Officers of the United States, shall be removed from Office on Impeachment for, and Conviction of, Treason, Bribery, or other high Crimes and Misdemeanors.

Article III
Judicial Branch

Section 1
Federal Courts

The judicial Power of the United States, shall be vested in one supreme Court, and in such inferior Courts as the Congress may from time to time ordain and establish. The Judges, both of the supreme and inferior Courts, shall hold their Offices during good Behaviour, and shall, at stated Times, receive for their Services, a Compensation, which shall not be diminished during their Continuance in Office.

Section 2
Extent of Judicial Powers

Clause 1: The judicial Power shall extend to all Cases, in Law and Equity, arising under this Constitution, the Laws of the United States, and Treaties made, or which shall be made, under their Authority;—to all Cases affecting Ambassadors, other public Ministers and Consuls;—to all Cases of admiralty and maritime Jurisdiction;—to Controversies to which the United States shall be a Party;—to Controversies between two or more States;—between a State and Citizens of another State; —between Citizens of different States, —between Citizens of the same State claiming Lands under Grants of different States, and between a State, or the Citizens thereof, and foreign States, Citizens or Subjects.

Clause 2: In all Cases affecting Ambassadors, other public Ministers and Consuls, and those in which a State shall be Party, the supreme Court shall have original Jurisdiction. In all the other Cases before mentioned, the supreme Court shall have appellate Jurisdiction, both as to Law and Fact, with such Exceptions, and under such Regulations as the Congress shall make.

Clause 3: The Trial of all Crimes, except in Cases of Impeachment, shall be by Jury; and such Trial shall be held in the State where the said Crimes shall have been committed; but when not committed within any State, the Trial shall be at such Place or Places as the Congress may by Law have directed.

Section 3
Treason

Clause 1: Treason against the United States, shall consist only in levying War against them, or in adhering to their Enemies, giving them Aid and Comfort. No Person shall be convicted of Treason unless on the Testimony of two Witnesses to the same overt Act, or on Confession in open Court.

Clause 2: The Congress shall have Power to declare the Punishment of Treason, but no Attainder of Treason shall work Corruption of Blood, or Forfeiture except during the Life of the Person attainted.

Article IV
The States

Section 1
Recognition of Each Other's Acts

Full Faith and Credit shall be given in each State to the public Acts, Records, and judicial Proceedings of every other State. And the Congress may by general Laws prescribe the Manner in which such Acts, Records and Proceedings shall be proved, and the Effect thereof.

Section 2
Citizens' Rights in Other States

Clause 1: The Citizens of each State shall be entitled to all Privileges and Immunities of Citizens in the several States.

Clause 2: A Person charged in any State with Treason, Felony, or other Crime, who shall flee from Justice, and be found in another State, shall on Demand of the executive Authority of the State from which he fled, be delivered up, to be removed to the State having Jurisdiction of the Crime.

Clause 3: No Person held to Service or Labour in one State, under the Laws thereof, escaping into another, shall, in Consequence of any Law or Regulation therein, be discharged from such Service or Labour, but shall be delivered up on Claim of the Party to whom such Service or Labour may be due.

Section 3
New States and Territories

Clause 1: New States may be admitted by the Congress into this Union; but no new State shall be formed or erected within the Jurisdiction of any other State; nor any State be formed by the Junction of two or more States, or Parts of States, without the Consent of the Legislatures of the States concerned as well as of the Congress.

Clause 2: The Congress shall have Power to dispose of and make all needful Rules and Regulations respecting the Territory or other Property belonging to the United States; and nothing in this Constitution shall be so construed as to Prejudice any Claims of the United States, or of any particular State.

Section 4
Guarantees to the States

The United States shall guarantee to every State in this Union a Republican Form of Government, and shall protect each of them against Invasion; and on Application of the Legislature, or of the Executive (when the Legislature cannot be convened) against domestic Violence.

Article V
Amending the Constitution

The Congress, whenever two thirds of both Houses shall deem it necessary, shall propose Amendments to this Constitution, or, on the Application of the Legislatures of two thirds of the several States, shall call a Convention for proposing Amendments, which, in either Case, shall be valid to all Intents and Purposes, as Part of this Constitution, when ratified by the Legislatures of three fourths of the several States, or by Conventions in three fourths thereof, as the one or the other Mode of Ratification may be proposed by the Congress; Provided that no Amendment which may be made prior to the Year One thousand eight hundred and eight shall in any Manner affect the first and fourth Clauses in the Ninth Section of the first Article; and that no State, without its Consent, shall be deprived of its equal Suffrage in the Senate.

Article VI
National Supremacy

Clause 1: All Debts contracted and Engagements entered into, before the Adoption of this Constitution, shall be as

valid against the United States under this Constitution, as under the Confederation.

Clause 2: This Constitution, and the Laws of the United States which shall be made in Pursuance thereof; and all Treaties made, or which shall be made, under the Authority of the United States, shall be the supreme Law of the Land; and the Judges in every State shall be bound thereby, any Thing in the Constitution or Laws of any State to the Contrary notwithstanding.

Clause 3: The Senators and Representatives before mentioned, and the Members of the several State Legislatures, and all executive and judicial Officers, both of the United States and of the several States, shall be bound by Oath or Affirmation, to support this Constitution; but no religious Test shall ever be required as a Qualification to any Office or public Trust under the United States.

Article VII
Ratification

The Ratification of the Conventions of nine States, shall be sufficient for the Establishment of this Constitution between the States so ratifying the Same. Done in Convention by the Unanimous Consent of the States present the Seventeenth Day of September in the Year of our Lord one thousand seven hundred and Eighty seven and of the Independence of the United States of America the Twelfth In witness whereof We have hereunto subscribed our Names,

---

George Washington, President and Deputy from Virginia

Delaware
> *George Read*
> *Gunning Bedford, Junior*
> *John Dickinson*
> *Richard Bassett*
> *Jacob Broom*

Maryland
> *James McHenry*
> *Daniel of St. Thomas Jenifer*
> *Daniel Carroll*

Virginia
> *John Blair*
> *James Madison, Junior*

North Carolina
> *William Blount*
> *Richard Dobbs Spaight*
> *Hugh Williamson*

South Carolina
> *John Rutledge*
> *Charles Cotesworth Pinckney*
> *Charles Pinckney*
> *Pierce Butler.*

Georgia
> *William Few*
> *Abraham Baldwin*

New Hampshire
> *John Langdon*
> *Nicholas Gilman*

Massachusetts
> *Nathaniel Gorham*
> *Rufus King*

Connecticut
> *William Samuel Johnson*
> *Roger Sherman*

New York
> *Alexander Hamilton*

New Jersey
> *William Livingston*
> *David Brearley*
> *William Paterson.*
> *Jonathan Dayton*

Pennsylvania
> *Benjamin Franklin*
> *Thomas Mifflin*
> *Robert Morris*
> *George Clymer*
> *Thomas FitzSimons*
> *Jared Ingersoll*
> *James Wilson*
> *Gouverneur Morris*
> *Attest: William Jackson, Secretary*

Amendments to the Constitution

The pages that follow contain the original text of the Amendments to the United States Constitution. Sections that are no longer enforced have been crossed out. The spelling and punctuation of the document remain in their original format. The headings are not part of the original Amendments.

Amendment 1 (1791)
Religious and Political Freedom

Congress shall make no law respecting an establishment of religion, or prohibiting the free exercise thereof; or abridging the freedom of speech, or of the press; or the right of the people peaceably to assemble, and to petition the Government for a redress of grievances.

Amendment 2 (1791)
Right to Bear Arms

A well regulated Militia, being necessary to the security of a free State, the right of the people to keep and bear Arms, shall not be infringed.

Amendment 3 (1791)
Quartering of Soldiers

No Soldier shall, in time of peace be quartered in any house, without the consent of the Owner, nor in time of war, but in a manner to be prescribed by law.

Amendment 4 (1791)
Search and Seizure

The right of the people to be secure in their persons, houses, papers, and effects, against unreasonable searches and seizures, shall not be violated, and no Warrants shall issue, but upon probable cause, supported by Oath or affirmation, and particularly describing the place to be searched, and the persons or things to be seized.

Amendment 5 (1791)
Life, Liberty, and Property

No person shall be held to answer for a capital, or otherwise infamous crime, unless on a presentment or indictment of a Grand Jury, except in cases arising in the land or naval forces, or in the Militia, when in actual service in time of War or public danger; nor shall any person be subject for the same offence to be twice put in jeopardy of life or limb; nor shall be compelled in any criminal case to be a witness against himself, nor be deprived of life, liberty, or property, without due process of law; nor shall private property be taken for public use, without just compensation.

Amendment 6 (1791)
Rights of the Accused

In all criminal prosecutions, the accused shall enjoy the right to a speedy and public trial, by an impartial jury of the State and district wherein the crime shall have been committed, which district shall have been previously ascertained by law, and to be informed of the nature and cause of the accusation; to be confronted with the witnesses against him; to have compulsory process for obtaining witnesses in his favor, and to have the Assistance of Counsel for his defence.

Amendment 7 (1791)
Right to Trial by Jury

In Suits at common law, where the value in controversy shall exceed twenty dollars, the right of trial by jury shall be preserved, and no fact tried by a jury, shall be otherwise re-examined in any Court of the United States, than according to the rules of the common law.

Amendment 8 (1791)
Bail and Punishment

Excessive bail shall not be required, nor excessive fines imposed, nor cruel and unusual punishments inflicted.

Amendment 9 (1791)
All Other Rights

The enumeration in the Constitution, of certain rights, shall not be construed to deny or disparage others retained by the people.

Amendment 10 (1791)
Rights of States and the People

The powers not delegated to the United States by the Constitution, nor prohibited by it to the States, are reserved to the States respectively, or to the people.

Amendment 11 (1795)
Suits Against a State

The Judicial power of the United States shall not be construed to extend to any suit in law or equity, commenced or prosecuted against one of the United States by Citizens of another State, or by Citizens or Subjects of any Foreign State.

Amendment 12 (1804)
Election of President

The Electors shall meet in their respective states, and vote by ballot for President and Vice-President, one of whom, at least, shall not be an inhabitant of the same state with themselves; they shall name in their ballots the person voted for as President, and in distinct ballots the person voted for as Vice-President, and they shall make distinct lists of all persons voted for as President, and of all persons voted for as Vice-President, and of the number of votes for each, which lists they shall sign and certify, and transmit sealed to the seat of the government of the United States, directed to the President of the Senate;

The President of the Senate shall, in the presence of the Senate and House of Representatives, open all the certificates and the votes shall then be counted;

The person having the greatest number of votes for President, shall be the President, if such number be a majority of the whole number of Electors appointed; and if no person have such majority, then from the persons having the highest numbers not exceeding three on the list of those voted for as President, the House of Representatives shall choose immediately, by ballot, the President. But in choosing the President, the votes shall be taken by states, the representation from each state having one vote; a quorum for this purpose shall consist of a member or members from two-thirds of the states, and a majority of all the states shall be necessary to a choice.

And if the House of Representatives shall not choose a President whenever the right of choice shall devolve upon them, before the fourth day of March next following, then the Vice-President shall act as President, as in the case of the death or other constitutional disability of the President.

The person having the greatest number of votes as Vice-President, shall be the Vice-President, if such number be a majority of the whole number of Electors appointed, and if no person have a majority, then from the two highest numbers on the list, the Senate shall choose the Vice-President; a quorum for the purpose shall consist of two-thirds of the whole number of Senators, and a majority of the whole number shall be necessary to a choice. But no person constitutionally ineligible to the office of

President shall be eligible to that of Vice-President of the United States.

Amendment 13 (1865)
Abolition of Slavery

Section 1 Neither slavery nor involuntary servitude, except as a punishment for crime whereof the party shall have been duly convicted, shall exist within the United States, or any place subject to their jurisdiction.

Section 2 Congress shall have power to enforce this article by appropriate legislation.

Amendment 14 (1868)
Civil Rights in the States

Section 1 All persons born or naturalized in the United States, and subject to the jurisdiction thereof, are citizens of the United States and of the State wherein they reside. No State shall make or enforce any law which shall abridge the privileges or immunities of citizens of the United States; nor shall any State deprive any person of life, liberty, or property, without due process of law; nor deny to any person within its jurisdiction the equal protection of the laws.

Section 2 Representatives shall be apportioned among the several States according to their respective numbers, counting the whole number of persons in each State, excluding Indians not taxed. But when the right to vote at any election for the choice of electors for President and Vice President of the United States, Representatives in Congress, the Executive and Judicial officers of a State, or the members of the Legislature thereof, is denied to any of the male inhabitants of such State, being twenty-one years of age,(See Note 15) and citizens of the United States, or in any way abridged, except for participation in rebellion, or other crime, the basis of representation therein shall be reduced in the proportion which the number of such male citizens shall bear to the whole number of male citizens twenty-one years of age in such State.

Section 3 No person shall be a Senator or Representative in Congress, or elector of President and Vice President, or hold any office, civil or military, under the United States, or under any State, who, having previously taken an oath, as a member of Congress, or as an officer of the United States, or as a member of any State legislature, or as an executive or judicial officer of any State, to support the Constitution of the United States, shall have engaged in insurrection or rebellion against the same, or given aid or comfort to the enemies thereof. But Congress may by a vote of two-thirds of each House, remove such disability.

Section 4 The validity of the public debt of the United States, authorized by law, including debts incurred for payment of pensions and bounties for services in suppressing insurrection or rebellion, shall not be questioned. But neither the United States nor any State shall assume or pay any debt or obligation incurred in aid of insurrection or rebellion against the United States, or any claim for the loss or emancipation of any slave; but all such debts, obligations and claims shall be held illegal and void.

Section 5 The Congress shall have power to enforce, by appropriate legislation, the provisions of this article.

Amendment 15 (1870)
Black Suffrage

Section 1 The right of citizens of the United States to vote shall not be denied or abridged by the United States or by any State on account of race, color, or previous condition of servitude.

Section 2 The Congress shall have power to enforce this article by appropriate legislation.

Amendment 16 (1913)
Income Tax

The Congress shall have power to lay and collect taxes on incomes, from whatever source derived, without apportionment among the several States, and without regard to any census or enumeration.

Amendment 17 (1919)
Direct Election of Senators

Section 1 The Senate of the United States shall be composed of two Senators from each State, elected by the people thereof, for six years; and each Senator shall have one vote. The electors in each State shall have the qualifications requisite for electors of the most numerous branch of the State legislatures.

Section 2 When vacancies happen in the representation of any State in the Senate, the executive authority of such State shall issue writs of election to fill such vacancies: Provided, That the legislature of any State may empower the executive thereof to make temporary appointments until the people fill the vacancies by election as the legislature may direct.

Section 3 This amendment shall not be so construed as to affect the election or term of any Senator chosen before it becomes valid as part of the Constitution.

Amendment 18 (1919)
National Prohibition

Section 1 ~~After one year from the ratification of this article the manufacture, sale, or transportation of intoxicating liquors within, the importation thereof into, or the exportation thereof from the United States and all territory subject to the jurisdiction thereof for beverage purposes is hereby prohibited.~~

Section 2 ~~The Congress and the several States shall have concurrent power to enforce this article by appropriate legislation.~~

Section 3 ~~This article shall be inoperative unless it shall have been ratified as an amendment to the Constitution by the legislatures of the several States, as provided in the Constitution, within seven years from the date of the submission hereof to the States by the Congress.~~

Amendment 19 (1920)
Women's Suffrage

The right of citizens of the United States to vote shall not be denied or abridged by the United States or by any State on account of sex.

Congress shall have power to enforce this article by appropriate legislation.

Amendment 20 (1933)
"Lame-Duck" Amendment

Section 1 The terms of the President and Vice President shall end at noon on the 20th day of January, and the terms of Senators and Representatives at noon on the 3d day of January, of the years in which such terms would have ended if this article had not been ratified; and the terms of their successors shall then begin.

Section 2 The Congress shall assemble at least once in every year, and such meeting shall begin at noon on the 3d day of January, unless they shall by law appoint a different day.

Section 3 If, at the time fixed for the beginning of the term of the President, the President elect shall have died, the Vice President elect shall become President. If a President shall not have been chosen before the time fixed for the beginning of his term, or if the President elect shall have failed to qualify, then the Vice President elect shall act as President until a President shall have qualified; and the Congress may by law provide for the case wherein neither a President elect nor a Vice President elect shall have qualified, declaring who shall then act as President, or the manner in which one who is to act shall be selected, and such person shall act accordingly until a President or Vice President shall have qualified.

Section 4 The Congress may by law provide for the case of the death of any of the persons from whom the House of Representatives may choose a President whenever the right of choice shall have devolved upon them, and for the case of the death of any of the persons from whom the Senate may choose a Vice President whenever the right of choice shall have devolved upon them.

Section 5 Sections 1 and 2 shall take effect on the 15th day of October following the ratification of this article.

Section 6 This article shall be inoperative unless it shall have been ratified as an amendment to the Constitution by the legislatures of three-fourths of the several States within seven years from the date of its submission.

Amendment 21 (1933)
Repeal of Prohibition

Section 1 The eighteenth article of amendment to the Constitution of the United States is hereby repealed.

Section 2 The transportation or importation into any State, Territory, or possession of the United States for delivery or use therein of intoxicating liquors, in violation of the laws thereof, is hereby prohibited.

Section 3 This article shall be inoperative unless it shall have been ratified as an amendment to the Constitution by conventions in the several States, as provided in the Constitution, within seven years from the date of the submission hereof to the States by the Congress.

Amendment 22 (1951)
Presidential Term of Office

Section 1 No person shall be elected to the office of the President more than twice, and no person who has held the office of

President, or acted as President, for more than two years of a term to which some other person was elected President shall be elected to the office of the President more than once. ~~But this article shall not apply to any person holding the office of President when this article was proposed by the Congress, and shall not prevent any person who may be holding the office of President, or acting as President, during the term within which this article becomes operative from holding the office of President or acting as President during the remainder of such term.~~

Section 2 This article shall be inoperative unless it shall have been ratified as an amendment to the Constitution by the legislatures of three-fourths of the several states within seven years from the date of its submission to the states by the Congress.

Amendment 23 (1961)
Voting in the District of Columbia

Section 1 The District constituting the seat of government of the United States shall appoint in such manner as the Congress may direct:

A number of electors of President and Vice President equal to the whole number of Senators and Representatives in Congress to which the District would be entitled if it were a state, but in no event more than the least populous state; they shall be in addition to those appointed by the states, but they shall be considered, for the purposes of the election of President and Vice President, to be electors appointed by a state; and they shall meet in the District and perform such duties as provided by the twelfth article of amendment.

Section 2 The Congress shall have power to enforce this article by appropriate legislation.

Amendment 24 (1964)
Abolition of Poll Taxes

Section 1 The right of citizens of the United States to vote in any primary or other election for President or Vice President, for

electors for President or Vice President, or for Senator or Representative in Congress, shall not be denied or abridged by the United States or any state by reason of failure to pay any poll tax or other tax.

Section 2 The Congress shall have power to enforce this article by appropriate legislation.

Amendment 25 (1967)
Presidential Disability and Succession

Section 1 In case of the removal of the President from office or of his death or resignation, the Vice President shall become President.

Section 2 Whenever there is a vacancy in the office of the Vice President, the President shall nominate a Vice President who shall take office upon confirmation by a majority vote of both Houses of Congress.

Section 3 Whenever the President transmits to the President pro tempore of the Senate and the Speaker of the House of Representatives his written declaration that he is unable to discharge the powers and duties of his office, and until he transmits to them a written declaration to the contrary, such powers and duties shall be discharged by the Vice President as Acting President.

Section 4 Whenever the Vice President and a majority of either the principal officers of the executive departments or of such other body as Congress may by law provide, transmit to the President pro tempore of the Senate and the Speaker of the House of Representatives their written declaration that the President is unable to discharge the powers and duties of his office, the Vice President shall immediately assume the powers and duties of the office as Acting President.

Thereafter, when the President transmits to the President pro tempore of the Senate and

the Speaker of the House of Representatives his written declaration that no inability exists, he shall resume the powers and duties of his office unless the Vice President and a majority of either the principal officers of the executive department or of such other body as Congress may by law provide, transmit within four days to the President pro tempore of the Senate and the Speaker of the House of Representatives their written declaration that the President is unable to discharge the powers and duties of his office. Thereupon Congress shall decide the issue, assembling within forty-eight hours for that purpose if not in session. If the Congress, within twenty-one days after receipt of the latter written declaration, or, if Congress is not in session, within twenty-one days after Congress is required to assemble, determines by two-thirds vote of both Houses that the President is unable to discharge the powers and duties of his office, the Vice President shall continue to discharge the same as Acting President; otherwise, the President shall resume the powers and duties of his office.

Amendment 26 (1971)
Eighteen-Year-Old Vote

Section 1 The right of citizens of the United States, who are 18 years of age or older, to vote, shall not be denied or abridged by the United States or any state on account of age.

Section 2 The Congress shall have the power to enforce this article by appropriate legislation.

Amendment 27 (1992)
Congressional Salaries

No law varying the compensation for the services of the Senators and Representatives shall take effect until an election of Representatives shall have intervened.

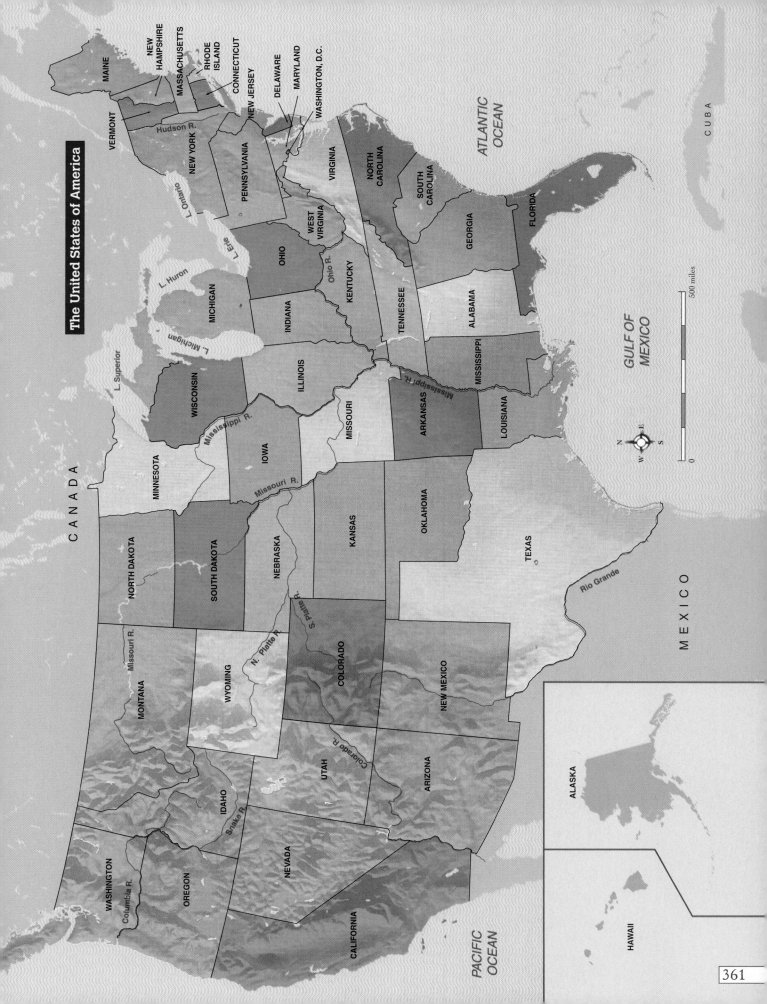

The United States of America

CANADA

MAINE

NEW HAMPSHIRE

VERMONT

MASSACHUSETTS

RHODE ISLAND

CONNECTICUT

NEW JERSEY

DELAWARE

MARYLAND

WASHINGTON, D.C.

Hudson R.

NEW YORK

PENNSYLVANIA

L. Ontario

L. Erie

WEST VIRGINIA

VIRGINIA

NORTH CAROLINA

SOUTH CAROLINA

GEORGIA

FLORIDA

ATLANTIC OCEAN

CUBA

L. Huron

MICHIGAN

L. Michigan

OHIO

KENTUCKY

TENNESSEE

ALABAMA

Ohio R.

INDIANA

ILLINOIS

L. Superior

WISCONSIN

Mississippi R.

MINNESOTA

IOWA

MISSOURI

ARKANSAS

Mississippi R.

MISSISSIPPI

LOUISIANA

Missouri R.

NORTH DAKOTA

SOUTH DAKOTA

NEBRASKA

KANSAS

OKLAHOMA

TEXAS

GULF OF MEXICO

500 miles

N
W   E
S

0

Rio Grande

MEXICO

Missouri R.

MONTANA

WYOMING

N. Platte R.

S. Platte R.

COLORADO

NEW MEXICO

Columbia R.

WASHINGTON

OREGON

IDAHO

Snake R.

NEVADA

UTAH

Colorado R.

ARIZONA

CALIFORNIA

PACIFIC OCEAN

ALASKA

HAWAII

361

Glossary/Index

Vocabulary definitions are shown in bold type.

Acknowledgements

Photo Credits

3 (t)©Bettmann/CORBIS, (bl)©Bettmann/CORBIS, (br)©Historical Picture Archive/CORBIS; 4 (t)©Michael Freeman/CORBIS, (b)©The Library of Congress, Prints and Photographs Division; 7 ©Bettmann/CORBIS; 8 ©The Library of Congress, Prints and Photographs Division; 9 ©The Academic Affairs Library, The University of North Carolina at Chapel Hill; 11 (t)©The Library of Congress, Prints and Photographs Division; 12 (l)©The Library of Congress, Prints and Photographs Division, (r)©CORBIS; 14 (t)©The Library of Congress, Prints and Photographs Division, (b)©CORBIS; 15 (t)©The Library of Congress, Prints and Photographs Division, (b)©The Library of Congress, Prints and Photographs Division; 16 (t)©Bettmann/CORBIS; 17 ©The Library of Congress, Prints and Photographs Division; 20 ©Bettmann/CORBIS; 21 ©Bettmann/CORBIS; 22 ©National Archives; 24 ©The Library of Congress, Prints and Photographs Division; 26 ©Bettmann/CORBIS; 27 ©Minnesota Historical Society/CORBIS; 28 (b)©CORBIS; 30 ©Bettmann/CORBIS; 31 (l)©Bettmann/CORBIS, (r)©Bettmann/CORBIS; 32 ©CORBIS; 33 ©The Granger Collection; 37 (t)©Bettmann/CORBIS, (bl)©The Library of Congress, Prints and Photographs Division, (br)©Bettmann/CORBIS; 38 (t)©James L. Amos/CORBIS, (b)©Bettmann/CORBIS; 39 ©Minnesota Historical Society/CORBIS; 40 ©The Library of Congress, Prints and Photographs Division; 41 ©CORBIS; 42 ©Bettmann/CORBIS; 44 (t)©Bettmann/CORBIS, (b)©The Library of Congress, Prints and Photographs Division; 45 (t)©CORBIS, (b)©Bettmann/CORBIS; 47 ©The Library of Congress, Prints and Photographs Division; 48 (t)©CORBIS, (b)©Bettmann/CORBIS; 49 ©Bettmann/CORBIS; 54 (t)©Getty Images, (b)©Bettmann/CORBIS; 55 ©The Library of Congress, Prints and Photographs Division; 57 (t)©The Mariners' Museum/CORBIS, (b)©CORBIS; 58 (t)©Bettmann/CORBIS, (b)©Bettmann/CORBIS; 59 ©Bettmann/CORBIS; 60 (t)©Schenectady Museum; Hall of Electrical History Foundation/CORBIS, (b)©Bettmann/CORBIS; 61 ©Underwood & Underwood/CORBIS; 64 (t)©Bettmann/CORBIS, (b)©Wisconsin Historical Society; 65 ©Bettmann/CORBIS; 66 ©David J. & Janice L. Frent Collection/CORBIS; 67 ©CORBIS; 71 (t)©Hulton-Deutsch Collection/CORBIS, (bl)©CORBIS, (br)©Bettmann/CORBIS; 72 (t)©David J. & Janice L. Frent Collection/CORBIS, (b)©CORBIS; 73 ©The Mariners' Museum/CORBIS; 74 (t)©The Granger Collection, (b)©Bettmann/CORBIS; 75 ©Naval Historical Center; 76 ©Getty Images; 77 ©Bettmann/CORBIS; 78 ©The Granger Collection; 79 ©The Library of Congress, Prints and Photographs Division; 80 ©Bettmann/CORBIS; 81 ©Bettmann/CORBIS; 82 ©Bettmann/CORBIS; 83 ©Bettmann/CORBIS; 84 ©The Granger Collection; 88 (t)©David J. & Janice L. Frent Collection/CORBIS, (b)©Bettmann/CORBIS; 90 ©CORBIS; 91 ©The Library of Congress, Prints and Photographs Division; 92 ©Getty Images; 93 ©Bettmann/CORBIS; 94 (l)©The Library of Congress, Prints and Photographs Division, (r)©Bettmann/CORBIS; 95 ©The Library of Congress, Prints and Photographs Division; 97 ©CORBIS; 98 (t)©The Library of Congress, Prints and Photographs Division, (b)©Underwood & Underwood/CORBIS; 99 (t)©Denver Public Library, Western History Collection, (b)©Bettmann/CORBIS; 100 ©The Library of Congress, Prints and Photographs Division; 105 (t)©CORBIS, (bl)©Bettmann/CORBIS, (br)©Bettmann/CORBIS; 106 (t)©Bettmann/CORBIS, (b)©Bettmann/CORBIS; 107 ©Bettmann/CORBIS; 109 ©Bettmann/CORBIS; 110 ©CORBIS; 111 ©The Library of Congress, Prints and Photographs Division; 112 ©CORBIS; 113 (t)©CORBIS, (b)©CORBIS; 114 (t)©CORBIS, (b)©Bettmann/CORBIS; 116 ©Duke University; 117 ©CORBIS; 118 ©Bettmann/CORBIS; 119 ©Bettmann/CORBIS; 122 ©CORBIS; 123 ©Bettmann/CORBIS; 124 (t)©Hulton Archive/Getty Images, (b)©The Robert Runyon Photograph Collection/The Library of Congress, Prints and Photographs Division; 125 (t)©Bettmann/CORBIS, (b)©The Granger Collection; 126 ©CORBIS; 127 ©Bettmann/CORBIS; 128 ©Hulton Archive/Getty Images; 131 ©Hulton-Deutsch Collection/CORBIS; 133 (t)©National Archives, (b)©Bettmann/CORBIS; 136 (t)©Bettmann/CORBIS, (bl)©Hulton Archive/Getty Images, (br)©Bettmann/CORBIS; 138 (t)©Minnesota Historical Society/CORBIS, (b)©CORBIS; 139 (t)©Underwood & Underwood/CORBIS, (b)©National Archives; 140 (t)©Hulton Archive/Getty Images, (b)©Bettmann/CORBIS; 142 ©Bettmann/CORBIS; 143 ©The Granger Collection; 144 (t)©The Library of Congress, Prints and Photographs Division, (b)©CORBIS; 145 ©The Granger Collection; 146 ©Peter & Melina Rodrigo 2004; 148 ©Hulton-Deutsch Collection/CORBIS; 149 ©Time Life Pictures/Getty Images; 151 ©FDR Museum and Library; 152 (t)©Hiroshima Collection/Lewis and Clark University, (b)©R.P. Kingston/Index Stock Imagery; 153 ©Bettmann/CORBIS; 154 ©Bettmann/CORBIS SYGMA; 155 ©Hulton-Deutsch Collection/CORBIS; 156 ©CORBIS; 157 (t)©Time Life Pictures/Getty Images, (b)©Bettmann/CORBIS; 159 ©Bettmann/CORBIS; 160 ©The Library of Congress, Prints and Photographs Division; 161 ©Bettmann/CORBIS; 162 (t)©Hulton Archive/Getty Images, (b)©Bettmann/CORBIS; 163 (t)©Time Life Pictures/Getty Images, (m)©Bettmann/CORBIS, (b)©Hulton Archive/Getty Images; 164 (t)©Bettmann/CORBIS, (b)©Hulton Archive/Getty Images; 165 ©Dorothea Lange/The Library of Congress; 166 ©CORBIS; 167 From *Farewell to Manzanar* by James D. Houston and Jeanne Wakatsuki Houston. Copyright © 1973 by James D. Houston. Reprinted by permission of Houghton Mifflin Company. All rights reserved; 171 (t)©Bettmann/CORBIS, (bl)©2000 Ding Darling Foundation, (br)©Bettmann/CORBIS; 172 ©Bettmann/CORBIS; 173 ©The Mariners' Museum/CORBIS; 174 (t)©Bettmann/CORBIS, (b)©Bettmann/CORBIS; 175 (t)©Time Life Pictures/Getty Images, (b)©Bettmann/CORBIS; 176 ©Bettmann/CORBIS; 177 (t)©Time Life Pictures/Getty Images, (b)©Bettmann/CORBIS; 178 (t)©Bettmann/CORBIS, (b)©Hulton-Deutsch Collection/CORBIS; 179 ©Hulton Archive/Getty Images; 180 ©Bettmann/CORBIS; 181 ©Marvin Koner/CORBIS; 182 ©Hulton-Deutsch Collection/CORBIS; 183 (t)©Time Life Pictures/Getty Images, (b)©Barbara Wichman; 184 ©Bettmann/CORBIS; 188 ©NASA; 189 ©Bettmann/CORBIS; 190 (t)©Bettmann/CORBIS, (b)©Getty Images; 191 (t)©Bettmann/CORBIS, (b)©Hulton Archive/Getty Images; 192 ©Bettmann/CORBIS; 193 ©Time Life Pictures/Getty Images; 194 (l)©Time Life Pictures/Getty Images, (r)©Time Life Pictures/Getty Images; 195 (t)©Bettmann/CORBIS, (b)©Rick Friedman/CORBIS; 196 ©The Library of Congress, Prints and Photographs Division; 197 ©Bettmann/CORBIS; 198 ©Hulton Archive/Getty Images; 199 (t)©Bettmann/CORBIS, (b)©Bettmann/CORBIS; 200 ©Bettmann/CORBIS; 205 (t)©The Image Bank/Getty Images, (l)©Getty Images, (r)©Getty Images; 206 (t)©Getty Images, (b)©Ron Kimball/Ron Kimball Stock; 207 ©Getty Images; 208 (t)©Getty Images, (b)©Charles E. Rotkin/CORBIS; 209 ©Time Life Pictures/Getty Images; 211 ©Time Life Pictures/Getty Images; 212 (l)©Archives, Hebrew Immigrant Aid Society, (r)©Bettmann/CORBIS; 213 ©Bettmann/CORBIS; 214 (t)©Bettmann/CORBIS, (b)©Dennis MacDonald; 216 ©Getty Images; 217 ©Getty Images; 218 ©Bettmann/CORBIS; 219 "Cesar Rosa" in *Mexican Voices, American Dreams: An Oral History of Mexican Immigration to the United States* by Marilyn P. Davis, Henry Holt, 1990; 222 (t)©Bettmann/CORBIS, (b)©Time Life Pictures/Getty Images; 223 ©David J. & Janice L. Frent Collection/CORBIS; 224 (tl)©Time Life Pictures/Getty Images, (tr)©Time Life Pictures/Getty Images, (b)©Georgia Tech Capital Planning & Space Management; 225 (t)©Getty Images, (b)©Time Life Pictures/Getty Images; 226 ©Underwood & Underwood/CORBIS; 227 ©Ed Eckstein/CORBIS; 228 (t)©Bettmann/CORBIS, (b)©Bettmann/CORBIS; 229 ©Getty Images; 230 ©Jacques Lowe-Woodfin Camp; 232 ©Bettmann/CORBIS; 233 (t)©NASA, (b)©Bettmann/CORBIS; 234 (m)©CORBIS, (b)©Bettmann/CORBIS; 235 ©Bettmann/CORBIS; 239 (t)©Bettmann/CORBIS, (m)©Bettmann/CORBIS, (b)©Time Life Pictures/Getty Images; 240 (t)©Bettmann/CORBIS, (b)©Associated Press, AP; 241 (t)©CORBIS; 242 ©Bettmann/CORBIS; 243 ©Bettmann/CORBIS; 244 ©LBJ Museum; 245 ©CORBIS; 246 ©The University of Southern Mississippi Libraries, McCain Library and Archives; 247 ©Getty Images; 249 ©Time Life Pictures/Getty Images; 250 ©Bettmann/CORBIS; 251 (t)©Time Life Pictures/Getty Images; (b)©Getty Images; 252 ©Time Life Pictures/Getty Images; 253 (t)©Bettmann/CORBIS, (b)©Bettmann/CORBIS; 256 ©Time Life Pictures/Getty Images; 257 ©Bettmann/CORBIS; 258 ©Bettmann/CORBIS; 259 ©Getty Images; 260 (t)©Jim Sugar/CORBIS, (b)©Ted Spiegel/CORBIS; 261 "What is Black Power?" from *Black Power*, by Stokely Carmichael and Charles Hamilton, copyright © 1967 by Stokely Carmichael and Charles Hamilton; 262 ©Morton Beebe/CORBIS; 263 (t)©Bettmann/CORBIS, (b)©Time Life Pictures/Getty Images; 264 (t)©Bettmann/CORBIS, (b)©Bettmann/CORBIS; 265 ©Bettmann/CORBIS; 266 Time Life Pictures/Getty Images; 267 ©Getty Images; 268 ©Bettmann/CORBIS; 269 (t)©Bettmann/CORBIS, (m)©Getty Images, (b)©Henry Diltz/CORBIS; 273 (t)©Bettmann/CORBIS, (bl)©The Bettmann Archive/CORBIS, (br)©Lurie; 274 ©Getty Images 275 ©Time Life

(t) top, (b) bottom, (m) middle, (l) left, (r) right

(t) top, (b) bottom, (m) middle, (l) left, (r) right